AF605884

NIGHTMARES OF THE NATIONAL IMAGINARY

Nightmares of the National Imaginary

Surveillance and Sousveillance in Canadian Literature

TOM HALFORD

UNIVERSITY OF TORONTO PRESS
Toronto Buffalo London

Toronto Buffalo London
utppublishing.com
Printed in Canada

ISBN 978-1-4875-6412-4 (cloth) ISBN 978-1-4875-6414-8 (EPUB)
ISBN 978-1-4875-6413-1 (PDF)

Library and Archives Canada Cataloguing in Publication

Title: Nightmares of the national imaginary : surveillance and sousveillance in Canadian literature / Tom Halford.
Names: Halford, Tom, 1983–, author.
Description: Includes bibliographical references and index.
Identifiers: Canadiana (print) 20250250381 | Canadiana (ebook) 20250250411 | ISBN 9781487564124 (cloth) | ISBN 9781487564148 (EPUB) | ISBN 9781487564131 (PDF)
Subjects: LCSH: Surveillance in literature. | LCSH: Canadian literature – 21st century – History and criticism.
Classification: LCC PS8101.S94 H35 2025 | DDC C810.9/355 – dc23

Cover design: Mark Byk
Cover images: (top) Betacam-SP/Shutterstock.com; (bottom) Maisei Raman/Shutterstock.com

We wish to acknowledge the land on which the University of Toronto Press operates. This land is the traditional territory of the Wendat, the Anishnaabeg, the Haudenosaunee, the Métis, and the Mississaugas of the Credit First Nation.

This book has been published with the help of a grant from the Federation for the Humanities and Social Sciences, through the Awards to Scholarly Publications Program, using funds provided by the Social Sciences and Humanities Research Council of Canada.

University of Toronto Press acknowledges the financial support of the Government of Canada, the Canada Council for the Arts, and the Ontario Arts Council, an agency of the Government of Ontario, for its publishing activities.

Canada Council for the Arts Conseil des Arts du Canada

Funded by the Government of Canada | Financé par le gouvernement du Canada | Canada

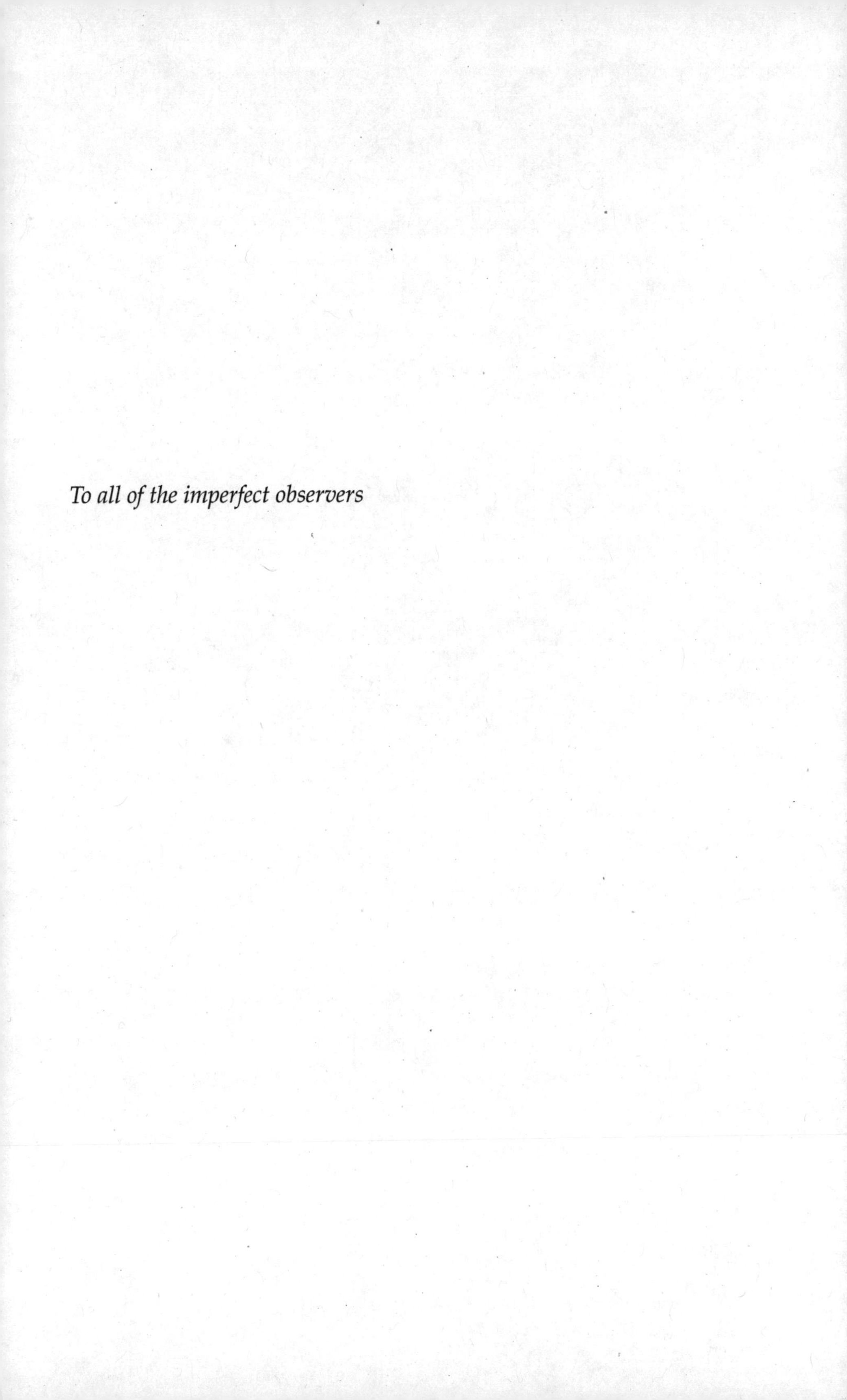

To all of the imperfect observers

Contents

Part Three: How Should We Look at Those Who Surveil?

Acknowledgments

I have learned so much from attending the Atlantic Canada Studies Conference and the Raddall Symposia. These gatherings feature established and emerging scholars. The opportunity to hear other academics speak has always been eye opening and inspiring. Corner Brook, Newfoundland, has a bright and supportive writing scene, and I find living there and interacting with its authors to be very helpful.

Portions of this book were previously published in the form of articles. An earlier version of the chapter on Michael Winter's *This All Happened* appeared in the *Journal of Newfoundland and Labrador Studies* in 2016. The chapter on David Adams Richards's *Principles to Live By* was published in *Studies in Canadian Literature* in 2018. I would like to thank the editors of both journals for permission to publish these chapters.

I would like to thank the following publishers for permission to include excerpts from the books of poetry discussed in part 1: Arsenal Pulp Press, New Star Books, Coach House Books, and Gordon Hill Press. I would also like to thank the poets: Ken Babstock, Larissa Lai, Rita Wong, and A.F. Moritz.

Writing is hard work. Thank you to all the authors who appear in this text.

There are many scholars who have helped me in one way or another. Here are a few of them: Larry Mathews, Danine Farquharson, Denyse Lynde, David Creelman, Herb Wyile, Cynthia Sugars, Peter Thompson, Paul Chafe, Alexander MacLeod, Christopher Armstrong, Shane Neilson, Randy Drover, Shoshanna Ganz, and Adam Beardsworth. If your name is not here, and you feel it should be, please give me a hard time about it.

I would like to thank my friends, family, and colleagues. I am grateful for every day that I can work at Grenfell Campus, Memorial University of Newfoundland. I am thankful for the kindness of friends and

I am blessed with the love and good humour of my family, especially Melissa, Violet, and Douglas.

I thank Mark Thompson for his guidance and patience. Thank you to everyone at University of Toronto Press for their help.

If I am being honest, I wrote this book for Inspector Tony Perry. I do not know if I will ever be able to fully explain why, but I think it is true. This is the best I can offer. I hope it does some good. May your memory live on.

Moreover, I do not have lived experience about some of the topics in this study. I am responding as a reader and writing about the kinds of opportunities that books provide. I respect the hard work of police officers and others who are tasked with surveillance. Speaking broadly, there are many people who are forced into difficult positions. I do not know your story, and there is more that I need to learn. I am writing from the perspective of a civilian, an important voice in the dialogue that is democracy.

Finally, I would like to say that I love Newfoundland and Labrador, and I love Canada. There is a small part of this earth that I can call home and where I can be myself. Wouldn't it be wonderful if we all could experience this feeling?

NIGHTMARES OF THE NATIONAL IMAGINARY

Introduction

The National Imaginary, Surveillance, Sousveillance, and Literature: The Last Word

When I lived in St John's, Newfoundland, my next-door neighbours were struggling to make ends meet. This was downtown where the houses are squished together, and our walls were connected. From time to time, even though we tried not to listen, my partner and I could hear them shouting at one another. We did not like the way they spoke to their boy, but it was not bad enough for us to call the police. Midway through the winter they used all the oil in their tank and could no longer afford to heat their house. On more than one occasion we turned a corner and found one of the parents asking us for money. Someone called child services, and their boy was taken away. Soon afterwards the parents moved out. I saw the father once. He was ahead of me in the line at a Tim Hortons. I waved, but he did not recognize me or he pretended not to see me. I did not really want to talk to him anyway. I cannot remember any of their names.

This is one example of what Gary T. Marx in *Windows into the Soul: Surveillance and Society in an Age of High Technology* would describe as an older form of surveillance. In this study I will refer to such an experience as *sousveillance*, or observing from below. Although I offer a theoretical and strategic form of sousveillance that creates a strong sense of indeterminacy and alterity, by and large, sousveillance is, as I hope my brief story indicates, not a perfect form of observation. As a multiform voice that has the potential to engage in dialogue with surveillance, however, it is an essential way in which people interact with their government and negotiate group identity. Community members observe one another. Sometimes this gaze is friendly and caring, but sometimes it is not. Groups create a series of expectations – ranging from the cultural to the legal – that people are supposed to follow. If those expectations are not met, there is an accompanying range of repercussions, and when an individual within the group is put in harm's way, then the state intervenes. Sousveillance and surveillance exist on a spectrum. Today, alongside traditional surveillance, digital surveillance projects a powerful gaze onto day-to-day life. G.T. Marx writes that "new surveillance may be defined as *scrutiny of individuals, groups, and contexts through the use of technical means to extract or create information*" (20; emphasis mine). This streamlined, ubiquitous, digital version of surveillance has significant influence on the lives of individuals, such as my neighbours. He writes: "[E]valuation systems initially were seen as means of controlling or managing the individual, but later categorizations identified individuals for favorable selection and treatment" (41). Such categories have an impact on life choices and heighten class division. It is worth noting that the place where my neighbours lived is now a hip espresso and gelato shop.

Contemporary surveillance gathers massive amounts of data that is used to simplify and sort individuals into categories. Since those who observe this data are often removed from the lives that will be influenced by this categorization, surveillance provides only a partial knowledge, data without the contradictions and complexities of day-to-day life. In *Scrutinized! Surveillance in Asian North American Literature*, Monica Chiu offers an important reminder that this data needs to be digested by human beings: "Information gathered by surveillance technology, for example, is limited by fallible human interpretation. More than merely observing the faces and actions of those it records, surveillance can reify, not eradicate, intractable ideologies" (12). Thus, no matter how comprehensive or how accurate the data, communities still carry with them a long history of assumptions, prejudices, and biases. Another fundamental issue is the fact that surveillance data funnels perception towards simplification and categorization. As Peter Marks points out in *Imagining Surveillance: Eutopian and Dystopian Literature and Film*, "Narrative identities produce personal stories, but categorical identities produce data, information that state and commercial agencies can use to classify, assess and otherwise administer all those whose information has been collected. Surveillance systems prefer categorical identities, which they do much to create as well as to monitor" (127–8). Narrative offers a necessary counterpoint which demonstrates that even though people might fit into categories, they are also far more nuanced and complicated than the way in which they are sorted. This is an important lesson not just for those who surveil but also for average people who read or hear about an individual in the news and assume they can define that person while ignoring the fact that there are generations of lived experience behind the headline. Some modes of observation tend to simplify as they sort, and other modes of observation tend to complicate and problematize categories. This book demonstrates how these modes can complement each other.

If surveillance can be understood as the methods that state and corporate entities use to look from above, then sousveillance can be understood as the methods that people use to look back from below. These two concepts exist on a spectrum: if civilians watch neighbours and telephone the police, then they connect themselves to the system of surveillance. Furthermore, from cellphone cameras to social media posts, there are now a host of ways that people can watch the watchers. Narrative, the focus of this study – specifically in the way that stories can help us critique ourselves, our communities, and our surveillance systems – is just one mode of sousveillance. We tell ourselves a story of who we think we are as individuals, and we also tell ourselves a story of who we think we are as a nation. On an individual level, some of these stories might be true and vital to our sense of self; others might be questionable and in need of a reality check. On a broad, cultural level, these stories accumulate into the national imaginary, or, in my case, the idea of Canada. For English-speaking Canadians, symbols such as the beaver, the Mountie, and the maple tree represent a shared sense of how we understand our nation. For example, at its best the Mountie (a member of the Royal Canadian Mounted Police, RCMP) – think of the characters Dudley Do-Right and Constable Benton Fraser (in the television series Due South) – represents the hope for safety and decency. The symbol of the Mountie also directly connects the national imaginary to surveillance in that it implies that Anglo-Canadians value the protection offered through the ideal of the good and morally upright observer. Much like surveillance, the national imaginary not only simplifies as it sorts, but also shapes identity in complex ways. Sousveillance is the attempt by individuals to negotiate these forces and to find spaces where people can create their own identities.

If nostalgic images of Mounties traversing pristine landscapes that teem with beavers and geese held any power in national and international discourses of what it meant to be Canadian, today it feels impossible to look past the oil pipeline running through that landscape or the fraught relationship between the RCMP and Indigenous Peoples. The idea of Canada is constantly shifting, and these changes are negotiated in – among other places – literature. In *Crosstalk: Canadian and Global Imaginaries in Dialogue*, Diana Brydon and Marta Dvořák define Canadian imaginaries as "the organizing structures of societal understanding within a nation-state" (1). The central argument of *Nightmares of the National Imaginary* is that literature challenges and complicates not only our national identity but also the ways in which surveillance and sousveillance simplify and sort individuals. From David Chariandy's *Brother*, which narrates the experience of an immigrant family interacting with urban policing, to David Adams Richards's *Principles to Live By*, which portrays the internal struggles of a fictional RCMP officer, literature presents an image of life in Canada that underwrites idealistic understandings of a nation state. Narratives that deal with representations of surveillance and sousveillance add nuance to the idea of Canada.

People might read a headline about a police shooting or about an immigrant family stranded in bureaucratic limbo, but narrative accounts bring these incidents to life. In an interview for Canada Reads 2019, "'Quietly Heroic Lives': Lisa Ray and David Chariandy Discuss His Novel Brother," David Chariandy and his interviewer, Lisa Ray, an actor and model, discuss how *Brother* might be considered a political novel. Essentially, *Brother* details the lives of people who are often reduced to sensational news stories. Lisa Ray asks: "It [*Brother*] is also a political novel, you know, I think just by telling this story of these people who have been under-represented in contemporary, mainstream Canadian literature – that's a political act. You know, giving them a voice, giving them agency, creating what I believe is almost like an opera around something, would be turned into a headline otherwise, you know?" ("Quietly Heroic Lives"). Chariandy responds with a question of his own: "How do we see the lives behind the bloody newspaper headlines?" From a news story detailing a tragic incident such as a police shooting, a reader might have a sense of what has happened, and the event might reflect or influence how the reader understands a particular part of the country. In a limited way, they might have a sense of the victim's final moments. Without lived experience, however, it is dubious that they could empathize with the agony of the victim's family and friends; this suffering happens long after the sensationalism of the event has faded. As a form, the novel, however, plods along, and a news story sprints ahead. Chariandy is adept at detailing the slow movement of grief. Novels are not the first or the loudest voices to speak in our national discourse. However, they are persistently there in the background, reminding us to think expansively and to contemplate people who might otherwise be ignored.

More cynical critics might dismiss Ray and Chariandy's discussion as part of the commodification of moralistic literature through celebrity and arbitrary prize systems. There is, however, an important kernel from their conversation that needs to be popped. They are suggesting that *Brother* might encourage readers to pause when they next see a gruesome headline and to consider the various lives affected by a traumatic event. This moment of hesitation and uncertainty resonates with the philosophy of ethical criticism as developed by European and Anglo-American critics such as Namwali Serpell, Emmanuel Levinas, Jacques Derrida, Martha Nussbaum, Simon Critchley, Wayne C. Booth, and Marshall Gregory.[1] From this rich tradition my study gains a focus on the Other, an acceptance of indeterminacy, and a philosophy of looking – all of which will be posited as a counterpoint to the gaze of state and corporate surveillance structures, which operate on certainty and on the categorization of human beings into strictly defined groups. Peter Marks also draws this connection between ethics, surveillance, and literature: "The sorts of choices characters are required and sometimes forced to make under the fierce scrutiny of surveillance systems ... project to readers and viewers what lived experience might be like in such systems, and the situations and developments by which such systems could be imposed" (16). In each one of the texts chosen for this study the gaze of the narrators and of the authors will be closely considered in all their amorphous potential. Some literary artists are hedonists, while others are far more invested in social responsibility. Thus, it will be essential to discuss the various ways that authors observe others and to stress the importance of indeterminacy, or the creation of moments where observers feel uncertain and must withhold judgment. Alterity, as the refusal to reduce the Other to sameness, will also be a key aspect of this study in reading about those who are vulnerable in Canadian society and in orienting a thoughtful gaze towards them.[2]

Aside from indeterminacy and alterity, these books create spaces for people to find moments of self-expression and self-creation, to explore thoughts and desires that they might not otherwise. In *Scandalous*

1 These texts include Namwali Serpell's *Seven Modes of Uncertainty*; Emmanuel Levinas's *Otherwise than Being* and *Totality and Infinity*; Jacques Derrida's *Writing and Difference; Martha Nussbaum's Poetic Justice*; Simon Critchley's *Infinitely Demanding* and *The Ethics of Deconstruction*; Wayne C. Booth's *The Company We Keep* and *The Rhetoric of Fiction*; and Marshall Gregory's *Shaped by Stories*.

2 For Sherene Razack, the identification of vulnerability can lead to its own set of problems. She writes that people must "move away from pity and towards responsibility" (126). Razack is writing from a legal perspective. In the world of literature, responses can be multiform and move in stages. It seems impossible and unethical to dictate how a reader might respond to a text. However, for individuals living with a system that favours some over others, Razack's insistence on responsibility is an important reminder.

Bodies: Diasporic Literature in English Canada, Smaro Kamboureli talks "of the subtle and not so subtle ways in which the desire-machine of the state socializes" (3). If the massive bureaucratic structure known as the Canadian government can be understood as a desire-machine that produces subjectivities, then literature is an important creator of hidden spaces and alternative desire-machines. Books, as Dionne Brand points out in *A Map to the Door of No Return*, are also desire-machines. They propel us to think and feel in new ways. For example, she talks about her experience of reading *The Black Napoleon*: "The book filled me with sadness and courage. It burned my skin. I lay asleep on its open face under the bed. It was the book that took me away from the world ... For days I lived with these people I found there ... In it I met a history I was never taught ... The book was a mirror and an ocean" (186–7). *The Black Napoleon* opened a space for her to desire and to imagine new ways of being.[3] Of course, desire-machines come in many forms, and they do not have to be literature. There are various modes that can be used to imagine new ways of being. For example, in *Black Like Who? Writing Black Canada*, Rinaldo Walcott emphasizes the importance of music (145). In this study, however, I focus on literary texts because they offer a depth to the human experience that does not necessarily exist in other art forms. I am using this depth as a counterpoint to the way in which surveillance simplifies and sorts. To be clear, I am not interested in rejecting or vilifying the desire-machine of the state. I want to find pockets of space for various types of imagining and narratives in which individuals discuss moments that they are being recognized and misrecognized; such expressions help people resist containment and control. I want to hear these expressions as clearly as I can, but I also want to highlight the fact that not everyone desires political resistance; readers are drawn to, among other things, the joy of language at play, the potential for escaping into the imagination, and the fun of spending time with fictional people.

In this study, specific modes of the literary gaze will be developed as a contrast to modes of observation enacted through surveillance. At the heart of many of the essays in *Surveillance | Society | Culture*, edited by Florian Zappe and Andrew Gross, is the conflict between data and

3 Desire is not necessarily definable for Brand; it is more like an energy that propels people forward. She writes: "I want to say something else about desire. I really do not know what it is. I experience something which, sometimes, if I pull it apart, I cannot make reason of. The word seems to me to fall apart under the pull and drag of its commodified shapes, under the weight of our artifice and our conceit" (*Map to the Door of No Return* 195).

narrative as ways of seeing the world. Ideally, narrative descriptions, as composed by literary artists, imbue readers with a richer representation of human life than the data gathered by surveillance systems. As narrative often demonstrates how people are more complex than the categories into which they fit, it is a strong contrast to data gathering that relies on sorting people into various, simplified categories.[4] Novels, in particular, demand that readers spend prolonged periods of time with characters who might seem to be a cliché at first glance, but by imagining the author's world, readers see how people are more than the categories they have been assigned. News stories and statistics begin the conversation, but literature has the last word.

The Canadian National Imaginary: The Dream of a Good and Decent People

Even though a nation is composed of people, institutions, and laws, Benedict Anderson's *Imagined Communities: Reflections on the Origin and Spread of Nationalism* articulates why a country will always have some abstract component. Anderson writes: "It is imagined because the members of even the smallest nation will never know most of their fellow-members, meet them, or even hear of them, yet in the minds of each lives the image of their communion" (6). As long as countries exist, abstractions of them will exist alongside. These imagined communities are constantly changing, however, and the metaphors that authors use to describe them change as well. One of the most compelling discussions of the national imaginary is in *Creative Subversions: Whiteness, Indigeneity, and the National Imaginary* by Margot Francis. She questions Anderson's construction of the nation and reformulates it as a type of haunting. Firstly, she points out the fact that countries exist largely as a result of the rule of law and the power of capital. Francis writes: "[D]espite Benedict Anderson's early analysis of the nation as the work of the imagination, much scholarship still assumes that nation-states are constituted primarily through law, rational discipline, and commodification" (157).

4 In *Transparent Lives*, Bennett et al. write: "A landmark study of Canadian police, for example, shows that policing was transformed in the late twentieth century by new technologies designed to identify and track risk. To perform this function, police use surveillance to watch people and then categorize them according to the level of risk they might pose. Once again, social sorting is the other side of the surveillance coin here. Proving one's 'innocence' becomes less easy for individuals falling into the wrong category, because the default position is suspicion of guilt until the system proves otherwise" (12).

One of the ways in which law, discipline, and commodification are sustained is through surveillance and sousveillance structures. The state imagines and observes us; we imagine and observe the state. As we observe one another and the state, we also always use our imaginations. Sometimes we see clearly. At other times we misrecognize and we make mistakes. As Chiu writes, "we look and look again to discover that how we see defines what we see and whom we overlook" (27). In these complex, imperfect ways, surveillance, sousveillance, and the national imaginary are constantly intersecting. The national imaginary is the illusion of who we think we are. Surveillance is the machine of bureaucracy categorizing and sorting identity. Sousveillance is the flawed human attempts at observing from below. As Francis develops her subversion of the national imaginary, she incorporates a new way of framing Anderson's work. She describes her national imaginary "as a palimpsest, or 'a parchment that has been inscribed two or three times, the previous text having been imperfectly erased and remaining therefore still partly visible.' This imperfect erasure, or the ways that the past continues to impinge on the present, has material and symbolic consequences" (163). Thus, our imagined community is not just those who are currently living in the same country as we are, but also those who have occupied the land in the past and those who will occupy it in the future. We are haunted and will continue to be so: "[T]he symbolic and material legacy associated with Canadianness points more towards a denied racist history that continues to reassert itself in the present day" (162–3). Although we have one sense of the national imaginary through children's books, popular media, and propaganda, Francis describes how radical art undercuts this cosy understanding and challenges Canadians to consider their national ethos with greater honesty. For Francis, the narrow-minded construction of the national imaginary necessitates resistance through spectacle. The visual art on which she focuses generally possesses qualities that should startle the viewer. Literary art also has the potential to shock readers, but in this study – with the exception of the play Foreign Radical and the true-crime work *Missing from the Village* – I am focusing mainly on how literature complicates perspectives and encourages hesitation before passing judgment. Thus, I tend to see the literary text and the moment of spectacle as working to a similar end but in disparate ways.

Surveillance largely operates through data, but the national imaginary functions on a symbolic level. Both tend to simplify, however, and literature – at its best – offers to complicate our conception of ourselves and our national ethos. My interest in the national imaginary lies in how it appears to function alongside surveillance structures to produce national subjects. The connections between concepts of ethos and the national imaginary are rich. The national imaginary is often a representation of the way in which we would like to see ourselves. Similarly, ethos is a sense of national character, more concretely grounded in our laws and customs. If ethos is character, then the national imaginary is persona. Narrative takes these images and complicates them. The RCMP is one of the classic emblems of the Anglo-Canadian national imaginary, but there are other kinds of police officers in Canada, namely those working in urban centres who are frequently placed in difficult positions. In this study, both Richards's *Principles to Live By*, which features an RCMP officer, and Katherena Vermette's *The Break*, which focuses in part on a member of the Winnipeg Police Service, are closely considered in the hopes of adding nuance to how such positions are perceived. Both ethos and the national imaginary influence how Canadians think about themselves and their institutions. Literary artists are in a unique position to influence perceptions of the state. Authors frequently communicate complex, often deliberately contradictory, forms of observation, and they do so through language that is rarely simple or easy to categorize. The literary gaze tends to add nuance and ambiguity to whomever or whatever it is directed. This nuance and ambiguity shows us that there is more to a story than what appears to be there at first glance.

No matter how talented and studied authors may be, they are writing for people who live with a host of prevailing assumptions about Canada and its institutions. Children are introduced to the Canadian national imaginary in many ways, but perhaps one of the more obvious ones is in "ABC" books. Depending on the book, *A* might be for the Arctic or for Alberta; *B* might be for beaver or for Baffin Island; *M* might be for maple syrup or for Mountie. These are the symbols that we use to teach our children about the country. These symbols shift and change, but the intent to define who we are as a people through sport, geography, food, agriculture, animals, and labour remains. This streamlining of identity can be challenged or fractured by the various genetic, cultural, and regional groupings in Canada. Brydon and Dvořák write: "Increasingly, Canadians are aware that in Canada there is more than one nation. Québec has officially been recognized as a distinct society. First Nations, Inuit, Métis, and non-status natives are increasingly visible as important communities with their own distinctive relationships to the Canadian state and the international community. As dual citizenships proliferate, some former immigrant communities are reimagining themselves within diasporic structures of imagination" (4–5). These diasporic structures are deeply important within communities that have historically been excluded from the national imaginary. Specific authors, such as Brand, have been influential in reworking shared understandings of Canada. As Paul Barrett points out in *Blackening Canada: Diaspora, Race, Multiculturalism*, "Brand's poetics breaks apart the seemingly stable and sutured national time to create a space for black diasporic subjects in the nation" (54). Within each community, representative images of Canada become emblematic. Historically significant national symbols, such as the Mountie, are reconsidered and redescribed. For better or for worse, they persist.

These representations of symbolic figures do not reflect the way that Canadians act; they reflect the way that Canadians would like to think about themselves. In *The Mountie: From Dime Store to Disney*, Michael Dawson argues that the Mountie is specific to English-Canadian nationalism (28). Writing of the national ethos in 1998, Dawson points out that "English-Canadians are electing governments that promise less intervention in the economy and decreased support for social programs. Yet television shows, like recent Mountie books and souvenirs, continue to celebrate a kinder, gentler Canadian ethic" (170). Thus, the symbols that nationals use to define themselves can seem hypocritical when compared to their behaviour. The national imaginary is not the national reality. As Daniel Francis argues in *National Dreams: Myth, Memory, and Canadian History*, this disparity between perception and reality can be extremely alienating. Yet, taken purely at the symbolic level, the Mountie is an excellent figure to attempt to unify national identity around law-abiding, dutiful citizens: "The early chroniclers described the Mountie as unassuming, patient, impartial, self-disciplined, sober, and completely incorruptible. Is it any wonder that Canadians decided to identify so closely with such a paragon?" (D. Francis 33). If one had to be surveilled, this ideal figure would be the number one choice. However, the history of the RCMP in Canada undercuts this myth. Francis writes: "As a frontier police force, the Riders of the Plains prepared the western interior for 'civilized' occupation. As an urban police force, the RCMP rooted out subversion and spied on political nonconformists. The benign image of the Boy Scout Mountie was the velvet glove in which the iron hand of the state wielded its power" (D. Francis 51). This figure has as much potential to alienate as it does to unite. Nevertheless, the myth of the Mountie persists: "Still, the traditional, upright image continues to resonate, or the Disney Corporation would not be interested in marketing it. It seems to stand for something deep in the Canadian character. It has become dissociated from the actual history of the force and stands alone as a symbol of how Canadians like to see themselves: honest, brave, modest, law-abiding, polite" (D. Francis 50). This is one of the many ways that surveillance, sousveillance, and the national imaginary intersect. Police officers do the hard work of enforcing surveillance structures; they have been idealized in the Anglo-Canadian imagination through the figure of the Mountie; certain authors and scholars have looked back at policing structures and demonstrated a more comprehensive, less idealized version of the RCMP. Knowledge of moments in which national institutions have worked against the best interest of Canadians might prove to be a vital counterpoint to our myth making, a way of humbling our national imaginary and providing a healthy dose of reality.

Despite the misleading nature of idyllic symbols, they remain an important marker to identify change and to spark discussion. In fact, these symbols often require reimagining if they are going to survive. Dawson highlights this point in relation to the Mounties: "Our past, like our government buildings and our highways, is often in need of renovation. A clear example of this was the renovation of the Mountie's image in the 1960s and 1970s. Faced with growing criticism of RCMP exploits in a world increasingly prone to questioning authority, what I describe as the class Mountie myth would no longer suffice" (29). These national symbols are flawed and problematic, but they also serve as a fundamental way in which we communicate what we would like to be. First we need to accept that the national imaginary does not reflect who we actually are as a people; these images reflect a mythology used to pacify ourselves that we are good and decent. Literature tells us a more complicated story.

Counter-Narratives of the National Imaginary: Nightmares of the Excluded Other

As Daniel Francis points out, national symbols unite and alienate. Historically the Canadian imaginary has worked to negate and exclude the Other. Charles Taylor presents the ethical imperative of developing a politics of recognition: "The thesis is that our identity is partly shaped by recognition or its absence, often by the misrecognition of others, and so a person or group of people can suffer real damage, real distortion, if the people or society around them mirror back to them a confining or demeaning or contemptible picture of themselves. Nonrecognition or misrecognition can inflict harm, can be a form of oppression, imprisoning someone in a false, distorted, and reduced mode of being" (25). If people want to live in a fair and just society, they must not only develop a politic but also observe and articulate what they see with care and accuracy. Taylor writes: "Within these perspectives, misrecognition shows not just a lack of due respect. It can inflict a grievous wound, saddling its victims with a crippling self-hatred. Due recognition is not just a courtesy we owe people. It is a vital human need" (26). One problem with the politics of recognition is that, when enacted by the Canadian state, it has contained, controlled, distorted, and exploited the Other. Ultimately the Canadian national imaginary relies on the construction of an exalted, compassionate self, which inevitably results in a contrasting figure of the Other. To move past a politics of recognition, discourse about the nation must look to the multiform expressions of those who have historically been excluded; surveillance needs to be understood as a massive misrecognition machine; average people need to accept their own luck and good fortune as opposed to a presumed cultural superiority; spaces need to be opened and protected for the Other to express and to create; these creations – generally speaking – should often be understood as an ever-changing multiform, not as an accumulation of a uniform identity that can easily be articulated and contained.

To combat a history of negation and exclusion, Black and Indigenous voices have highlighted specific moments in Canada's past that they refuse to forget; simultaneously, they critique the politics of recognition as a way of containing and silencing diverse voices. As Rinaldo Walcott writes, in *Black Like Who? Writing Black Canada*, "Erasing all evidence of any other presence (First Nations and Black) is crucial if the myth of two founding peoples is to hold the crumbling nation of Canada together in the face of Quebec's ever-impending separation and declaration of nation status" (50). The process of building a national identity, for Walcott, derives from the dominant groups' own anxiety related to negation and erasure. If a government can cultivate a coherent, admirable national identity, then it has a greater opportunity to grow patriotic citizens who will maintain its culture and structure. This development of a national imaginary comes at a cost for those who do not fit the narrative. We are not talking solely about feelings of alienation; the state actively destroys concrete connections to the past. For example, in *Crow Gulch* poet Douglas Walbourne-Gough has written eloquently on the erasure of a largely Indigenous community in Corner Brook, Newfoundland. Similarly, Walcott describes the removal of Blackness from Canadian history: "The long and now broken silence in St. Armand, Quebec concerning the slave cemetery almost ploughed over, which the locals call nigger rock; the destruction of Africville in Nova Scotia; the demolition of Hogan's Alley in Vancouver in the '60s'; in Ontario the changing of the name of Negro Creek Road to Moggie Road in 1996; all suggest a willful attempt to make a black presence absent. These moments are complex ones because they occasion what we might term, after Jimmie

Durham, the absented presence of blackness in Canada" (136). It feels important to stress that a politics of recognition is a progression from a politics of negation and exclusion. With Walcott and Walbourne-Gough, the individuals who have been alienated by the nation-building process have space and time to articulate their idiosyncratic perspectives. Recognizing the work of poets such as Walbourne-Gough and critics such as Walcott is an important place to start. There are, however, so many ways to misrecognize.

For Smaro Kamboureli, the politics of recognition might shift the discourse away from negation and erasure, but it does so in a deeply flawed way. In *Scandalous Bodies: Diasporic Literature in English Canada*, she aptly critiques the way in which the Other is often reduced to a containable and controllable subject. She writes: "I am concerned here with the ways ethnic subjectivity is produced by the media, by the Canadian state, and by the philosopher Charles Taylor. The cultural politics that emerges from my examination of media representations of multiculturalism points to a tendency towards the management and commodification of ethnic subjectivity. This tendency is not unlike that manifested in the Canadian Multiculturalism Act, which legitimizes ethnic difference" (xvi). The containment of the Other is a way for the state to dominate those in the margins through polite observation. Kamboureli writes: "The emphasis is placed on reproducible and therefore reductive heritage images, precisely because they are seen as reflecting a past irrelevant to Canada's and therefore of little, if any, political pertinence to Canadian culture. Such displays of difference promote a fetishization of ethnic imaginaries: they cast minority Canadians as objects of national voyeurism by keeping them, as it were, under surveillance" (109–10). Kamboureli's criticism poses compelling problems. The state attempts to enact a politics of recognition but ultimately socializes and surveils its subjects into specific categories. This amounts to state-sanctioned misrecognition, manipulation, and distortion.

One could argue that the national imaginary in Canada has shifted and grown to incorporate the voices and history of Black, Indigenous, and people of colour (BIPOC). However, Sherene Razack and Sunera Thobani each argue that certain constructions of the national imaginary are not simply alienating but racist and xenophobic. Established Canadians might tell themselves a story about their progressive national character – how welcoming and kind they are – often as a contrast to other groups and other nations; in doing so, they inevitably misrecognize. In *Looking White People in the Eye: Gender, Race, and Culture in Courtrooms and Classrooms*, Razack explains how the construction of the

Canadian national imaginary depends on the development of contrasts that are ultimately flattering for white Canadians. For Razack, Canadians negotiate their history against the United States. She pinpoints specific elements of the ideal Canadian, writing: "Canadians define themselves as unimplicated in the genocide of Native peoples or the enslavement of African peoples, a position of innocence that is especially appealing because it enables Canadians to imagine themselves as distinct from Americans. Canadians also mark themselves as the peacekeepers of the world, as living in a country that welcomes immigrants and as having few imperialist pretensions" (89). Originally published in 1998, Razack's critique still rings true even if Canadians have become more conscious of their troubled history. Razack demonstrates how Canadians frame the national imaginary against other countries and regions, particularly in relation to the concept of a vulnerable Other. She writes, "Oppressed Third World women, particularly the passive, downtrodden Indian woman and the veiled Muslim one, are recurring and familiar images in Canadian public discourse" (100). Identifying vulnerable people is not in and of itself a negative practice. However, if the observer sees the vulnerable Other without any recognition of the damaging nature of colonialism, then this will inevitably lead to misrecognition. Razack writes: "[R]elations among unequals are powerfully shaped by the histories and contemporary realities of oppression. ... powerful narratives turn oppressed peoples into objects, to be held in contempt, or to be saved from their fates by more civilized beings" (3). Similarly, in *Exalted Subjects: Studies in the Making of Race and Nation in Canada*, Sunera Thobani highlights how in exalting the Canadian subject as an ideal figure, discussions of national identity create an excluded Other. She writes that nationals are often considered to be "responsible citizens, compassionate, caring, and committed to the values of diversity and multiculturalism. Having overcome great adversity in founding the nation, these subjects face numerous challenges from outsiders – 'Indians,' immigrants, and refugees – who threaten their collective welfare and prosperity" (4). For Thobani, this creates a discourse of good self and bad Other, which implies that Canadian identity is forged in racism, Eurocentrism, and xenophobia. Whatever Canada and Canadians might aspire to be, "underneath the sanitized garb of a postmodern, multiracial, multiethnic 'tolerant' Canada, beats the heart of a stubbornly colonial national-formation, sharing a common imaginary with other white settler societies" (Thobani 29). Even when there are more positive representations of the Other, Thobani argues that this positivity is often framed within their similarities to the Canadian subject. Both critics desire that we move away from an exalted self and imagine a nation that no longer treats the Other as a contrast to the self-described progressive Canadian subject.

This politics of false recognition combined with the exalted self results in an exploitive and insidious relationship between the Canadian government and the Other. Glen Coulthard's *Red Skin, White Masks: Rejecting the Colonial Politics of Recognition* articulates the manipulative and reductive ways in which the Canadian state observes and interacts with Indigenous communities. Even though the government appears convivial and apologetic for past wrongs, it still imposes an insidious form of power through colonialism. Coulthard writes: "[I]n situations where colonial rule does not depend solely on the exercise of state violence, its reproduction instead rests on the ability to entice Indigenous peoples to identify, either implicitly or explicitly, with the profoundly asymmetrical and nonreciprocal forms of recognition either imposed on or granted to them by the settler state and society" (25). As opposed to having a relationship formed out of mutual respect and reciprocity, Indigenous people are still not seen as equal and independent of the Canadian state. Coulthard highlights how the politics of recognition can be profoundly damaging: "Thus, much like Hegel before him, Taylor argues that human actors do not develop their identities in 'isolation.' Rather they are 'formed' through 'dialogue with others, in agreement or struggle with their recognition of us.' However, given that our identities are formed through these relations, it also follows that they can be significantly deformed when these processes go awry" (Coulthard 29). For Coulthard, there is no possible way that a government that exploits land to extract resources can coexist in a healthy way with Indigenous communities. He argues: "For Indigenous nations to live, capitalism must die. And for capitalism to die, we must actively participate in the construction of Indigenous alternatives to it" (173). The state can attempt to be as convivial and apologetic as possible, but if its interests are asymmetrical to Indigenous ways of being, then there is no possibility for a beneficial politics of recognition.

Moving away from the exalted subject involves taking an honest look at Canada's history and highlighting BIPOC authors, among others. These identities are complex and multiform, and they trouble the idea of fixed or uniform group identities. For example, Walcott writes: "[W]hen I use the term blackness, I mean to signal blackness as a sign, one that carries with it particular histories of resistance and domination. But blackness is also a sign which is never closed and always under contestation" (27–8). An eminent Black scholar might articulate how Blackness is multiform and complex, but the state and its citizens impose a gaze that simplifies and categorizes. This is just one way in which identity is imposed on people through misrecognition. Phanuel Antwi, in his essay "Rough Play: Reading Black Masculinity in Austin Clarke's 'Sometimes, a Motherless Child' and Dionne Brand's *What We All Long For*," is evocative here:

> Through the multitude of literary and cultural texts circulating in mainstream consciousness, we quickly become aware that the singularity of an individual black man's performed subjectivity easily becomes obscured; the multiple faces that differentiate us barely emerge, or upon emergence, quickly get re-categorized as more alike than distinct. Because we do not quite know when we will become the suspicious black (male) subject under the eye of the law or when we will escape the fishbowl phenomenon of being watched, many of our movements tend to be calculated and guarded, so guarded that each movement seems strangely immobile. How can it be otherwise, when most of our parents remind us, daily, how dangerous it is "out there" for black folks? (Antwi 194)

Observing the disparity between the self-expression of BIPOC and the identities imposed on them is a vital step towards fighting misrecognition. If I am hearing Antwi clearly, however, the problem runs much deeper. BIPOC communities cannot really aspire towards self-expression and self-creation in the same way that non-BIPOC communities can. They have to negotiate their identities under "the eye of the law."

Thus, if there is going to be space for self-creation and self-expression, the idea of Canada and its surveillance structures needs serious reimagining. Barrett reworks historical failings of the national imaginary. Those who are not white have traditionally been on the margins of the nation-building process. This problem results not only from the erasure of Blackness but also from Canadian multiculturalism. In the imagining of the nation as welcoming and tolerant, he points out that "whiteness and racism in Canada are equally unmarked and invisible" (6). To rectify this lack of self-awareness, Barrett posits the importance of narrative in telling a more comprehensive story of Canada. He writes, "This blackening of the nation's history explicitly links the poetics and politics of these writers in an effort to intervene in the public sphere and to alter the meaning of blackness in the Canadian imaginary" (24). Narrative, in all of its contradictions, might offer a fuller representation of the country and its peoples. Not only do stories from Black authors encourage readers to listen to people who have often been ignored, but also they redescribe the national imaginary. Barrett writes, "Their narratives transform black absence into a transgressive form of presence that rewrites the nation from a black perspective" (25). One of the main battles for redescribing the Canadian national imaginary has been fought over representations of surveillance and policing. Barrett takes up the killing of Albert Johnson as one of his strongest examples: "Within the Canadian public sphere, Johnson's body becomes contiguous with black deviance and criminality. [Dionne] Brand and [Austin] Clarke transform the depiction of his body by imbuing him with a history and character that exceeds the mainstream media depiction of him as 'immaculate with his disaster' (Brand, *thirsty* ix)" (Barrett 21). For Barrett, narrative functions to critique and add nuance to the national imaginary. It offers not only an image of Blackness but also an image of whiteness from a Black perspective. If Canadians want to build an image of the country that unites more than it alienates, if they want a national identity that does not negate, exclude, pacify, or contain the Other, then they must listen closely.

Another way to counter a politics of false recognition is through a diasporic imaginary. Kamboureli, for example, discusses her conception of the diasporic critic as one whose "ethnic background cannot be reduced to a stable and essentially 'true' past, so her national identity as Canadian resists simplification" (22). Walcott also stresses the importance of diasporic sensibilities: "Diaspora sensibilities do something to that writing that is active and resistant. Diaspora sensibilities use the nation to make ethical claims and demands for social justice. Diaspora sensibilities speak to nations' limitations and demands nations be remade in a constant and restless ethical search for home. Home, in the diasporic framework, is an ethical place, not a narrative of containment" (23). Walcott resists limiting Blackness to one national discourse. He writes, "Nation-centred discourse can only be a trap that prohibits black folks from sharing common feeling, especially when common actions and practices of domination seem to present themselves time and again in different spaces/places/nations" (147). My study desires to incorporate this diasporic sensibility while also – perhaps contradictorily – accepting that we live in a massive bureaucratic structure known as Canada that profoundly influences the lives of those who live inside and outside of its borders. Books are remarkable pockets of space and time into which people can escape, into moments of self-expression and self-creation that amount to, among other things, alternative ways of being.

The national imaginary and the politics of false recognition are embedded within the metaphor of surveillance in that they function to simplify and sort. I find aspects of the theory behind Taylor's politics of recognition to be extremely persuasive. Kamboureli and Coulthard, however, dissect the ways in which this philosophy has malfunctioned when put into practice. For my part, I question the idea that I can accurately recognize the Other. I have faith in the processes of extended reading and writing, but I am also dubious about the idea that they grant me clear, functional understanding of individuals within a group. I am more confident that these processes help me identify the ways in which I have misrecognized and misunderstood others. The more I read, the more I realize how little I know. Therefore, instead of recognition, a politics of alterity, nuance, and indeterminacy guides my readings of the texts in this study.

Surveillance as Social Sorting: Categories Change the Future

The intersections of literature and surveillance are rich, but the essential distinction in this study is that surveillance simplifies as it sorts. Like the national imaginary, it provides the illusion of clear identity. Literature complicates these categories. Definitions of surveillance are contested, but any discussion of this topic must involve a close consideration of the relationship between those who observe and those who are observed. The authors of *Transparent Lives: Surveillance in Canada* define *surveillance* as "any systematic focus on personal information in order to influence, manage, entitle, or control those whose information is collected … Surveillance is a dominant organizational practice that often results in people being categorized in ways that facilitate different forms of treatment for different individuals. From Google to Homeland Security, from Revenue Canada to the RCMP, this sort of surveillance is central" (Bennett et al. 6). Maintaining national security, discussing individual privacy, and enforcing the law all fall into discussions of surveillance,[5] and discussions of policing and of surveillance

5 My hope for this book is that it takes a broad consideration of surveillance in contemporary society as represented through fiction. Surveillance studies sometimes risk becoming overly abstract, considering all forms of observation – anything from the television shows people enjoy to the data recorded in a history browser – to be surveillance. In this study I respect that surveillance has polymorphous qualities, but I also try to be as concrete as possible. The living, breathing individuals who act as the first point of contact between the state and human beings are police officers. Calls for defunding the police in texts such as Desmond Cole's *The Skin We're In* and Robyn Maynard's *Policing Black Lives* push this topic to the forefront of our national discourse. By bracketing the world of policing with the discourse on surveillance, I hope to give full consideration not just to those who are observed but also to the thoughts and feelings of those whose job it is to observe. Surveillance is more than just mining data; it is a system of government and corporate entities. Police services are tasked

are interconnected.[6] The key distinction is that policing is an apparatus of surveillance. Importantly, however one defines surveillance, the focus needs to be on the relationship between the observer and the observed. In "Struggling with Surveillance: Resistance, Consciousness, and Identity," John Gilliom argues: "[Surveillance] is a watching over, which means that there must be both watcher and the watched. A tour of the field suggests that we have been particularly good at studying the watchers – the police, the CCTV operators, etc. – but not so good at the necessarily messier, less institutionalized, and exploratory but absolutely crucial job of studying the watched" (126). Gilliom stresses the harmful effect of surveillance on those who are being observed, simplified, and sorted. The observer tends to be part of an organization or institution, and the observed tends to be an individual or a group of individuals who have been profiled in some way. Thus, there is a clear power dynamic to surveillance in that categories and definitions have implications. The eye of surveillance looks down from above; those who are being watched often feel unfairly defined by the way they are being observed. It reduces the amount of agency they feel in the creation of their own identities.

Social sorting negatively affects certain groups far more than others. In "Forgotten Surveillance: Covert Human Intelligence Sources in Canada in a Post-9/11 World," Steve Hewitt wryly observes: "To put it in more real-world terms, I as a white, Euro-Canadian, middle-class male with slightly left-of-centre political views and agnostic religious beliefs have, through privilege, little to fear from blanket surveillance. Conversely, a change to one or several of those characteristics, such as religious belief, and suddenly a convergence can occur with the characteristics of a marginalized category that has been mapped onto the notion of a 'threat' by structures of power. As a result, this shift can lead to far more intrusive surveillance and direct consequences as opposed to simply the collection of data" (46).

My own categories are almost exactly the same as Hewitt's description. I do not have to fear surveillance on a personal level. However,

with so much more than protecting people; they are sometimes forced to protect government and corporate entities instead of those people. In considering surveillance from the perspective of those who surveil as well as those who are surveilled, this study hopes to push the discourse on Canada's national identity to complex, perhaps uncomfortable discussions about the types of assumptions we make.

6 Jean-Paul Brodeur and Stéphane Leman-Langlois discuss, in "Surveillance Fiction or Higher Policing," how surveillance has been traditionally viewed as part of the policing apparatus.

in *The New Politics of Surveillance and Visibility*, Richard Ericson and Kevin Haggerty highlight that not all Canadians have this privilege: "Although surveillance is now directed at all social groups, not everyone is monitored in the same way or for the same purposes. Different populations are subjected to different levels of scrutiny according to the logic of particular systems. Among the more contentious population categories used by surveillance systems are racial or ethnic identities" (14). Despite the fact that I have little to worry about on an individual level, as a nation we should still aspire to be ethical even if we have not been so in the past. Surveillance as it currently influences the life choices of BIPOC and LGBTQ+ (lesbian, gay, bisexual, transgender, and queer)[7] communities is profoundly unethical. Therefore, the damage caused by these systems needs to be clearly articulated, and the systems themselves need to be recalibrated.

Even though Hewitt's and my own categories allow us to avoid intense scrutiny, social sorting is still closely connected to identity formation and is worthy of attention. Some of these descriptors are political. Instead of *Euro-Canadian*, one might choose to say *settler Canadian* in order to highlight Canada's colonial past. Furthermore, one might not be satisfied by how much a category confines one to a particular moment. For example, I might shift throughout my life between agnosticism and Christianity. Again, I have nothing to fear from making public my own wavering religious belief, but my faith is deeply important to my sense of self. As the authors of *Transparent Lives* write: "Having a sense of control over our public persona is vitally important, as are the ways in which we are profiled and categorized, because such processes have an impact on our life chances and choices. We are treated differently depending on our profiles, and such treatment, in turn, changes our present and our future. This is social sorting" (Bennett et al. 4). Thus, while this book focuses on the people who are the victims of surveillance and sousveillance, this topic is relevant to all Canadians on the basic level of identity formation. The consequences of social sorting are more drastic for some than for others, but it modifies everyone's behaviour.

For those who exist outside of the strictly observed categories, surveillance might be frustrating, but for those who exist within them, surveillance is infuriating, frightening, and life altering. In *Dark Matters: On the Surveillance of Blackness*, Simone Browne demonstrates how surveillance in America results in systemic racism, particularly on Black

7 I am using *LGBTQ+* over other terms because in the time that I have been working on this book, the preferred letters and symbols have fluctuated. Placing an emphasis on the + feels like the smartest option to highlight inclusivity.

communities. She states that "black men between the ages of twenty and twenty-four are imprisoned at a rate seven times higher than white men of that age group," highlights "the various exclusions and other matters where Blackness meets surveillance, and then reveals the ongoing racisms of unfinished emancipation" (13). The consequences are not abstract or theoretical. They are concrete and life changing for all those who are simplified and categorized by their race. Browne is careful to focus on the ways in which race intersects with other categories such as gender, class, and location, which ultimately results in some people being more harshly observed than others. Too often these advantages and disadvantages are historically embedded in our society. Part of her project involves bringing these imbalances to light. In order to do so, she offers the concept of dark sousveillance, which "plots imaginaries that are oppositional and that are hopeful for another way of being" (21). Browne frequently but not exclusively looks to literary art, citing such authors as Dionne Brand and Lawrence Hill. These imaginaries might seem meagre in the face of massive and powerful bureaucratic structures, but they are vital for individuals and for communities who need to find hope in the future. In *Dear Science and Other Stories*, Katherine McKittrick highlights that digital surveillance in America not only sorts people into groups but also might lead to certain outcomes: "What we have is a system wherein black people are dehumanized in advance, and this dehumanization is hardened and made objective by mathematical codes" (113). To support her argument, she discusses the tragic story of Davonte Flennoy, an African American male deemed to be extremely high risk, and despite efforts to help him prove a predictive model wrong, he was shot and killed in 2012. McKittrick shows that in reducing people to categories, surveillance frames possibilities and channels behaviour. If not race and ethnicity, then one might worry about surveillance based on one's income bracket and location. Gilliom discusses his research of poor, rural, welfare mothers and argues that "for the [compliant] … [a surveillance program] is a beneficial or inconsequential gaze, for the [non-compliant] … it is a system of detection, judgment, and, often, punishment aimed at limiting freedom and channeling behaviour" (125). For those who are not white and male, the gaze of state is more intense. Davonte Flennoy's story is a haunting example of the predictive power of surveillance. It does not just observe; it creates environments and shapes our futures. To be fair, the state – whether it be Canada or the United States – needs to categorize and sort citizens; government organizations have distinct protocols and rules that they deem necessary to function and to maintain safety. However, it is logical and fair to expect some kind of dialogue. There need to be voices in our national conversation that complicate and add nuance to the voices that simplify and categorize. These are the voices whom I understand to be sources of a critical sousveillance.

Sousveillance as Dialogue: Looking Back at the Powerful

In the chapter on Lynn Coady, I discuss three different modes of sousveillance: community, literary, and digital. Until that chapter I am largely developing an ideal version of sousveillance, one that adds nuance and texture to state and corporate surveillance. One goal of sousveillance is to help the powerless resist feeling dominated by those in power. The pioneer of sousveillance is Steve Mann, but in his original conception Mann risks overlooking his own privileged position as an observer. In "'Sousveillance': Inverse Surveillance in Multimedia Imaging," Mann writes: "The term 'sousveillance' refers both to hierarchical sousveillance, e.g. citizens photographing police, shoppers photographing shopkeepers, and taxicab passengers photographing cab drivers, as well as personal sousveillance (bringing cameras from the lamp posts and ceilings, down to eye-level, for human-centered recording of personal experience)" (620). Mann views his own efforts in the field of sousveillance as an artistic practice, one that will hopefully inform and influence the surveillance industry (622). The exciting possibility here is that if one has access to particular technology and training, then one can observe the observers. However, some caution needs to be applied to Mann's original conception of sousveillance. Mann has time and money to make use of such materials. Not everyone can afford to take part in his artistic practices. Furthermore, he has altered his appearance and world view based on his own individual preference. He writes that "through simply a personal desire to live in a computer mediated world, [I] encountered hostilities from paranoid security guards, seemingly afraid of being held accountable" (625). Some people are sorted into categories at birth. They do not choose to draw attention to themselves. This distinction between choice and the absence of choice is key to the discourse on surveillance and sousveillance. Some people do not want and cannot afford to have any more attention directed their way, while others delight in experimentation. Contrary to this original example of sousveillance, there are stronger models of resistance. Jan Fernback, in "Sousveillance: Communities of Resistance to the Surveillance Environment," highlights, "the Tony Blair watch, a sousveillance collective created by The Guardian to monitor Blair; ihollaback.org, a resistance movement using mobile technologies to end street harassment of women and LGBT individuals; and resistance efforts in Ghana whereby voters who were prevented from voting used mobile phones to report their experience to call-in shows on local radio stations" (20). The key difference between these instances and Mann's version of sousveillance is that Mann's practice has a whiff of decadence, whereas Fernback discusses examples that are far more urgent. Nevertheless, sousveillance is multiform and dynamic. Whether or not the observer is privileged, if they create the potential for discourse with the state and corporate entities, then they are practising sousveillance.

At its core, sousveillance is really about the possibilities of watching from below. The state simplifies and categorizes. Those who sousveil observe and describe this social sorting, highlighting the misrecognized. An essential, often contested component to the theory of surveillance and sousveillance is the panopticon as developed by Jeremy Bentham and much later by Michel Foucault. Essentially, the panopticon was first conceived as a prison system where the few could watch the many. This structure makes it incredibly difficult for the observed to look back. Foucault's conception of the panopticon became a metaphor to describe the way in which citizens feel scrutinized and alter their behaviour. The basic contrast between Bentham and Foucault is that Bentham thought that being watched could help people to be positive contributors to society (Bentham 200), but Foucault considered observation to be restrictive to identity formation (Foucault 207). A host of scholars such as Browne and McKittrick demonstrate that Foucault's conception of the world remains pertinent. His panopticon articulates the ways in which the state dominates the identities of its subjects. Thomas Mathiesen, in "The Viewer Society: Michel Foucault's 'Panopticon' Revisited," observes one way that average people look back. In his description of synopticism Mathiesen discusses "a striking parallel to the panoptical process, and concurring in detail with its historical development, we have seen the development of a unique and enormously extensive system enabling the many to see and contemplate the few" (219). Although sousveillance is indebted to this concept of synopticism, I also want to consider whether or not those who surveil on behalf of the state experience power in simple or uniform ways. Some must feel like they have little choice or control over their own sense of self. Furthermore, it seems that the perspective of Bentham has been distorted over time.[8] In his description of the panopticon, the few are

8 For an extended critique on the ways in which Bentham has been misread in contemporary surveillance studies, David Rosen and Aaron Santesso's *The Watchman in Pieces: Surveillance, Literature, and Liberal Personhood*, particularly the chapter "The Liberal Panopticon," is an excellent resource.

not necessarily in positions of power. Whatever Bentham's concept for prison reform became, it started as a way for people from all parts of society to observe and take part. In "Outline of a Plan for the Management of a Panopticon Penitentiary-House," Bentham writes: "[B]y that peculiarity of construction, which, without any unpleasant or hazardous vicinity, enables the whole establishment to be inspected almost at a view, it should be my study to render it a spectacle, such as persons of all classes would, in the way of amusement, be curious to partake of; and that not only on Sundays at the time of divine service, but on ordinary days at meal times or times of work: providing thereby a system of inspection, universal, free, and gratuitous, the most effectual and permanent of all securities against abuse" (200). Bentham is not solely talking about a prison guard being the watcher; he is talking about observers being from every part of society. Foucault's panopticon is a way of imagining how the powerful use observation to maintain control over society; sousveillance is not simply an inversion of surveillance; while acknowledging the limits of the gaze from below, sousveillance also strives to observe with indeterminacy, nuance, and alterity.

To use books to enact sousveillance might seem problematic. It is debatable whether or not the written word actually allows readers to observe the Other. Books might just indoctrinate and pacify us. Deeply informed by Foucault's work, D.A. Miller's landmark study *The Novel and the Police* argues that as a form the novel operates through clear demarcations between the normal and the deviant. Those who are deviant are punished, and those who follow the rules of the status quo are rewarded. In this way, novels encourage readers to evaluate their own desires and conform to the values in the world of the novel (216). Readers imagine they are being watched and adjust their behaviour accordingly. In this sense Miller demonstrates how Foucault's argument on panoptic discipline can be applied to the novel. Browne articulates how the control offered by the panopticon is distinct from spectacle and functions in a similar way to how Miller describes the power of literature: "The Panopticon would allow for a disciplinary exercise of power. Such exercises of power are not ones of pomp and pageantry, like a queen's coronation, a state funeral, or a royal wedding, or of the overt kind of spectacular violence that often accompanies sovereign power. Instead, in this instance, power is covert and achieved by a play of light" (Browne 34–5). In this sense the slow, subtle persuasion of the panopticon is distinctly literary in its influence. Although Miller's observations of the Victorian novel might be accurate, the novels in this study often break down social norms and challenge the status quo. Authors spend considerable amounts of time demonstrating how an action might be perceived as deviant by the state or the community but might be necessary or understandable based on an individual's situation. If Foucault's panopticon is substituted for Bentham's original descriptions – in which members of a community observe – then books might rightfully be considered a source of sousveillance. In spending prolonged periods of time contemplating the interiority of others, novels have potential to help readers be more thoughtful and sympathetic. Miller positions the reader as a prisoner within their own society, but the desired outcome of my study would position readers as part of a community of observers who direct their gaze not only at the powerful but also at the Other in its various manifestations.

Indeterminacy, openness, and alterity are the focus of this ideal version of sousveillance, which seeks to break down categories and to add nuance. Questioning the power of literature as a path to understanding the Other, Dionne Brand argues that the Western tradition falsely presents itself as a rational project ever reaching towards a better, kinder world. However, the qualities of literature that hook readers are often related to their passions and anxieties. She states: "Writing is an act of desire, as is reading. Why does someone enclose a set of apprehensions within a book? Why does someone else open that book if not because of the act of wanting to be wanted, to be understood, to be seen, to be loved?" (*Map to the Door of No Return* 192). To understand the Other, one does not simply pick up a handful of books and read. The act of reading and writing is far more complicated than a direct transfer of the knowledge the author intends to communicate. Readers have personal histories, idiosyncrasies, anxieties, hopes, and fears that all influence how a book might alter or enrich their views. Brand argues that, instead of a direct transfer of knowledge, "books leave gestures in the body; a certain way of moving, of turning, a certain closing of the eyes, a way of leaving, hesitations. Books leave certain sounds, a certain pacing; mostly they leave the elusive, which is all the story. They leave much more than the words" (*Map to the Door of No Return* 191). In this sense, reading and writing are far more about desire than about understanding the Other and improving the self. For Brand, desire can never be rationalized or fully understood. Therefore, the changes resulting from the act of reading and writing cannot be reduced to simple description. Nevertheless, spending time with specific books encourages certain types of desiring, and for critics such as Wayne C. Booth and Marshall Gregory books are a particular type of company that change the self in tiny increments.[9]

9 Gregory writes: "As we respond to the world's invitations in this way or that way, we make up a self out of these responses because such responses configure – or, more accurately, they consistently reconfigure – our intellects, our beliefs, our emotions, and our ethical judgments" (*Redefining Ethical Criticism* 291).

Desire might resist being understood, but it can be pointed in specific directions, such as a desire to observe vulnerable people. For Jacques Derrida and Emmanuel Levinas, the imperative of philosophy is to give oneself to the Other.[10] One of the differences between scholars fitting into the Anglo-American tradition such as Booth, Nussbaum, and Gregory, or European philosophers such as Derrida, Levinas, and Critchley, is that one group tends to look for sameness and the other group tends to seek difference. This focus manifests as a search for empathy (Booth, Nussbaum, and Gregory) or alterity (Derrida, Critchley, and Levinas). I want to scrutinize empathy, as the possibility that I might think and feel as the Other. The possibility that a white, middle-class male living in Atlantic Canada might read a novel like *Brother* and feel exactly what Michael, the narrator, feels is delusional. My experience is mediated through the text. I feel safe and warm as I observe the narrator suffering through a cold and slushy Scarborough winter. However, if I respect the difference of the Other through alterity, then I might feel something like a measured sympathy. If readers consistently spend time imagining unfamiliar lives, they will hopefully see how people are more complex and textured than the stereotypes offered in the news and in other forms of popular media. They might understand how little they knew before. Reading texts gives us the opportunity to engage with the Other for extended periods of time,[11] and even though I might not be able to experience empathy, I might, as Namwali Serpell argues, make the leap towards it as I am reading, even though I will always fail. Serpell argues for "an extreme movement between empathy and alterity" (44), a kind of "flinging of the self toward the other that nevertheless recognizes its own futility and thus neither dissolves the self nor appropriates the other" (58). Thus, this book aims to contribute to the national imaginary and to the national ethos through a particular way of seeing. To actually look with care and clear eyes, one needs to acknowledge the intractable force of desire, the limitations of the self, and the impossibility of knowing the Other. As Serpell demands, however, we must always take the leap. That leap is the ideal of sousveillance.

---

10 Here I am thinking specifically of *Otherwise Than Being* and *Totality and Infinity* by Levinas; and "Violence and Metaphysics" by Derrida. I am also thinking of Critchley's *Ethics of Deconstruction*. What I derive from these texts is an ethical imperative to never reduce the Other to sameness.

11 Martha Nussbaum's *Poetic Justice* influences my thinking here in her argument that people can enjoy stories that narrate the lives of vulnerable people. There are many reading acts that do not have to involve engagement with the Other, and desire as it is articulated by Brand is far more powerful than rational thought. Nevertheless, there is great value to reading about people whose lives are different from our own.

Overview of the Book's Parts

In the first part I expand on the ethics of sousveillance and develop a theoretical framework for the multiple, conflicting ways in which narrative might inform readers. The literary gaze offers key insights into the ethics of watching and being watched. Michael Winter's *This All Happened* exemplifies how the literary gaze, despite its occasional cruelties, often escapes categorizing and simplifying. State and corporate surveillance function by defining and sorting people into groups. However, the literary text, with its ambivalence and uncertainty, is always subject to new and amorphous interpretations. Winter's novel will be presented as an example of sousveillance when it is actually put into practice. His narrator, Gabriel English, exemplifies the opportunities and pitfalls of sousveillance for literary artists who desire to observe the contemporary surveillance state. In the first chapter of this part, *This All Happened* will be used to cultivate a philosophy of sousveillance, not exclusively as an idealistic counterpoint but as an important voice in a broader discourse about Canada.

In the second chapter of part 1, the aesthetic strategies of four poets will be discussed to show different ways in which sousveillance can disrupt or inform the gaze of surveillance. In Ken Babstock's *On Malice* and A.F. Moritz's *The Garden*, both poets highlight the trouble with distance between the observer and the observed. Personal data of private citizens is gathered from afar by corporations and government agencies, not by people who know and care for those who are being observed. Babstock's poem "Perfect Distant Blue Objects" critiques William Hazlitt's nuanced but idealistic argument in "Why Distant Objects Please." Resembling encrypted intelligence, Babstock's text is dense and challenging, which frustrates the attempt to easily find meaning, and instead encourages indeterminacy and an intense close reading. There appears to be a host of impossible metaphors that problematize the attempt to make sense of the data gathered. Moritz, by contrast, wrestles with his detachment from news of racialized violence while also still feeling drawn to consider it in some meaningful way. He writes, "The very fact of the television news, but also its obvious inadequacies, its partialities and limitations of viewpoint, emphasized to me my own troubling co-presence with and separation from the unrest" (71). Taken together, these two texts will be used to discuss key issues in contemporary aesthetics as they relate to distance and surveillance. Distance, however, can be beneficial. Larissa Lai and Rita Wong use distance as an opportunity to safely compose their thoughts and to critique the status quo. Wong and Lai are female minorities who are openly queer. To these two poets, even when we are away from one another, we are always connected through objects, through technology, and through animals. Breaking down the boundaries of distance through digital and literary sousveillance involves giving oneself over to new ways of imagining the self.

In the third chapter of part 1, Lynn Coady's work demonstrates shifts from community sousveillance to literary sousveillance to digital sousveillance. The concepts of autonomy and responsibility are employed to discuss the oscillation that people often go through in the process of identity formation. *Strange Heaven* follows Bridget Murphy as she attempts to resist a repressive and strictly gendered community gaze. Inevitably, when one looks with care at one person, other individuals are ignored. Coady's *Mean Boy* and *The Antagonist* articulate how writers can be at once caring and sympathetic in their gaze to some but cruel and dehumanizing to others. The narrator in *Mean Boy* desires to be a celebrated author, and in order to achieve this greatness, he believes he must free himself of all influence from writers whom he once considered his heroes. *Mean Boy* is a Künstlerroman with satirical qualities, in which the young artist moves from adolescence into maturity. *The Antagonist* shifts this gaze from the writer to someone who has been written about. Rank, the narrator of *The Antagonist*, describes the pain of being misrecognized by a friend. In "Someone Is Recording," Coady narrates an increasing divide between two influencers on opposite ends of a political spectrum. The polarizing gaze of digital sousveillance is critiqued in this short but powerful story. Sousveillance is no simple panacea to surveillance and can be just as dismissive and repressive in specific situations. In part 1, these texts will be used to cultivate a philosophy of seeing and being seen. However, the narrators, the characters, and the authors are not always the people who need to worry most about how and why they are being watched. Aside from Lai and Wong, they tend to be straight, white, and middle class. The tension and the anxiety expressed is significant and deserves attention. However, the stakes are higher for BIPOC and LGBTQ+ Canadians.

The second part of this study considers how, for BIPOC and LGBTQ+ individuals living in Canada, direct contact with surveillance and with police can be stressful and intimidating. Officers have the difficult job of observing citizens and arresting people who break the law. However, the gaze of Canadian police is overly directed at young, male minorities.[12] When interactions between young, male minorities and police

12 In "Disproportionate Minority Contact in Canada," Robin T. Fitzgerald and Peter J. Carrington write: "First, disproportionate minority contact was reported by this nationally representative sample of Canadian youth aged 12–17 years. Specifically,

turn violent, Canadians might read about a young man being shot by the police, but they cannot really appreciate how the victim's family struggles long after the headlines have faded from mainstream media. As studied in chapter 4, Chariandy's *Brother* brings such headlines to life. He articulates how one group of young, Black men feel about being unfairly watched. This surveillance from the police, which leads to the death of Francis, the narrator's brother, results in a long and painful grieving process. In *Brother*, Chariandy highlights the anger from feeling unfairly scrutinized, while paradoxically encouraging Canadians to observe a broken family after the moment many would look away.

Where *Brother* narrates the interaction between young men of colour and the police, Sharon Bala's *The Boat People* is about a group of migrants coming into contact with the full force of the Canadian government and the media, as we will see in chapter 5.[13] Mahindan, a Sri Lankan

---

youth belonging to a high-risk visible minority category (that is, youth identified as Aboriginal, Black, and West Asian racial/ethnic origin) were approximately three times more likely than other youth to report having had contact with the police in the past year. We feel that this is a conservative estimate of DMC in Canada, given that other Canadian research has demonstrated significant overrepresentation of particular minority groups at different stages of the justice system. For example, the odds of an Aboriginal person being identified by the police as an offender were nearly seven times higher than the odds for a non-Aboriginal person in a central Canadian city (Fitzgerald and Carrington 2008); the representation of Aboriginal people in … custody in Canada is generally about seven times greater than their representation in the population (Beattie 2006; Brzozowski et al. 2006; La Prairie 1992; Roberts and Melchers 2003); and the representation of Black people in federal incarceration is over three times greater than their representation in the Canadian population (Wortley 1999)" (472).

13 In *Refugee States*, Vinh Nguyen and Thy Phu provide helpful distinctions between the terms *migrant*, *refugee*, and *immigrant*: "Consider, for example, 'migrant,' a term that intersects with and yet is often considered distinct from 'immigrant' and 'refugee.' Indeed, not all migrants are immigrants, the latter usually understood as subjects who enter the nation-state through legally sanctioned mechanisms and who are expected to contribute to the economic and social development of the nation and to remain indefinitely – a process that refugees can also undergo. Migrant is a term often employed to designate those who are undocumented, or stateless, or holding temporary or precarious legal status, among other categories. Refugees are, at times, understood as migrants. At highly politicized moments, however, refugees are considered distinct from migrants. The relationship between the two categories is contentious. The term 'economic migrant' is used in many instances to deny refugee claims, according to national protectionists who seek to disqualify applicants on the grounds that migrants who move for better economic opportunities cannot be considered refugees, who are deemed to be politically persecuted. Given these conflations, refuge(e) must be considered neither in hermeneutic isolation nor as historically fixed categories, but rather as porous concepts and flexible subjectivities" (7).

refugee, falls for the dream of Canada, but he is confronted by the cold machine of the Canadian state that places him behind bars and brands him a potential terrorist. Sharon Bala brings the system of government surveillance to life, one that sorts those who are welcomed into this country and those who are not. Readers are encouraged to critique the idea of Canada as a warm, inviting place and to rivet their eyes to the cold bureaucracy of the state. *The Boat People* is an act of sousveillance, looking back at this country from below.

Justin Ling's *Missing from the Village* is the sole work of non-fiction in this study. It demonstrates the real-life stakes of surveillance and of policing vulnerable groups. Detailing the search for a serial killer in Toronto's queer community, Ling's text also focuses on the way in which the LGBTQ+ community has been unjustly observed by the Toronto Police Service. *Missing from the Village* intersects with *The Boat People*, because multiple victims of the serial killer were immigrants to Canada. Ling has the opportunity to conclude his book, as a work of non-fiction, with a convincing argument for concrete changes to the Toronto Police Service and to public policy, while also acknowledging the good work that many police officers do. Overall, my study operates under the comfortable assumption that fiction helps people imagine the lives of others. When they are observing victims in *Missing from the Village*, more is asked of readers. There is a sense that one might be trespassing and gawking. True crime should haunt readers with the aura of lives traumatically altered.

One of the strengths of Ling's *Missing from the Village* is the way he balances his criticism of the Toronto Police Service with praise of specific officers. My study strives for a similar approach in part 3 by looking with a generous gaze at those who surveil. Richards's *Principles to Live By* represents a shift in the study, in chapter 7, in that it considers the effect of the public eye on the mental health of police officers. If sousveillance is a worthy response to surveillance, then the repercussions of this gaze should be fully considered. In Richards's imagined world some officers rise to the pressure of being watched and others crumble. A dichotomy is developed between the heroic officer John Delano and the corrupt Sergeant Melonson, who abuses his position of power. John struggles with post-traumatic stress disorder (PTSD), and he can be read as the archetype of the contemporary fictionalized police officer – overworked and on the edge.

Katherena Vermette's *The Break* narrates the investigation of a sexual assault against a young girl, Emily Traverse. Through her descriptions of the police Vermette narrates the way in which the Canadian government surveils Emily's family members, who mainly live in Winnipeg's

North End. Chapter 8 contextualizes the novel among a broader debate in Canada about how the settler state interacts with Indigenous people, highlighting its troubled history of surveillance and policing. It also traces the significance of one officer's Métis identity in his connecting with the victim and her family during the investigation. Vermette narrates the experience of a young officer, Tommy Scott, who believes in the work he does, but at the same time he has to fight against racism in his own police department.

Dealing largely with digital surveillance and terrorism, *Foreign Radical,* produced by Theatre Conspiracy, encourages viewers to take part in the performance. As the only study of a play in this book, chapter 9 will consider the importance of performance and audience in relation to surveillance and the literary arts. In situating the audience in the decision-making process, this participatory play challenges readers and viewers who detach themselves from the ethical and moral implications presented by a text and by their country. *Foreign Radical* allows us to return to the idea of the didactic spectacle. If we pay close attention, we might struggle to think of ourselves as innocents in the world of surveillance.

PART ONE

Developing an Ethics of Sousveillance

1 Michael Winter's *This All Happened*: The Artist as Imperfect Model for Sousveillance

Those who are subject to the gaze of a literary artist might find the experience pleasant; others might find it distressing. So much depends on the author and on the person being watched. Michael Winter's *This All Happened* exemplifies the complex, slippery nature of the literary gaze. Structured as a fictional diary, with the narrator, Gabriel English, penning daily entries about his life in St John's, Newfoundland, Winter's novel teases an autobiographical allure that is akin to gossip. The voyeuristic qualities of the novel caused somewhat of a stir in St John's when it was first published. In "The Rock Observed: Art and Surveillance in Michael Winter's *This All Happened*," Chris Armstrong writes that Winter's friends and family felt they had been unfairly written about and they were offended: "'Fiction' like this didn't sit well with real people in St. John's, especially those acquainted with the author; one member of Winter's circle threatened him with a punch in the nose for prying and publishing" (37–8). As time has passed, diverse responses to Winter's journal à clef have emerged. Some people were upset; others were indifferent, and some were flattered (Mathews). For example, in *This Is My Country, What's Yours?* Noah Richler reports a conversation he had with two people who were the basis for one of Winter's characters:

> "What Michael did brilliantly ... is that he put so many of the St. John's characters and experiences into the book and yet never has anyone ever felt kind of like – well, *the next time I see him ...*"
>
> "The next time I see him, what?"
>
> "The next time I see him – *you know*."
>
> "Nobody feels that," said the one. (Richler 330)

Critics of *This All Happened* tend to describe the observations of Winter and of his narrator as a source of surveillance. An alternative reading through the metaphor of sousveillance questions how Winter's novel might signal a way for a private citizen to live strategically with contemporary surveillance. The literary impression parodies surveillance as an experience that is constantly subject to new interpretations; it is an amorphous thing that can never be fully captured and sorted.

Surveillance is a recurring theme in Winter's writing, and critics have read his work through this lens. Chris Armstrong, Paul Chafe in "Beautiful Losers: The Flâneur in St. John's Literature" and Peter Thompson in "Surveillance and the City in Michael Winter's *This All Happened*" have examined the observational practices of Gabriel in *This All Happened*. In Winter's *The Big Why*, Rockwell Kent is under the watch of the government for professing his love of German culture during the First World War. David Twombly gets a "no-fly caution" in *The Architects Are Here* when he says "something sarcastic about blowing up the plane" (132), and in *The Death of Donna Whalen* the actions of the Royal Newfoundland Constabulary are scrutinized. Surveillance takes many forms in Winter's novels, and one of its frustrating or intimidating elements tends to be its sorting and reducing of citizens into types. Surveillance technologies, such as CCTV (closed-circuit television), create the illusion of a concrete perception through the video recording of moments that could only otherwise be recalled through memory. Individuals can rewind to an event and witness it repeatedly; it appears as a real experience despite the fact that it lacks the interiority and the confusion of immediate perception. If a by-product of surveillance is ethical or moral certitude, then indeterminacy and irony frustrate the belief that what one sees or records is absolutely true. Although it may sound as though I am contrasting visual and verbal media, my overarching focus is on the relationship between artistic modes and governmental modes of observation. This chapter focuses on the literary impression because it tends to invite complex representations of character and to disrupt moral certainty. As Martha Nussbaum writes in *Poetic Justice*, "When simplified conceptions of the human being are in widespread use for predictive purposes, it is all the more important to keep reminding ourselves of the richer picture of human life to which such simplified models are ultimately accountable" (47). My definition of indeterminacy for this chapter is a moment or moments in which an observer cannot be certain of what he or she sees; this definition derives from Mikhail Bakhtin's usage of the term in "Epic and Novel" when he discusses how "the novel inserts into … other genres an indeterminacy, a certain semantic openendedness, a living contact with unfinished, still evolving contemporary reality (the openended present)" (Bakhtin, *Dialogic Imagination* 6–7). In contrast to the novel form, surveillance technologies tend to sort and categorize (Armstrong 48), and they "eliminate the variability of territory" (Thompson 73). My definition is also informed by Wolfgang Iser's "Indeterminacy and the Reader's Response in Prose Fiction" since I follow his argument that indeterminacy is cultivated through specific aesthetic choices that encourage reader participation (6). I am using Linda Hutcheon's definition of irony in "Irony, Nostalgia and the Postmodern" as the moment "when two meanings, one said and the other unsaid, come together, usually with a certain critical edge" (par. 15). The indeterminacy of the present and the irony of the reading experience permeate *This All Happened*. Readers are actively encouraged through the author's – and occasionally the diarist's – aesthetic choices to participate in critiques of how one writer observes and describes his world.

Criticism on *This All Happened* characterizes Gabriel's diary as a source of surveillance, and one question that tends to be asked about this text is whether or not Gabriel is an ethical observer. Armstrong and Thompson both consider art's compliance with or resistance to the ways in which societies observe and judge citizens. Armstrong expands on Paul Chafe's representation of Gabriel as a flâneur, or one who "is amongst the crowd, but not part of it ... both participant and recorder, a roving reporter who maintains critical distance even as he threatens to melt into the masses" (Chafe 119–20). Analysing the ways in which surveillance stifles class mobility, Armstrong uses *This All Happened* to question whether or not literary artists can compete with the ever-growing technological eye of judgment. Thompson highlights the ways in which Gabriel uses art to further his own interests and to gain control over his friends and family in social situations. For him, Gabriel represents a figure transitioning from the old ways of surveilling people to newer forms such as CCTV. My central point of contention to these esteemed and perceptive critics is that surveillance is not the best metaphor to describe Gabriel's and Winter's observations. Art can certainly be a tool of social coercion, as Chafe, Armstrong, and Thompson all show; however, Gabriel generally adds texture through his observations of others. Even though he receives state funding through an arts grant, his allegiances are to his craft and to his aesthetic sensibilities, not to his government or to a corporation. This obsession with his writing makes him occasionally snobbish and even cruel but not an agent of state or corporate supervision. Thus, I will consider whether or not authors can be a source of sousveillance, a far more appealing concept for those who are interested in resisting abuses of social control or in productively cooperating with the powers that be when it might prove beneficial.

Armstrong questions whether or not artists have the capacity to resist the stifling elements of surveillance through their creative action. He demonstrates the effects of various kinds of observation in *This All Happened*, and he elucidates the systemic problems of surveillance technologies. Acknowledging that contemporary society depends on surveillance to produce a sense of security, he points out that it becomes problematic when it is used as a tool by those who are in positions of power to reinforce hierarchical social structures (Armstrong 39). Armstrong is not confident about the potentiality of art as a means of opposition to ways in which visual technologies define and objectify human beings: "I want to view Gabriel's aesthetic stance alongside the threats to identity and personhood posed by electronic surveillance, specifically, the electronic (video and digital) data-image, while also suggesting that the prospects of resistance staged in the precincts of art, at least for Gabriel and perhaps his fellow cultural producers, seem severely limited, and dubious at best" (Armstrong 48–9). One response to the technological objectification of human beings through surveillance would be a textured and subjective account of an individual's experience. Even more appropriate, this literary resistance would concern the individual's idiosyncratic contemplations of various forms of surveillance. Armstrong anticipates this argument and rejects it: "In Gabriel's implicitly social vision, the artist collects and transforms moments of experience in his art, redistributing them in the primitive social currency of the gift. Exchanged by mutually authoring subjects, the literary impression, moreover, contrasts the data image and the electronic network, with the latter's one way transmission of information, its categories confined to observed (not lived or shared) action, and its potentially wide dispersion and destructive effects" (50). Armstrong's cynicism about this form of resistance is rooted in Gabriel's representation of himself as a specific type of artist. In this sense, Armstrong echoes a similar critique to Chafe's observation of Gabriel as a flâneur. The fact that the artist can be identified as a type frustrates the attempt to be a unique recorder of experience. For Armstrong, Gabriel is not simply a flâneur but also, expanding on the various types, "a clownish misfit, a portrait of the artist as media cliché or commodity, at best perhaps an ironized romanticism" (51). His experience loses its subjectivity and its individuality as a result. He becomes a composite of the available data on artist types rather than a unique and idiosyncratic creator. The texture of his experience is reduced to a minor variation on a major cliché. Ultimately, however, Armstrong is ambivalent about the potentiality of art as a form of resistance to ubiquitous surveillance technologies. Although he is dubious about Gabriel, he offers some hope in Winter's authorial position: "Winter senses the limitations of art and of a humanistic response to surveillance, yet despite its deficiencies art satisfies the socially instituted pleasures of seeing and being seen, of knowing and being known" (Armstrong 51). To redirect this thread of Armstrong's argument, this chapter emphasizes the way in which Winter develops *This All Happened* to encourage irony and indeterminacy.

While Armstrong focuses on the potentiality of art as a form of resistance, Thompson illustrates the ways in which Gabriel uses writing as a method to gain control over his surroundings. He argues that Gabriel represents a transitionary phase in theories of surveillance, from the subjective interpersonal note-taking of individuals to the objective data gathering made possible by new technologies such as CCTV: "[Winter's] … protagonist in *This All Happened* finds in surveillance a strategy for preserving traditional forms of community and sealing off Newfoundland to outsiders. The text offers on the one hand a critique of the impersonal nature of contemporary forms of surveillance and an uneasy analysis of Newfoundland's 'ironic' urban culture on the other" (Thompson 72). Where Armstrong is dubious about the use of art as a form of resistance to visual technologies, Thompson sees journal writing as an outmoded tool of social control. Textured subjectivity does not reveal human fallibility or the hypocrisy of one individual's gaze. Instead, the literary impression elucidates the ways in which people use art as an avenue to gain power and influence: "While his obsession with surveillance is closely related to his aesthetic vision – he tells Lydia at one point that his binoculars 'make colour appear' and 'create sound' (70) – Gabe seems less interested in the way in which this activity informs his writing and more concerned with using the information he gleans from observing the city to his advantage in social situations" (Thompson 77–8). Thompson brings up a valid concern in relation to the importance of art as a form of resistance to surveillance technologies. If art provides writers with cultural authority or interpersonal advantages, then there will be people who will abuse these benefits. However, the construction of *This All Happened* invites readers to observe Gabriel in his authorial position. In this sense, Winter encourages a certain vigilance against those who seek control through their observational and descriptive practices.

To shift Armstrong's and Thompson's observations of *This All Happened*, I will use sousveillance rather than surveillance to describe the writing of Winter and of Gabriel. Like *surveillance*, *sousveillance* is an ambivalent term. However, it does have more positive connotations in the placing of greater power in the hands of individuals who feel disenfranchised by surveillance technologies. If citizens become more aware of how they watch and are watched by others, then these citizens will have more choice in how they want to interact with various manifestations of surveillance and sousveillance. Two qualities in Winter's text that encourage a productive sense of watching and being watched are indeterminacy and irony because they invite readers to consider what Nussbaum might call "the richer picture of human life" (47). At no point do I suggest that sousveillance is absolutely opposite and separate from surveillance. A synonym for *sousveillance* in this book is *parodic surveillance*. In using *parodic*, I am not referencing its comedic connotations as a type of burlesque (Abrams 26); I am referencing Linda Hutcheon's definition in "The Politics of Postmodernism: Parody and History": "What I mean by 'parody' here is not the ridiculing imitation of the standard theories and definitions that are rooted in eighteenth-century theories of wit. The collective weight of parodic practice suggests a redefinition of parody as repetition with critical distance that allows ironic signalling of difference at the very heart of similarity … this parody paradoxically enacts both change and cultural continuity: the Greek prefix para can mean both 'counter' or 'against' AND 'near' or 'beside'" (Hutcheon, "Politics of Postmodernism" 185–6). Thus, when I use the terms *sousveillance* or *parodic surveillance*, I aim to reference how sousveillance is counter but also cooperative and even complicit with surveillance. In one sense, Gabriel represents a clinging to traditional forms of communal observation, but he also makes use of newer surveillance technologies when necessary.

As argued in the introduction, the impersonal and the placeless eye of government and corporate surveillance can be supplemented by the ground level observations of people who value indeterminacy and irony. In "The Generalized Sousveillance Society" Jean-Gabriel Ganascia writes: "[T]he notion of a surveillance society, which many of our contemporaries still dread, does not seem to characterize the present state of our postmodern societies … This does not mean that surveillance has disappeared, but instead that the global organization of the surveillance society has been replaced by a new social organization, more flexible and fluid, where surveillance and what we can call 'sousveillance' coexist" (491). If private citizens have an increased potential to observe and to be aware of how they are observed, then this shift could put more agency in the hands of individuals who feel stifled and subjugated by surveillance. However, sousveillance does not truly counter power with power; it is a steady redefinition of power from below. To borrow Hutcheon's definition of parody, sousveillance might be best thought of as an "ironic signalling of difference at the very heart of similarity" (Hutcheon, "Politics of Postmodernism" 185). If people cannot balance the power to observe, then at least they might be able to parody the ways in which surveillance operates. Winter does this throughout *This All Happened* in his varied idiosyncratic descriptions of surveillance technologies. My hope is that this book does something similiar.

In this period of multilateral observation the literary impression could inform readers about the effects of watching and being watched. Novels reveal the nuances and the complexities of observation and description. However, the affect and the social influence of the novel are contested. Although Bakhtin argues that reading encourages a sense of openness in how one sees the world, we should return briefly to D.A. Miller who argues that the novel form creates stifling behavioural expectations. Even if the technological eye of judgment is multilateral, Miller in *The Novel and the Police* argues that the novelistic eye of judgement is typically unilateral. Miller's theory derives from Foucault's concept of panoptic discipline. Through a clear demarcation between the normal and the deviant, fiction imposes a set of traits onto the supposedly free, liberal subject. This discipline "provides the novel with its essential 'content'" (Miller 18) and makes fiction "the very genre of the liberal subject, both as cause and effect" (Miller 216). On the one hand, in his characterization of the novel, Miller represents the author as the individual lurking inside this three-tiered panoptic structure. On the other hand, one classic theoretical assumption about the novel is that it infuses static worlds with the openness and the uncertainty of the present. Despite the benefits of surveillance, one drawback is that observers who watch others via data collection or CCTV cameras do not experience their subjects' day-to-day lives. Bakhtin theorizes in "Epic and Novel," however, that when the novel intermingles with forms like the epic, it challenges the elevated nature of time-honoured stories, and it makes heroic characters far more human (Bakhtin, *Dialogic Imagination* 14). Essentially, the novel grounds readers in a contemporary and an indeterminate reality as opposed to the epic's basis in a concrete and distanced past: "[T]he entire world and everything sacred in it is offered to us without any distancing at all, in a zone of crude contact, where we can grab at everything with our own hands" (26). In this sense, Bakhtin's argument is prescient in its focus on the novel as a zone of contact between different realities. If Gabriel has the authority to demarcate the normal and the deviant, he does not have the comfort of a unidirectional gaze. He is under observation not only for what he writes but also for his position as an observer. Rather than an unseen official imposing a strict demarcation between the normal and the deviant, he is something closer to Bakhtin's characterization of the reader in novelistic discourse, an individual in "a zone of crude contact" subject to a host of competing wills (Bakhtin, *Dialogic Imagination* 26). In *This All Happened* the diary form is also being novelized alongside surveillance. The discourse of *This All Happened* suggests that diaries and fictional diaries parody surveillance technologies. They are not parodic, because they are more coherent or authentic than other forms of observation; they are parodic because they invite readers to observe the indeterminacies and the ironies of one individual's daily life.

To further demonstrate why sousveillance is a strong metaphor to understand *This All Happened*, Gabriel's style and the overall construction of Winter's text must be shown to possess elements of irony and indeterminacy. Both Armstrong and Thompson present convincing arguments about the literary artist as a source of surveillance. However, as I hope this chapter has shown so far, there are more optimistic ways to characterize the work of creative writers. The ironies of *This All Happened* are not always obvious, and they are generally not ones that Gabriel is aware of, but they highlight the fact that certain things are deliberately left unsaid by Winter. *This All Happened* asks readers to consider the overarching irony that even though Gabriel observes others, his life comes under the closest and most prolonged scrutiny because they are privy to his journal. When someone observes others in this text, he or she usually ends up being observed, and in this sense the very idea of observation becomes ironic. In contrast to the ironic elements of this novel, Gabriel is cognizant of the indeterminacy of certain moments, and the writing of these moments is often infused with metaphors. Description has the power to transform the way in which these moments are remembered; when these described moments are read or interpreted, they are transformed yet again. What results is an endless process of transformation. The categorizing and sorting mechanisms of state and corporate surveillance are opposite to this lively, amorphous, and liberating quality of literary language. Sousveillance is a far more apt description of the observational gaze created by Winter and by Gabriel.

As Gabriel more than any other character in *This All Happened* is under the closest scrutiny, his tendency to watch others is underwritten with a sense of irony. The text begins with a preface, written by Winter, in which he signifies Gabriel as a writer and a fictional character: "Gabriel English was the protagonist in a book of stories I wrote entitled *One Last Good Look*. Let me tell you about Gabriel English. He is a writer" (xii). Readers are thus encouraged from the beginning to observe Gabriel as an author figure and as a construction of Winter's imagination. His journal is one flawed individual's intimate and occasionally humiliating account of a year in his life. Imagine that you are looking into a window, and you see someone staring at you. The two of you are complicit in this gaze. The difference is that the person looking out is gazing into a public space, whereas you are gazing into a private world. As readers, we are gawking at an intimate window into Gabriel's life. Even if the narrator is not aware of his flaws and shortcomings, readers are invited to perceive them in his journal. Although he organizes and describes these moments, each reader has the opportunity to be sceptical about the ways in which this writer portrays himself. The gap between Gabriel's perceived self and the self he reveals through his actions is ironic, but it also encourages the reader to doubt the claims that Gabriel makes through writing. Part of the experience of reading This All Happened involves witnessing the ways in which one individual abuses his position as a powerful observer. James O'Rourke argues in *Sex, Lies, and Autobiography* that "literary works are uniquely capable of challenging the narratives that give our lives a sense of ethical coherence when their polysemic qualities – their ironies, ambiguities, and indeterminacies – falsify the central premise of moral philosophy, the presumption of a discernible continuity from ethical principle to practice in everyday life" (O'Rourke 1–2). Winter makes Gabriel's failings and occasional creepiness an observable element of the text. In the preface Winter states that Gabriel "confesses his failings, copies overheard drunken conversations ... [and] reports gossip" (xii). Gabriel's unethical practices of observation are a recurring theme of the text. This point becomes clear when he talks about spying on his girlfriend through a pair of binoculars. Sometimes he uses his position as observer to his own advantage, but he also describes these moments in his journal, which readers then observe. Stories such as *This All Happened* reveal that even though a person views himself as essentially good and decent, actions suggest otherwise: "This story of the good self is a narrative of interiority that centers on the feelings and intentions of the autobiographer ... this narrative of the good self is shadowed by an account of acts and consequences in which the autobiographer profits from the misfortunes of others and plays some role in the production of those misfortunes" (O'Rourke 2). The irreconcilability of these two selves invites a sense of uncertainty in how the narrator is understood, and it indicates that something is not being said about the way the narrator watches his community.

As the note-taker and composer of his journal, Gabriel would resemble Foucault's version of the panoptic, unidirectional watcher if not for the fact that he is marked as a writer. As the novel repeatedly demonstrates, those who observe tend to make themselves objects of scrutiny.

Since people know that Gabriel is an observer, they return his gaze and attempt to use him to their own ends. Winter writes: "[Oliver] is telling me this story because he knows I'm a writer. He is telling me this so I'll write it down. It's as though he knows Maisie Pye [Oliver's wife and Gabriel's friend] is writing about him and he wants to have a piece of the action" (Winter, *This All Happened* 42). Oliver wants to influence Gabriel's perception. As a writer, Gabriel becomes a potential conduit for Oliver to air private grievances in a public forum. Furthermore, Gabriel lives in a community where other people are observing and writing about their own experiences. Maisie Pye is a novelist, and Lydia Murphy, Gabriel's girlfriend, has a journal in which she records her own observations (89). More directly, Gabriel discusses how watching others can result in being watched: "I've been told that I have a critical eye. Some people mistake my gaze for judgement. When all I'm doing is looking into your eye" (23). Sometimes sousveillance is confrontational and antagonistic, but it is also playful and convivial. For example, Lydia gives Gabriel a doll in his likeness, and he is flattered. "I cry laughing," he writes (66). Alex Fleming, a love interest, gives him a Christmas present that encourages him to contemplate what it means to watch people: "The box has a glass front that's been sandblasted except for an eye, which you can look through. At the back of the box is another eye. It is a photograph of my eye" (269). In contrast to Miller's theory, novelistic discourse lacks the panoptic structure as discussed by Foucault if the author figure is a flawed individual who observes, manipulates, plays, and experiments while he is observed, manipulated, played upon, and experimented with – who is in crude contact with other human beings in their various complexities. As Gabriel narrates "the story of the good self" (O'Rourke 2), readers are invited to sousveil his actions, both good and bad. One of the most likely ways to make oneself a subject of observation is to be an observer. In this sense, observation itself takes on an ironic aspect. Thus, in many ways, if the writer is inside of a panoptic structure, then it would be Bentham's panopticon, and it is the various readers who serve as the community of watchers.

Aside from the overarching irony in the way that the text is constructed and the observers are almost always observed, there are subtler ironies. For example, Gabriel longingly describes the ways in which people in a small community watch each other. This description of Heart's Desire confides a nostalgia for an older Newfoundland,[1] one

1 This nostalgia might be surprising for some, but this scene in particular strikes me as one that captures a way of life in Newfoundland that is still held dear:

that existed before various technological innovations made contemporary surveillance possible. Armstrong writes: "Gabriel, clearly, yearns for a form of community in which surveillance figures as concern and care … this kind of yearning for community … can be read against the sinister and depersonalizing effects of (post)modern surveillance" (44). Likewise, Thompson uses this scene to highlight Gabriel's nostalgia for older forms of observation and of recording: "Gabe goes to great lengths to present himself in his diary entries as an 'ethical observer' interested in guarding traditional forms of social monitoring that exist in small communities" (83). Even though Gabriel yearns for these older ways of watching, his actions suggest that he also appreciates and values newer forms. For example, he writes on his laptop about this community. Winter has constructed this moment in the text to encourage readers to see that something is not being said by the narrator: Gabriel is posturing; he values new technology as a means to observe and record information. Yearning for and guarding the old ways of watching are outward elements of the diary; the reliance – sometimes begrudging reliance – on new ways of watching is an irony constructed by Winter. The use of a laptop to type up one's nostalgia for a time less reliant on electronic devices signifies Gabriel as a figure of parodic surveillance. He desires to be counter to the intrusions of contemporary society, but he is inevitably implicated in that which he aims to resist.

Further emphasizing his parodic relationship with surveillance, Gabriel relies on technological devices and on government supervision as a form of help. He and Lydia realize that someone is breaking into her house. CCTV cameras prove to be an annoyance, but they ultimately allow the police to catch the intruder. Furthermore, the police officers who installed them are portrayed sympathetically: "They are polite, ashamed if they have to do a little damage to the mouldings. The cameras are tiny, with high resolution. Apparently, there are three, though as soon as they are installed I cannot see them" (Winter, *This All Happened* 195). Gabriel's description of surveillance devices might seem oppressive and upsetting. However, Gabriel and Lydia both know where these cameras have been placed. Although Gabriel expresses

---

Josh [a boy Gabriel befriends] comes by on his bike with no handlebars. You like fish? He is steering with a set of vice grips clamped to the front fork.

I eat nine pieces of fish with slices of hot homemade bread. The fish is served from the stove. On the table are jars of tomato and rippled pickle slices. I have a mug of boiled water in which I can put a tea bag or a spoonful of instant coffee. There's a can of evaporated milk.

Josh's mom, Doreen, is rolling cigarettes at the table. (Winter, *This All Happened* 21)

annoyance about the cameras, he is subdued and his complaints are reasonable: "We eat with our fingers. Lydia says we can shut off the video system while we're in the house. But even so I feel monitored. There is one camera on the front door, one in the living room, and one in the kitchen" (201). This experience with surveillance does not appear to be a completely negative interaction. Gabriel does not wish to simply supplant newer forms of state supervision with traditional, communal observation; he values a human-centred way of observing others, but he cooperates with his government, and he makes use of new technologies. Surveillance and sousveillance coexist in *This All Happened*. Both ways of seeing are neither simply good nor bad but are complex forms of watching and being watched with distinct purposes, risks, and opportunities.

The style in which Gabriel chooses to describe his surroundings highlights the indeterminacy and the subjectivity of perception. Descriptions of events and of place are often fused with a secondary image. For example, when Lydia flies into St John's, she describes the waves as looking "like a thousand white sandwiches at a funeral" (Winter, *This All Happened* 36). Similarly, when Gabriel watches a city tractor piling snow against his fence, he writes, "The pickets lean and splinter, buttons on a fat man's gut" (62). When people watch, they make associative leaps, and visuals take on a metaphorical aspect. The view flying into St John's has connotations of death and loss, whereas the snow-clearing scene implies a sense of excess. The descriptions of these scenes communicate that there is an emotional and a subjective inner world of the observer. If the same moments were recorded via CCTV, they would lack this metaphorical aspect and this interiority. The literary language emphasizes the human centredness of sousveillance. What each person sees is radically subjective and influenced by their thoughts and feelings; one's inner world is powerful enough to transform waves into sandwiches or a fence into a fat man's gut. Winter's use of metaphor invites readers to think of observation and description not as a simple recording of events but as a transformative act. Thus, one should not be certain that what others write actually happened. Instead, such metaphorical language encourages a sense of indeterminacy.

Not only does Gabriel infuse the setting with metaphorical imagery, but also he states that writing is always a form of remembering. Perception is full of unexpected associative leaps, and the immediate moment of seeing is specifically characterized as indeterminate. Gabriel writes: "When you describe an experience what you are recounting is your memory of the act, not the act itself. Experiencing a moment is an inarticulate act. There are no words. It is in the sensory world. To recall it and to put words to it is to illustrate how one remembers the past" (Winter, *This All Happened* 273). He stresses the fact that everything he writes is a subjective attempt to relate his memory of events, never the official story. The moment in which one experiences an event can never be fully or clearly enunciated. This disparity results in a gap between observation and description. He may have observed events in one way, but he is explicit about the fact that everything he writes is a subjective description of his memories, not a direct or perfect account of a moment. Immediate perception is beyond language, and writing about these moments does not relate what actually happened. Literary language creates its own happening.

The way in which Gabriel discusses his own writing might clarify how authors appear to record events from their lives but, upon closer analysis, are actually creating new, literary moments. When Gabriel watches his friends and writes about them, he is not doing so exclusively to further his writing career or to gain control over them. Nevertheless, real life sneaks into fiction: "I should be writing the novel, but instead I concentrate on Lydia. Remembering how she smelled a pair of gloves and knew who owned them. How can I turn that into a historical moment? Moments never attenuate. Moments are compressed into the dissolve of real time. I will never forget how she looked when she smelled those gloves … I will have Rockwell Kent's wife have this ability. But Kathleen Kent is nothing like Lydia" (Winter, *This All Happened* 34).

Gabriel's observations of his friends and his girlfriend filter into his writing, but he often watches with an affectionate, caring eye. He records in order to cling to specific moments with people whom he loves. Assuming that Lydia Murphy equals Kathleen Kent is not only wrong but it reduces Gabriel's observational desires to a cold and utilitarian impulse. Although the living person does not directly translate into the fictional person, however, real-life details cultivate an allure of gossip. It seems as though the author is talking about his friends and family even though he is only using their outlines to animate new people. Using these outlines is no sinister act, but it is not an altogether innocent one either. Sometimes fiction becomes truth: "[Maisie Pye is] making a novel about what's happening now. It's thinly veiled autobiography. Except she's pushing it. The Oliver character has an affair, and her friends, when they read it, think Oliver's cheating on her. He's not, she says. People believe if you write from a tone of honesty, conviction, and sincerity, if you capture that correctly, then readers will be convinced it all happened that way" (Winter, *This All Happened* 29). As the novel progresses, Maisie Pye's fiction becomes reality when it turns out that Oliver is having an affair. This subplot to the text carries a darkly comedic message about making things up: language has the power to transform imagined events into reality. Authors might feel that they have concealed details from real life or that they have "captured" a moment, but when a story is published, it is no longer under their control. Likewise, Winter's novel is less about what did or did not happen in real life but more about being transposed into a literary world. The answer to the question of what actually happened in Winter's novel might not satisfy readers who are looking for a bit of gossip. The only honest answer is that Winter's novel happened; Lisa Moore concludes her introduction to *This All Happened* on a similar point: "What this means is that if this has not really all happened, it will, and will again and again, for every reader" (x). Moore's introduction indicates a specific reading of *This* in the novel's title. *This* refers to the fragile relationship between reader and text and to the imaginative power that this interaction holds to create an experience that is its own indeterminate moment.

Before concluding, I need to address the fact that Gabriel is able to focus on writing as a result of a government arts grant. It presents a potential flaw in my argument because it implicates him directly in state supervision. Chafe, Armstrong, and Thompson all tend to view Gabriel as a type of cultural official whose position as a writer reinforces stagnated class divisions. The most troubling scene occurs at Coleman's grocery store when Gabriel observes people "paying with Government of Newfoundland blue cheques that require MCP and SIN and theyre [sic] worth $301.50 and theyre [sic] buying cases of Pepsi, Spaghettios, tins of vienna sausages, cold pre-fried barbecue wings, I can barely write this it's all so cliché" (Winter, *This All Happened* 117). Armstrong explains how Winter uses his writer character to communicate the troubling gaze of the artist at the poor (Armstrong 47). Gabriel is uninterested in impoverished people, due to their lack of imagination (47), and this point for Chafe is compounded by the hypocritical detail that the only reason Gabriel can distinguish himself from people on welfare is the fact that he is a writer with an arts grant (Chafe 135). However, this scene should also be read within the broader context of the novel's cultural and economic contingencies. Gabriel lives and writes in what Herb Wyile describes as a region that is dependent on tourism and that tends to struggle economically (Wyile, *Anne of Tim Hortons* 4). Furthermore, Thompson points out that "Gabe's hostility toward the tourists he sees … [is] part of a wider cultural and literary backlash toward the unequal relationship between residents and visitors created by the tourism industry in Atlantic Canada" (Thompson 84). In the acknowledgments section at the back of the book Winter ironically refers to tourism: "Much of *This All Happened* was written and edited during time funded by the Cabot 500 Year of the Arts program. May you all visit Newfoundland" (*This All Happened* 287). In doing so, he playfully casts his readers as literary tourists taking a break from their everyday lives to watch this struggling artist and his quirky friends. Thus, the scene at Coleman's should also be read as an invitation for tourists to glimpse a version of Newfoundland that will never be mass produced by the tourism industry. Furthermore, despite the fact that Gabriel is implicated in state supervision, his gaze is communicated through first-person, subjective narration. His observations can still be discussed as a form of sousveillance because he writes from eye level and, perhaps more importantly, because his gaze can be scrutinized by others. Readers and critics have the opportunity to critique the way he observes and to consider how they have observed in similar situations. My point in this chapter has been to argue not that Gabriel is an ideal author figure who never participates in surveillance but that his actions are most accurately thought of as parodic surveillance, as counter but also cooperative and even occasionally complicit in reducing people to clichés.

Gabriel's descriptive practices and his stylistic choices highlight the subjectivity and the indeterminacy of perception. No matter what data might be available to the observer, something has been left unsaid. Where the gaze of surveillance technologies appears to be ubiquitous, irony is a constant reminder that there is always something not said and not seen. Gabriel's indeterminate descriptive practices highlight the fact that observing and describing are never simple or direct. Creative uses of language have the power to transfigure an object or a person into something or someone new. It is true that the title of Winter's book *This All Happened* exploits an autobiographical allure (Armstrong 37), but not enough people have asked what *This* refers to. If This stands for the experience of reading a novel and not for a series of actual events that happened in St John's, then what it means for Gabriel and for Winter to observe needs to be reconsidered. *This All Happened* is not going to save victims of state or corporate observation, but the concepts of irony, indeterminacy, and sousveillance could add texture to the detached, placeless strategies employed by surveillance technologies. Even if Gabriel's aesthetic philosophy is about capturing honest moments or latently using an artistic gaze to gain control of his surroundings, Winter's is not. Winter creates a metaphoric world that feels immediate and conflicted, similar to lived experience. The fact that readers can critique Gabriel's behaviour encourages them to become participants in what

Bakhtin would describe as "a zone of crude contact" (26). The distance of contemporary surveillance denies this contact, and that is a problem that needs to be addressed in a society that wants to be democratic. Literary artists such as Gabriel and Winter could be one among many models for the way in which people choose to respond. At the very least, it is worth taking a look.

2 Please Tell Me What the Poets Are Saying: Cyborgs, Flowers, and Impossible Metaphors in the Poetry of Ken Babstock, A.F. Moritz, Larissa Lai, and Rita Wong

In the previous chapter I argued that Gabriel English was best thought of as an author who practised sousveillance rather than surveillance. In this chapter I demonstrate specific strategies that authors employ to practise sousveillance against the simplifying gaze of surveillance. Authors have the ability to put readers into "a zone of crude contact" (Bakhtin 26). However, if we think about the reading act, we generally experience the text at a remove from whomever or whatever has been observed by the author. In criticism on contemporary surveillance, distance has been problematized because it allows those who surveil to sort from above without ever coming into contact with those whom they observe. In *Surveillance and Space*, Francisco Klauser writes: "Whether we are talking about video surveillance, drones or satellites, sensors inbuilt in urban infrastructures or handheld self-tracking devices, the key point is that information is being recorded somewhere and subsequently transferred, accumulated and analysed elsewhere" (131). Those who have been tasked with surveillance, such as CCTV operators, have complained about the fact that they "are not organically connected to monitored individuals, unable to establish ties of locality and occupation of the same space or be approached by human senses" (Klauser 134). This disconnect from the observed individuals reduces the quality of the observations that can be made. When distance coincides with social sorting, surveillance contributes to class imbalances: "[T]echniques for the accumulation and analysis of information also allow the categorization, profiling and thus differential treatment of individuals and social groups" (143). Thus, distance contributes to the simplification of data gathered, and it sorts people into reductive categories. Massive amounts of data gathered at a remove dehumanize those who are being observed through simplifying and sorting.

The poets in this chapter offer methods to respond to the simplifying gaze of surveillance through their own distinct methods of sousveillance. In *Blackening Canada*, Barrett articulates the ways in which literary art can function as an interruption to the national imaginary. In particular, he focuses on Black Canadian writers and their work in describing neglected histories of the country. He writes: "*thirsty*'s poetic structures of delay, prolongation, repetition, and caesura cut into the temporal present of the nation to insist that the present is haunted by unacknowledged and inarticulable histories. The broader project of thirsty to return to the traumatic and erased history of Black people in Canada via the exemplary figure of Alan represents Brand's intervention in the progressive myth of the nation" (56–7). These interruptions are grounded in specific aesthetic strategies, such as the caesura, that cut through myths and wake us up from national dreams that are exclusionary and alienating. The poets in this chapter use specific aesthetic strategies to disrupt the categorizing and simplifying gaze of surveillance. To do so, they develop metaphors that throw us into states of profound thought, focus our attention on specific people or issues, and show us how we are interconnected with a host of other categories. However, quite often they also observe and create from afar. As this chapter will show, distance is neither uniformly good nor bad. If one acknowledges its drawbacks, then observing at a remove presents certain benefits.

Even though distance between those who watch and those who are watched allows the observer to simplify and sort without understanding the complexities and the nuances of a person's life, the categories into which one fits are still an essential component to identity. When one willingly fits into a particular category, one can often articulate the various nuances within it. When a category is imposed onto a person, it sometimes feels as though nuance is lost. Oddly enough, the race, gender, and sexual identities of these poets influences their relationships to distance and to collaboration. Even though a person is more than their category, it would be narrow minded to ignore that there are commonalities among certain groupings and that these groupings can affect behaviour. To state the relevant categories as bluntly as possible, Ken Babstock and A.F. Moritz are white men, and Rita Wong and Larissa Lai are women of Asian descent who identify as queer. Babstock and Moritz work mainly in isolation, but Lai and Wong are more comfortable collaborating. Moritz is invested in the European tradition of the poet as the guiding light of the common life, whereas Lai and Wong engage with Eastern philosophy. Furthermore, cyborg theory informs the work of both Wong and Lai; in contrast, Babstock's poetic descriptions of a machine consciousness is bewildering and frightening. One poet's way of seeing is not objectively or uniformly better than another's. Each one takes on specific strategies that allow them to practise sousveillance in its multiform variations from their distinct subjective positions.

Babstock and Moritz use aesthetic strategies to problematize distance. While Moritz reverts back to traditional yet persuasive conceptions of the poet as compassionate observer, Babstock articulates a wild sneer of resistance and outrage. In contrast, Wong and Lai overcome distance through technological means in order to connect and collaborate. By speaking in impossible metaphors or by dwelling on the helplessness of viewers who are exposed to near-constant mediated violence, Babstock's *On Malice* and Moritz's *The Garden* both interrupt the gaze of surveillance by communicating underlying problems in relation to observation and distance. Lai's and Wong's poetry, both collectively and individually, might offer a way of rethinking these issues and offering potential benefits to observing and communicating from afar. In *Automaton Biographies*, Lai writes on everything from cyborgs in *Blade Runner* to her own childhood growing up in Newfoundland.[1] Distance is not a dilemma; it is an escape and an opportunity to speak back from a position of safety. In *sybil unrest*, Lai writes alongside Rita Wong in a text that was originally composed via email, employing what could be called digital sousveillance. Once again, distance contributes to the poet's ability to communicate with like-minded people and to speak back to the powerful. Their speaker longs for "electric release" (21) in which giving oneself over to technology might provide an escape from the quotidian. Lai and Wong suggest that to counter the problems created by distance one must take advantage of the opportunities that technology creates. In *Iron Goddess of Mercy*, Lai implodes the binary of cyborg and self in an increasingly polarized world, and she imagines new machines that readers might become.

Both Babstock and Moritz attempt to interrupt surveillance through critique and metaphor, but whereas Babstock presents a scathing

1 Essentially a cyborg is one who is not bound by traditional binaries between human and machine or human and animal. In "A Cyborg Manifesto: Science, Technology, and Socialist Feminism in the Late Twentieth Century," Donna Haraway calls attention to a concept of the self that desires unity and counters it with the cyborg who resists binaries and lives in the space between them: "certain dualisms have been persistent in Western traditions; they have all been systemic to the logics and practices of domination of women, people of color, nature, workers, animals – in short, domination of all constituted as others, whose task is to mirror the self. Chief among these troubling dualisms are self/other, mind/body, culture/nature, male/female, civilized/primitive, reality/appearance, whole/part, agent/resource, maker/made, active/passive, right/wrong, truth/illusion, total/partial, God/man" (178).

revision of an idealistic philosophy of observation, Moritz offers an ethics of unrelenting care and love from the gaze of the seemingly detached observer. Babstock's poem "Perfect Distant Blue Objects" critiques William Hazlitt's nuanced argument in "Why Distant Objects Please." Resembling encrypted intelligence, Babstock's text is dense and difficult to understand, which frustrates the attempt to find meaning easily, instead encouraging a measured uncertainty and an intense close reading. The distance between the observer and the observed makes it extremely difficult to define the subject being watched. In contrast, A.F. Moritz's The Garden contemplates the necessity of believing that a connection can be made between the observer and the observed even from great distance. Whereas Babstock's work critiques the surveillance state, Moritz's work imagines the ways in which a viewer might be an ethical witness to racialized violence even when it is mediated through a screen.

In critiquing the idealization of distance in William Hazlitt's "Why Distant Objects Please," Babstock's "Perfect Distant Blue Objects" is a furious nightmarish vision of whoever or whatever is surveilling average people. In Babstock's work there appears to be a host of impossible metaphors. For example, he writes, "Remembrance sometimes smells longer than a chain of visible servers" (60). The aesthetics cannot simply be explained by synaesthesia. Another head scratcher is "During snow, North Americans hang out in my mouth. I have a winter interval" (60). The gaze of the individual is fused in often confounding ways with technology, creating a strong sense of indeterminacy towards categorization; the speaker is not simply human or inhuman but is something altogether new, strange, and unsettling. Whereas Lai and Wong employ cyborg theory to think through philosophical impasses, Babstock's cyborg is a terrifying vision of how we observe and are observed. In a way, reading Babstock's reworking of Hazlitt is like viewing scattered data mid-transfer – like a computer program that is attempting to understand a human argument. In "Between-Space, Beforehand and Unseparated: Ken Babstock's On Malice," David Swartz writes: "Babstock shows how one's sense of smell and sound and vision contribute to the perception and recollection of objects, including oneself … 'When I smell that mind I want home' or 'the smell of scarcity and perpetuation.' According to William Hazlitt 'Sounds, smells, and sometimes tastes, are remembered longer than visible objects, and serve, perhaps, better for the links in the chain of association.' Babstock fills these links by appropriating Hazlitt's own text with surprising results."

On the one hand, in his essay Hazlitt talks about the smell of a brick kiln, which is not necessarily a pleasant memory but it possesses a kind of utility in that he can make sense of the past in relation to the present.

He can call on the memory and use it to explain himself. On the other hand, Babstock references the smell of a brain, scarcity, and perpetuation. Wires become crossed in the senses, and worry ensues about the ways in which technology observes human beings. We can be confusing in our attempts to describe our memories and our sensory experiences through metaphor; if surveillance structures became sentient, how bewildering would we be?

One of Hazlitt's central arguments is that distance allows the viewer to overwrite what he or she sees with the imagination and to resist the baser instincts that one might feel when directly confronted with a place or thing. Hazlitt writes, "Distant objects please, because, in the first place, they imply an idea of space and magnitude, and because not being obtruded too close upon the eye, we clothe them with the indistinct and airy colours of fancy" (219). In overwriting what one sees in the distance with the imagination, Hazlitt proposes that human beings can fight their baser instincts and instead call upon nobler emotions. He writes, "Our feelings, carried out of themselves, lose their grossness and their husk, are rarefied, expanded, melt into softness and brighten into beauty, turning to ethereal mould, sky-tinctured" (219). When people view things from a distance, they are able to impose their imagination in the most pleasing ways, leaving nature untouched physically but lovelier in the mind. This is an idealistic and generous way of thinking about the human imagination and about the implications of distance in space. Although it is more fanciful than critical, it is not the worst way to observe objects from afar. Importantly, Hazlitt argues that distance of space improves our impression of places and things but not of people. To appreciate other people the observer needs to be close to them. He writes:

> I will conclude the subject of the Essay with observing that (as it appears to me) a nearer and more familiar acquaintance with persons has a different and more favorable effect than with places or things ... Suppose ... your adversary turns out a very ugly man, or wants an eye, you are baulked in that way: he is not what you expected, the object of your abstract hatred and implacable disgust. He may be a very disagreeable person, but he is no longer the same. If you come in a room where a man is, you find, in general, that he has a nose upon his face. (Hazlitt 235–6)

When it comes to objects, Hazlitt argues that distance might actually be beneficial in certain respects. It allows for a kind of generous imagining to overwrite the object. However, when it comes to people, Hazlitt warns that the imagination is dangerous, that it simplifies and distorts, and instead, observers need to be confronted by a face-to-face interaction with another human being.

In certain ways Babstock inverts Hazlitt's aesthetics of distance. Whereas Hazlitt argues that distance of time can dull the pain of a particular moment, that one might think of future possibilities to ease painful memories, Babstock writes that thinking of the future is "not a good effacement of memory" (54). In fact, for Babstock, distance of time is often overwritten with a kind of regret, not an ease of pain. Perhaps the more striking differences between the two authors, however, becomes obvious in the ways in which they discuss distance between people. In "'The Secular Prophet': A Review of Ken Babstock's *On Malice*," Alex Porco writes: "Physical proximity produces intimacy and sympathy, according to Hazlitt ... Proximity to flaws and quirks is humanizing. Surveillance and capture, on the other hand, are dehumanizing practices performed at a remove. The particular body is subject to generalization, and the individual subject is reduced to data." (par. 16). Porco emphasizes an essential criticism of the way in which distance can dehumanize. Moving into closer proximity is often offered as a counterpoint, but the speaker of Babstock's poem rejects this notion as well. Perhaps most strongly articulated by Emmanuel Levinas, the face-to-face interaction becomes an important practice to humanize whoever is being observed. In *On Malice* the observer might move closer to the observed, but perception always distorts human beings. Not only does Babstock create indeterminacy towards Hazlitt's optimistic assumptions, but also he demonstrates how quickly the face-to-face interaction can turn nasty. Babstock writes:

Respect
for like men
might turn as the ugly eye turns, not balked at
but put out.
He is an abstracted object, not in the way
of expected
disagreements; he and his distance are an implacable
disgust,
hatred in a long room where the same person is
a face with no nose and a general to man. He found
you alone with your diversions, your sympathies, alone
he seems contemptuous, he has nothing, and says
stupidity
conceived him over a laugh. You heard something laughing
as he laughed. (Babstock 69)

This apparent face-to-face interaction is overwritten with the language of computer programing in that abstracting an object is a way of simplifying data to ensure that a program works more efficiently. Once again, technology infuses itself into language as a way of seeing. Whereas, on the one hand, Hazlitt relies on an agreed-upon reality – the quasi-comedic point that we might all notice each other's noses and recognize a shared humanity – on the other hand, Babstock highlights how easy it can be to see past the Other's human traits, that a face can have no nose, that an object can be abstracted if that allows the observer to process more efficiently their conception of the world.

At the root of Babstock's revision of Hazlitt's philosophy of distance are contrasting assumptions about how human beings process reality. Hazlitt presents a complex picture of how individuals understand their worlds; however, he assumes that perception is an accurate reflection of reality, and he believes that looking for shared qualities tends to be a positive strategy to resolve differences of opinion. These two assumptions frustrate Babstock's speaker. He writes, "Distance entertains us only partially, and people / entertain / compounded simplicities then work out guesses in answer to nothing derived from reality" (Babstock 71). Babstock insists that perception is mere guesswork, instead of the knowing or true understanding of one's world, and that by the time we process reality, there is really nothing much of reality left. All this processing amounts to a series of moments, some of which are remembered but most of which are not. All of that is to say – to abstract my own data – that distance from other people is clearly a problem if one hopes to observe them fairly, but seeking out a closer proximity is not an easy solution. People are too good at looking past another person's nose when it is convenient for them to do so.

In contrast to Babstock's intense, disorienting critique of distance, Moritz argues that distance must be overcome through an undying compassionate attention to the Other. In "Three Kings: 1992, 1968, 2020," Moritz highlights the cyclical, seemingly endless racialized violence that viewers observe through a television screen. One cannot help but think of Thomas Mathieson's synoptic gaze and how the many have the opportunity to observe the few. The key difference here, however, is that even though Moritz has the opportunity to observe, he is left with a profound sense of confusion and helplessness. He observes shocking abuses of power and racialized violence, but his watching does nothing to lessen the pain of others. The recording of Rodney King being beaten by police officers is "in- / forming us / over and over, the images, / replayed, remade / on television, now / that it was news again" (Moritz 2, lines 16–21). One of the many disturbing aspects of the video from the perspective of the viewer is how clearly it demonstrates police brutality despite the fact that the officers were deemed to be not guilty. The viewer connects the beating of King to Martin Luther King, Jr., to Jesus Christ, and eventually to the murder of George Floyd. He writes: "So they were left / the unworthy, the failed / regents of justice here, / of that banished poetry. / Were you there when they crucified / my Lord?" (4, lines 48–53). Being able to track this violence as a prolonged history gives more weight to the claims. Simultaneously, however, the timeline highlights the speaker's inability to effect change. All he can do is observe. The speaker pleads for this suffering to stop: "Lord, / don't let it be / that your being / lynched on a tree / ever and again as on a loop / in hell, a video we repeat / of a being beaten" (5–6, lines 62–8). The poet expresses the contrast between the reality of his society and what he desires it to be; in his doing so, these images of racialized violence demonstrate the cruel power dynamic articulated through news media. Pleading for change, the speaker acknowledges his own peculiar relationship to the violence through his role as viewer. He says: "O don't let it be / the image of what we are, / of what we always must do. But establish / the justice, the poetry that you were / and are to be, / the poetry that they / that we / kill you for" (6, lines 69–78). Poetry here takes on a complex, metaphorical meaning in the sense that the images make the viewer feel a profound stimulation, alive with the stark awareness of this injustice. The closing line serves as a haunting reminder that the viewer is not innocent; he keeps this endless loop alive through his insistence on the viewing. Through implicating the speaker and the viewer, Moritz resists casting them as exalted subjects; they are not ideal but part of the problem.

For Moritz, poetry is of and among the people. This means that poets need to be open to all that is around them through the creative process and that they are not able to choose what or whom they observe. In "The Garden in the Midst" the speaker writes: "[P]oem and garden, / walled off, are pierced, penetrated, / and are helpless, open to everything / seen and unseen" (Moritz 7, lines 3–6). Thus, if a poet sees injustice mediated through the news, they are struck by it, called to respond. This openness to feeling can be understood through the binary of the material and the poetic. The material includes the distant sound of aeroplanes and tires on concrete but also of the human beings who populate the world. He writes of "humans / who roll over one another, composing de- / composing ceaseless motion / that doesn't move/ in the worldwide eye" (7–8, lines 14–18). What is human is not necessarily ideal or divine but a kind of movement and energy: "[T]he world material / in which the human wave passes as a form / of torsion, of anxiety" (8, lines 23–5). Outside of the garden of calm that is poetry, an image of an amorphous teeming, material energy emerges. Importantly, the literary counterpoint to the hustle and bustle, the getting and spending of the world at large, does not possess an equal force. It offers a fragile, weak response. The speaker says: "[W]hile poetry/ and the garden in the midst / stretch out their roots and leaves: / their action is no stronger than a flower" (9, lines 30–3). This meagre but honest representation of poetry in the world positions a poem as something that needs to be tended, protected, loved. The barriers between the material world and the poetic are porous. Nevertheless, there is something sacred that not only must be observed in the poetic but also helps us to sousveil the material with some semblance of care.

The literary gaze might seem like a weak response to the massive machine of state and corporate surveillance, but the speaker highlights how the delicate objects that grow in the garden are capable of a particular kind of strength in that they are part of a larger, natural, interconnected world. Moritz writes of the marigold that "swallows the sun / and brings it here: the sun that in / a torture that never terminates, / or almost never, burns the elements, / so that sun fire / can linger in the marigold" (10–11, lines 6–11). The metaphor that he builds is one of a magical symbiosis. Not only does the flower harvest the sun, but also it gathers from the earth. It "eats the smother / and rot within wet earth, / and brings them up here in its veins, / into the surface of flower: brings up / saps that flowed around broached caskets, / ichors that lay cooking on the inner melt / compressed by the weight / of everything that year by year / falls and is buried / by all that falls and is / buried later" (12, lines 22–32). The tremendous power of an object so weak and delicate speaks to the tenuous life of poets and their poetry. In "The Human Flower" the fickle brittleness of our bodies is highlighted. Moritz writes: "[Y]ou have / no other body, nothing / but this making you / determined: potency that is perfect, / motionless, enchained, unfolding / death. And poetry and the garden / where it's made are nothing / but a flower in this sense" (21, lines 27–34). The metaphor of poetry as flower is made explicit, and the garden is highlighted as a unique space where poetry lives. The power of the literary gaze lies not only in its wild interconnectivity but also paradoxically in its vulnerability and its weakness. In its openness to feeling, it encourages others to experience pain, sympathy, and a host of other complex, contradictory emotions.

Once Moritz has established his speaker's vision of poetry's existence in the world, he returns to the problem of observing injustice from a distance. First and foremost, Moritz feels a sense of helplessness and frustration at the obvious lie that he and other observers are being fed. He writes: "Suburban Simi Valley held the jury / that held the African was never beaten, / is not poor and has no reason" (24, lines 29–31). To fight against this impotence Moritz offers close scrutiny of the scene and a public rebuttal. Even if the powers that be might not hear him, he needs to state that he is aware of the lie presented through the news. Referencing William Blake's *Visions of the Daughters of Albion*, Moritz positions the poet within a tradition of the sensitive observer. Through the story of Oothoon, Blake attempted to show his solidarity with women and their continued fight for equality. Moritz implies an important aspect of the literary gaze through the concept of the ally – that individuals can still observe with care and they can offer their support. Yet, even with the concept of the ally to pacify his sense of impotence, he must still tackle the problem of distance.

The fundamental belief on which Moritz insists in relation to sousveillance is that there are profound moments and sincere expressions that cut through time and space. Moritz writes: "Let no one lie: that the poem's nothing, / and nothing to you, and far away, / never known by you, entered / by you – that it brands / foreign names in white scars on black continents / and stars. The poem / is in you who sing, / who most magnificently have / sung in disaster. It sings in you / its eternity, what flowers in blood and lights / in the eyes, what is made – in hands, on lips, / in the garden of all moments / of our lives: our hopes" (44, lines 34–47). In Moritz's idealistic but persuasive vision, the literary artist offers to create an experience that grants access to the profound emotion that connects us together. Importantly, for Moritz, the literary artist gives light and life where too many are numb to the pain and suffering of others. Moritz writes: "[I]t's you / working with remorseless / love bringing all that / to birth in you / so everything / may flower and sing" (45, lines 52–7). The literary gaze as rich soil for growth and compassion might not be a new idea, but through the strong feeling with which Moritz posits his belief, his metaphor makes distance feel briefly and fleetingly surmountable.

In the essays that follow his poems Moritz expands on his aesthetic philosophy and on his doubts about the potential of poetry, which yet again distinguishes him from the exalted subject. He questions his own distance from the events that he has observed. He writes: "Someone with the luxury of sitting in his garden for seven days: is there sense in his thinking about poetry's isolation from the poor? And what poetry? What poetry is isolated from the poor? Isn't it only the poetry of the rich? Or rather, of the 'middlesort', the clerkly class, which serves the rich, and which is tempted to arrogate to its own sort of poetry the sole title of Poetry?" (72). The literary arts might not be the preferred mode of communication for the common people. A certain level of education or informal training is necessary to understand the various subtleties and nuances of poetry. Reading through both Moritz's and Babstock's work is deeply challenging. And yet, in Moritz's own experience of sousveilling media related to the 1992 Los Angeles uprising, a poet did cut through time and space. Some thirty years afterwards, an unnamed poet still occupies Moritz's thoughts: "Immediately after the uprising, an edition of ABC News's Nightline program originated from South Central Los Angeles: May 4, 1992. At the neighborhood meeting that ABC had organized in the hall of a local church, one of the speakers was a poet: a street poet, an oral poet" (76). This poet articulates a message that no one else can communicate: "The street poet's poem makes us see that we will never understand the people who provoked the riot, police and jurors and their encouragers, and we will never understand the people who participated in it and suffered from it, the inhabitants of South Central Los Angeles, unless we listen to them in a certain way, a poetic way: attention to the whole reality. But this truth is occluded by police barricades, gated communities, segregated zip codes, massive imbalance of wealth and power" (Moritz 82). This brief moment of literary expression might seem meaningless and ephemeral, but it stands out like the metaphorical flower, breaking down the distance of time and space. Moritz highlights the importance of unknowingness. He does not exalt himself as a profoundly compassionate observer. Instead he emphasizes the profound challenge of attempting to see the Other.

There is a risk that Moritz's aesthetic philosophy of distance possesses a misguided arrogance and ignorance. He might think he cares, but what if he misrecognizes? How much can a person care about others if they are detached and distant from the day to day – the sights, sounds, and smells – of their lives? Does Moritz propose to be compassionate without any of the complexities of being face to face with the Other? Literary art might offer an important reminder of how we have the potential to look with care but also how easily that gaze can be flawed, how it can see past certain human traits, how it can unfairly simplify when it should aspire towards generosity and complexity. Although Moritz offers hope, his metaphor of the flower and the garden is a risky strategy to interrupt the gaze of surveillance. Even if Moritz resists exalting himself, his insistence on the poet as compassionate observer exalts the literary gaze. Winter's representation of Gabriel offers a fuller understanding of the flaws that authors have and the ways in which they use their status as observer to wield power over others, but Moritz provides more of an inspirational flourish. Sometimes we need to see clearly; at other times we need a spark of encouragement in order to keep going.

Whereas Moritz presents the power of literature to cut through time and space, Lai and Wong posit a constantly shifting identity, one that resists the simplifying gaze of surveillance, resulting in indeterminacy towards categorization. Lai's work, in particular, is often discussed in relation to the concept of the cyborg.[2] In his "Dystopia Now: Examining the Rach(a)el's in Automaton Biographies and Player One," Kit Dobson discusses how in the film Blade Runner "eyes reappear throughout the film, not only in the artificial owl's blink, or simply in the repeated images of eyes, but also in the Voigt-Kampff test that Deckard and others like him administer to suspected replicants in order to test their humanity" (401). Importantly, the test needs to be performed close up. If Rachel could keep her distance, then she would not be sorted and simplified by the powerful. Despite the fact that Rachel is indeed not human, Dobson points out an important shift from the film to Lai's text. He writes, "That Rachel is not a human does not, however, lead her to feel inferior in Lai's rendition; quite the reverse" (401). For Lai, it is better to be the cyborg because the very idea of being human allows the powerful to simplify and sort individuals. In "auto matter" the cyborg offers to be an aesthetic interruption in a couple of ways, one of which is the insistence on a constantly shifting identity. Lai writes: "[I]ndecent indices suggest / it was that way too / both lands either / or / the score at airport lounge / twists revolution's hope against cap's scope / we float our 'i' / right between the eyebrows" (162, lines 1–7). This floating "i" resists the simplifying gaze of surveillance and creates indeterminacy towards categorization. By breaking down borders and binaries, this constantly shifting identity can never be sorted. Even though the state dehumanizes with ease, the cyborg perpetually escapes containment.

sybil unrest, which Lai composed with Rita Wong, emphasizes the need to be constantly creating multiple selves and to be aware that we are always constructed in relation to the world around us. In "'Infiltrate as Cells': The Biopolitically Ethical Subject of sybil unrest," Sonnet L'Abbé argues that "*sybil unrest* proposes political action and resistance as occurring at the moments where the subject literally composes herself – nutritionally, affectively, and narratively – as living material, functionally interdependent on and with all other living material on the planet" (L'Abbé). L'Abbé demonstrates how closely connected the text is to Haraway's concept of the cyborg in this breaking down of various

2 See Sharlee Reimer's "Troubling Origins: Cyborg Politics in Larissa Lai's Salt Fish Girl," and Tatjana Milosavljevic's "The Cyborg Continuum: From Myth to Techno-capitalism in Larissa Lai's *Salt Fish Girl*."

borders between the human and essentially everything else. Among other things, there is a blending between male and female and human and animal. Lai and Wong write: "[N]erves want a happy ending / organism organizes / dreamt the experiment was just a dream / dreamt i was a butterfly drowned in butter / dreamt i was a man / codes switched" (Lai and Wong 8, lines 3–9). A person is not a distinct and separate category but an interdependent being. This interdependency ironizes the categories into which people are forced. However, Wong and Lai also seem to highlight one glaring problem with this interdependency. We might escape simplification and classification, but we are also tapped into an electronic landscape that changes us and manipulates us from a distance. In "Sedimenting the Past, Producing the Future: An Interview with Larissa Lai on the Poetics and Politics of Writing" (Krüger), Lai talks about how she and Wong felt implicated in the news coverage of the SARS epidemic and the American invasion of Iraq: "[I]t was hard not to feel a sense of responsibility for the unjust violence that was taking place in Iraq. So we would be sitting at our hotel room watching CNN and the BBC World Service feeling helpless and wanting to do something. And obviously not really having the power to do much, except pass a notebook back and forth across the room. That was how *sybil unrest* started" (Krüger 100). Sounding an awful lot like Moritz, Lai and Wong desire to engage with the mediated images they have of the world, but where Moritz attempts to articulate deep emotion, Wong and Lai employ a strategy of resistance dependent on irony and an attentiveness to language.

Since Lai and Wong accept that they are altered by the technology that surrounds them, they seek to articulate non-compliant, shifting identities within it. They write: "[T]elevised revulsion / armed patrols / against anadromous androgynes / pixelated shot at black hair / signals amber, red light / distract the gaze / from canada's expert destruction corporation" (Lai and Wong 17, lines 1–7). Although they clearly critique the way in which mass media attempts to manipulate and change them, they also acknowledge that they are a part of it. Lai and Wong imply that we are all complicit in what we watch. They write: "[D]rink the vision / watch the scream / dream the snuff / congratulate the contradiction / we couldn't have done it without you" (18, lines 16–20). As a contrast to Moritz who views poetry as separate from mass media, Lai and Wong present a deliberate effort to think from inside the machine. They write: "[M]achines R us / our cables couple on sexed insertions / aliens invaded ages ago / we adore their rapid rate / thru veins / brain this love story / intimate hybridity / we gorge on microchips" (32, lines 1–8). They add: "[R]ecovery of our collective / cyborg consciousness /

resist the transistor / sister or let radio waves / flag your heart down" (32, lines 11–15). For Lai and Wong, thinking from inside the machine breaks down this distance between the supposedly moralistic observer and the unwilling/willing participant. The cyborg accepts their complicity, embraces collaboration, creates indeterminacy, and resists exalting their position.

Despite the emphasis on all things that are not the self, Lai's career as a writer has also featured multiple stand-alone texts. Even though collaboration can be fun and meaningful, an author can also cultivate a multivalent self, which is not really a singular being but a shifting "i." In an interview with Fazeela Jiwa, when asked about the way in which collaboration influences the self, Lai says: "I am really interested in forms of consciousness that emerge from entities other than the self, and collaboration is a way of engaging this. Rita and I know things together that we might not know individually. This is political because it gets away from the Enlightenment self, the competing self, the consuming self and so on. Not to mention the academically productive self … It is fun, and empowering too" (Jiwa). Thus, for Lai there is not a contradiction in creating work collaboratively and creating work on her own. In *Iron Goddess of Mercy* Lai seems to be suggesting that this complicated sense of various selves is another way of escaping the gaze of an observer who desires to simplify and sort. It is difficult not to think of Haraway's closing claim in relation to Lai's latest book of poetry, in which she states, "I would rather be a cyborg than a goddess" (Haraway 181). In this final claim Haraway creates a binary in contrasting the cyborg with the goddess. To dissolve this binary Lai blends the two, letting them steep as the work progresses. There is the non-human and the human, the divine and the concrete, the tough and the gentle. Nevertheless, as much as one might want to resist borders and binaries, it is hard not to see that the online world has created increasingly entrenched political binaries (Hills and Menczer). Lai references this divide through the concept of the echo chamber, or a group that only has dialogue with people who already agree with them, and as a result their politics becomes increasingly extreme. She writes: "Dear Echo Chamber, the difference between the Japanese Imperial and Japanese Canadian swims an ocean pacific's specific as the frump in lumpen" (Lai, *Iron Goddess* 145). She adds: "Can't have it out on twitter as Echo flits from circuit to circus, rages from body to machine to body to dream seeking the feather coat shed as flesh hoping she could leave it by the mirror pool just long enough to get clean" (144–5). Being inside this machine would only lead to a hardening of borders. Thus, if one enters the machine, one might paradoxically move away from the ideal of the cyborg. Perhaps the only way to change the machine is to become more aware of the binaries that escaped even Haraway in her early argument. She asks: "Dear Machine, can one machine be medicine for another machine? When the biopolitic sticks when the necropolitic kicks, I ache for liberal love" (*Iron Goddess* 51). In persistently recreating the self, one also breaks down the distance between polarized groups. Haraway encourages the possibility of becoming a cyborg; with Lai, we already are part of a system, not distinct entities; the categories are an illusion imposed on us by surveillance structures.

The poets in this chapter offer different manifestations of literary sousveillance. Moritz strives to connect to various communities through a poetic gaze, and he imbues his observations with an intense, passionate sincerity. He embodies the tradition of the poet as the guiding light of the common life. Babstock's poem sneers at finding a human connection even in the face-to-face interaction. With Moritz, we might have to delude ourselves into feeling hope, but with Babstock we are left with a distraught, solipsistic isolation. Lai and Wong's collaborative efforts grant a way of moving past the individual author as great observer and communicator of feeling. It is the awareness of how we are already interconnected that is of deep significance in the work of Lai and Wong. When we become specific types of machines, ones that are constantly breaking down boundaries, creating indeterminacy, feeling intensely, reducing distance between polarized groups, and perpetually seeking to observe with care, then we interrupt the reductive gaze of surveillance. When we strive for these goals, we practise an ideal form of sousveillance through the reading act. An ideal is not often realized, but at least it is something nice to observe in the distance.

3 Different Modes of Sousveillance in Lynn Coady's Writing: Community, Literary, and Digital

In the first chapter of this section I demonstrated how authors are imperfect observers but are still models of sousveillance. In the second chapter I showed how four authors respond to the simplifying gaze of surveillance. Now I want to move away from talking about sousveillance as a reading or writing strategy, and I want to divide the subject into three categories to highlight the ways in which looking from below works in different situations. In this chapter I further develop an ethics of sousveillance, and I highlight the shifts from a society that mainly employed community sousveillance to one that also employs literary and digital sousveillance. In "As for Me and Me Arse: Strategic Regionalism and the Home Place in Lynn Coady's *Strange Heaven*," Herb Wyile credits Coady with interrupting depictions of the Atlantic Canadian regional imaginary. In *Strange Heaven*, readers follow the story of Bridget Murphy, a teen mother who has given up her baby. The reductive and repressive gaze of family, friends, and townspeople is closely observed and scrutinized. In this sense, literary sousveillance is used to critique community sousveillance. As an author Coady is perpetually turning back on previous texts to critique what she has written in the past. For example, when read together, *Mean Boy* and *The Antagonist* detail the cruelty of literary sousveillance. She offers satirical and parodic representations of creative writers, the figures who, I have argued, are representative of sousveillance. Even though digital sousveillance offers a counterpoint to literary sousveillance, Coady's "Someone Is Recording" details the increasingly polarizing world being created by influencers. There is no ideal mode of observation; each way of seeing has its own potentialities and flaws. However, a close consideration of the concepts of autonomy and responsibility might prove to be helpful in understanding how these various modes of sousveillance can be restrictive or helpful to identity formation. In her depiction of these various modes of observation, Coady's work can be employed to ironize sousveillance in its various manifestations.

In its tendency to simplify and sort, surveillance reduces the complexity of human beings, but those who are categorized can look back at the institutions that attempt to define them. To be fair, though, communities and individuals sometimes observe in far more reductive ways than does the state. To further complicate this issue, we sometimes choose to associate ourselves with specific groups and categories, even at times accepting a simplifying category if we feel it suits us. To take a step back, every aspect of our personalities is not nuanced, textured, and complicated. There are times we might need to resist connections to group identity through parody, satire, or critique even if these aspects of identity are important to us. There are other times we might need to highlight how we do not fit into specific aspects of local, regional, or national narratives that are available to us. To put it simply, sometimes we need to seek autonomy from group identity, and at other times we feel an unavoidable responsibility to it. In these texts by Lynn Coady sousveillance often results in an oscillation between autonomy and responsibility. Sousveillance sometimes brings people together, and at other times it pushes them apart. Autonomy is not isolating oneself from all influence but finding a way to cultivate the self on one's own terms. Those who seek autonomy are often ironists. Richard Rorty describes the ironist in *Contingency, Irony, and Solidarity* as one who "is looking for … a redescription of … [a personal] canon which will cause it to lose the power it has" (97). Ironist writers push back against the weight of social norms, and they desire to create themselves in a way that feels new. Responsibility is not a simple duty to others but a complicated and contentious embrace of what it means to live and think with other people. It bears similarities to the way in which Lai and Wong discuss the interconnectivity of all things. In *Giving an Account of Oneself*, Judith Butler describes responsibility as being "in our skins, given over, in each other's hands, at each other's mercy" (101). For Butler, "this is a situation we do not choose. It forms the horizon of choice, and it grounds our responsibility" (101). Depending on one's life situation, there are advantages to seeking out autonomy and to seeking out responsibility. In a stage in one's life where one feels confined by the past while simultaneously being exposed to new ways of being – perhaps at university and away from home – the opportunity to experiment with new selves can prove to be an intoxicating and liberating experience. As a counterpoint, there are also clear advantages to being aware of the fact that we owe something to the people who care about us. In another sense, if we have been described by someone else in such a way that we feel misunderstood and powerless, we might need to call them not only to their mistaken interpretation but also to the fact that we all exist only in relation to one another. Mari Ruti's *The Call of Character: Living a Life Worth Living*, articulates how responsibility and cultivating the self need not be antithetical: "[S]elf-cultivation is not a matter of nurturing an essential core of being that makes us who we are, but rather of dwelling in the world in ways that allow us to add ever new layers of meaning into an identity that is always in the process of forming itself. That is, I start from the premise that our self is not a private possession (or achievement), but rather something we construct gradually through our engagement with our surroundings, including other people" (x). Although Ruti is incredibly apt, lived experience does not always allow for the merging of these two concepts. People are often pushed and pulled between responsibility and autonomy depending on their life situations. For example, if one feels deeply misunderstood, then one might strive for autonomy and redescription. Responsibility to a closed-minded community can lead to a repression of identity formation.

In Coady's *Strange Heaven*, Bridget Murphy feels stifled and misrecognized by the people in her town. She suffers from a feeling of responsibility to her family even though she desires to break away from the social norms that are imposed on her. In Bridget's small Cape Breton town there are tight lines between normal and deviant behaviour. Wyile argues: "Bridget's sense of being scrutinized, assessed, under surveillance is a crucial effect of the juxtaposing of Bridget's life inside and outside the institution. Just as Bridget was monitored, interviewed, even videotaped in the hospital, after her release she is monitored both by her concerned family and by the community at large, institutions similarly desiring to identify and regulate deviant behaviour" (5). Bridget experiences one form of social control and surveillance in the mental institution, but the force and scope of surveillance pale in comparison to community sousveillance in Bridget's town where people are constantly observing each other. When someone sees someone else, a reductive life history frames the interaction. Coady writes: "In small towns, thought Bridget, you are always aware that everybody knows your business and is thinking about you to some extent. When they see you on the street they consult the brief information roster they carry inside their brains. Like: George Matheson. Jeezless punk. Got busted once for possession. Called his mother an old slut. Threw a punch at the principal in grade eleven. That sort of thing" (*Strange Heaven* 180). Within the gaze of the community, people are simplified and sorted into types. There might not be a digital record, but people talk, and they seldom forget. Thus, part of the project of *Strange Heaven* is adding nuance to the way in which people observe a young woman such as Bridget. Coady has discussed the absence of female literary voices at the time she began writing, saying, "Most of the Cape Breton and Maritime writers were male, and I hadn't seen anything that reflected my experiences as a female in the Maritimes, or more specifically, in small town Cape Breton" (Steeves 233). Therefore, this type of literary sousveillance is designed to critique and to add texture to community sousveillance, encouraging a measured sympathy by spending time with the inner thoughts of a young woman.

In Bridget's town strict gender roles are maintained through community sousveillance. Wyile argues, "Bridget's physical and psychic development takes place within what Judith Butler describes as a framework of regulatory social practices that serve to reinforce polarized and essentialist gender identities and to obscure the fundamentally performative nature of gender" (*As for Me and Me Arse*, 3). The combination of constant scrutiny and extreme conservatism shatters lives. The narrative of *Strange Heaven* is haunted by a traumatic incident in which a young man kills a young woman with whom he had been in a romantic relationship. As Bridget's resentful, obsessive ex-boyfriend Mark is always looming in the distance, the threat of domestic violence is also a steady undercurrent to the narrative. The various social pressures imposed on women come to the forefront in a conversation with her brother, Gerard. Bridget asks: "'Lookee here, Gerard. I'm a tramp. I'm one, right? At least by your criteria, aren't I?'" (Coady, *Strange Heaven* 113). Her brother pauses to think about it, ultimately telling her "'not anymore'" (113). Coady writes: "This was not exactly Gerard trying to be kind. This was the mathematics of Gerard's mind. She could almost hear the calculations going on" (113). Gerard's perspective is not unique and idiosyncratic but reflective of his culture. Bridget's truly deviant behaviour, according to the community, involves leaving Mark after the pregnancy because she lacks the maternal desire to build a home for the prospective child. She knows from experience that if she fails to meet cultural expectations, then she will be branded a tramp and sent to a mental institution. The expectations for extreme passivity of women and extreme aggressiveness of men create dangerous consequences. One of Bridget's friends, Dan Sutherland, explains: "'[If] you are a male with good grades and interests that do not even remotely involve a jock strap or helmet or stick of some kind, you may as well get all your teeth removed at the dentist's office" (121). While women are supposed to follow passively the social order, men are expected to dominate others through physical force. These strict gender binaries exacerbate the spectre of domestic violence. In the world of the novel, responsibility to the community comes not only with a reduction in one's idiosyncratic identity but also with the likelihood of physical and psychological harm.

Breaking out of these binaries entails being deemed a deviant figure by the community. Although Bridget seeks allies to help her find autonomy from the confines of her town, ultimately she is alone. For Bridget, people in the community will always misrecognize and simplify. Coady writes: "She plowed up the Street toward the pharmacy, thinking about people thinking about her. People thinking about her in relation to themselves and other things. Using her to support their own theories, to consolidate their outlook" (*Strange Heaven* 182). Community sousveillance does not offer nuanced observation of distinct personalities; for Bridget, it simplifies and sorts in a way that is reminiscent of surveillance. In a stunning scene at the end of the novel Bridget finds herself obsessing over fake eyeballs. Coady writes: "When she was fourteen, she took one look around her room at all her dolls and stuffed animals, counted around twenty-five sets of fake eyes looking at her, and shoved the lot of them up the cubbyhole in the attic" (191). Bridget begins to realize that people who seem to be looking are only doing so superficially, seeing whatever they want. The only person who might be able to understand Bridget with some level of nuance is Alan Voorland, an outsider figure from Ontario. Similarly to Gabriel English, Alan is a recorder and an observer of people in the community. He practises literary sousveillance: "He was from Guelph and wandered around town examining and exclaiming at everything like an anthropologist" (32). In contrast to community sousveillance, Alan appears to value idiosyncrasies and difference among people. Coady writes: "He took out a notebook and said it was full of character sketches he had written about all his interesting friends" (36). Alan is appealing to Bridget as an individual who appears to consider thoughtfully the lives of others rather than reducing them to simplified categories. Ultimately, however, he leaves for Guelph and distances himself from Bridget. The full scope of his narrative suggests that even though he cares for Bridget, he is also a hedonist who takes advantage of a teenager at a vulnerable moment in her life. Bridget comes to a point where she can redescribe Alan; if he is an ally, it is only in his shared desire to seek autonomy. Although Alan gives off the appearance of responsibility, it proves to be false. He is a figure who savours the ironic detachment he experiences while observing a quaint town before returning to his actual life. In the end, her interactions with Alan only further solidify Bridget as a deviant figure in the eyes of the community.

One response to misrecognition and simplification is to narrate the interior world of the person who has been misunderstood and to highlight precisely why they seek autonomy. Sometimes this takes a novel; at other times, it can occur in a flash of insight. Two of Bridget's friends come to visit her while she is in a mental institution, and one suddenly realizes that he has not fully considered her point of view. Coady writes, "It might have occurred to Stephen [Cameron] that he'd been listening to only one side of the story for a very long time" (*Strange Heaven* 71). These moments in which a person pauses and considers their own ignorance have the potential to create nuance and to encourage the withholding of judgment. Stephen Cameron, however, might shift his perspective slightly, but he persists in his condescending and misguided efforts to reconnect Bridget with her ex-boyfriend. The novel as a whole can be read as an attempt to add complexity to a figure – the Maritime teen mother – who is deemed by her community to be deviant. More broadly, Coady's narrative is, as Herb Wyile describes it, a "parodic commentary on folk culture" (*As for Me and Me Arse* 10). Yet, there are moments of intense sincerity suggesting that certain figures within the community can help people within it. They might not be able to reconfigure the culture, but they have access to ways of helping vulnerable people. In these types of closed communities there is an ethics to privacy. Certain information about people needs to be withheld in order to protect them. If this information gets out, people risk being simplified, categorized, and punished. Bridget has an impromptu conversation with her family doctor who tells her that he wishes they would have talked about birth control. She would not have wanted her parents to know, but he says, "'I would have respected your privacy'" (Coady, *Strange Heaven* 182). This moment in Strange Heaven is a sober reminder of the vital importance of confidentiality. If Bridget had been allowed this discussion with her doctor, she could have avoided the trauma that resulted from an unwanted pregnancy. In this particular situation a private conversation hidden from the judgmental ears of the town seems to be one of the few responses to community sousveillance. People need these kinds of spaces and moments if they are going to be able to cultivate their identities without being dismissed or deemed to be deviant.

While *Strange Heaven* effectively works to critique community sousveillance, *Mean Boy* and *The Antagonist* focus readers' attention on literary sousveillance. Coady is an astute observer of the ways in which people attempt to control the behaviour of others and the ways in which people react when they feel misrecognized. *Mean Boy* demonstrates how writers develop their own insular and exclusionary groups, and *The Antagonist* narrates the ways in which literary sousveillance can also be cruel and reductive to people outside of literary communities.

Coady is starkly aware of the types of tensions that occur when someone feels that biographical details have been used unethically by creative writers. The fictional poet and professor Jim Arsenault of *Mean Boy* bears similarities to the poet John Thompson, who had died suddenly at the age of thirty-eight but still managed to leave his mark on the Canadian literary scene.[1] Coady spoke later of an incident that occurred at Mount Allison University: "There were people [at the reading] who still remembered him [Thompson] and revered him very much and a couple of them kind of jumped up during the Q&A period … and gave me hell for using his life" (Ahearn 4). She justified the use of Thompson's biography by arguing that fiction was always a blend of lived and imaginary experience: "[P]eople didn't seem to know what made them angry, or that the character had so much in common with John Thompson but that the character, at the same time, wasn't like John Thompson … And that's kind of what fiction is" (Ahearn 7–8). Although Coady was technically right, the people who criticized her also had a valid point. They felt that she used details about their dead friend to develop a character in a novel. This ethical dilemma results, in part, from the limited and flawed perspective that authors have when they attempt to narrate other peoples' lives. There will always be someone in the periphery, someone who feels unfairly characterized even when an author strives to observe with care and compassion. Coady's initial response downplays the frustrating nature of quasi-biographical details in fiction. To people who remember Thompson, her novel implies that he repeatedly made a fool of himself and took advantage of students. One could argue that she should have reworked this character to hide the similarities, and even though these similarities are also a way of spreading Thompson's story, Coady's initial response feels inadequate, perhaps because her full consideration of these ethical issues comes in the form of *The Antagonist*. This work invites readers to consider the intricacies of using quasi-biographical detail and the inevitably limited perspective of literary sousveillance.

In *Mean Boy* the narrator, Larry Campbell, dreams of becoming a revered writer. His fantasy of being a literary artist, however, is not

1 Peter Sanger's entry in the *New Brunswick Literary Encyclopedia* is telling here: "John Michael Thompson (1938–1976) has become one of the most influential twentieth-century Canadian poets. His second book, *Stilt Jack*, a sequence of thirty-eight ghazals published posthumously in 1978, inspired and inspires the fashion of writing ghazals and nonce-ghazal couplet forms which has become one of the more common stylistic markers of English Canadian poetry during the last three decades" (Sanger par. 1).

simply about finding time and space to create but also about trying to act out a fantasy self, one that he has seen in the media. He assumes that in order to write great poetry, he needs to behave like Lord Byron and drink like Dylan Thomas. In attempting to escape the constraints of his friends and family, Larry unintentionally alienates people who care about him. One of his friends, Charles Slaughter, is a stereotypical testosterone-fuelled "meathead." Coady seems to return to this character in *The Antagonist* through her narrator, Rank, in order to flesh out and complicate some of these simplifications. Even though Rank is different from Slaughter, they share enough similarities to warrant comparison. In many ways Slaughter is an entertaining and compelling figure in *Mean Boy*, but he also borders on cliché; in contrast, Rank, whose full name is Gordon Rankin, is a complex and multidimensional narrator. To an extent, *The Antagonist* can be read as Slaughter's response to Larry after he finishes reading *Mean Boy*. Using email, Rank attempts to write back to his novelist buddy, Adam Grix, and explain exactly how reworking the past into fiction is a kind of trespassing. By focusing on a peripheral character in someone else's Künstlerroman, *The Antagonist* becomes a parodic reworking of this subgenre. Rank expresses the pain and frustration of being indirectly written about in a friend's novel. When read together, these two texts articulate a responsibility towards the observed; they communicate an ethics of literary sousveillance.

In *The Antagonist* and *Mean Boy*, Coady disentangles assumptions about writers, one of which is the notion that authors are special observers. At least since the Romantics, prominent writers in Western literature have positioned themselves as close observers of the quotidian. In the preface to *Lyrical Ballads*, Wordsworth proposes that the poet has a unique gift of insight: "The principal object, then, which I proposed to myself in these Poems was to choose incidents and situations from common life, and to relate or describe them, throughout, as far as was possible, in a selection of language really used by men" (59). From Wordsworth we understand the literary artist as the one who finds meaning in the quotidian. When this emphasis on the everyday is paired with an extravagant sense of one's own purpose and a breaking free from responsibility to others, it can result in an aloof, self-entitled world view. This dangerous mixture can be found in the motif of the "artist as hero," which was best articulated by Maurice Beebe in *Ivory Towers and Sacred Founts: The Artist as Hero in Fiction from Goethe to Joyce*: "As long as art was considered chiefly a matter of imitation, the artist seemed less important than his subject. When he claimed a special faculty – the imagination – which permitted him to perceive deeper truths than those known to the less visionary, he made the one who sees more important than what is seen" (26). Authors do not have to throw away this notion of being special observers so long as they infuse this identity with humility and self-critique. In *Infinitely Demanding: Ethics of Commitment, Politics of Resistance*, Simon Critchley contrasts the concept of a tragic self with that of a comic self. For Critchley, these distinctions apply to the ethical demand of giving oneself over to the Other. However, this same dichotomy can be applied to authors and their diverse aesthetic goals. One can be a tragic hero or a comic hero. At the risk of being reductive, the tragic is essentially "too heroic," whereas the comic "is a more minimal, less heroic form of sublimation" (Critchley, *Infinitely Demanding* 63). The comic is couched in perpetual failure. One might possess the ability to observe the common life and articulate the quotidian in ways that are distinct and special, but that does not mean that anyone will notice or care. It also does not mean that this ability to observe makes one more important than others. For both Bridget Murphy and Larry Campbell, this process might be necessary if they hoped to cultivate a distinct sense of self. However, in *Mean Boy* and *The Antagonist*, Coady demonstrates how certain ways of seeking autonomy are toxic. Profoundly influenced by literary mythologies, Larry in *Mean Boy* observes others with blind self-interest and unintentional cruelty. When confronted by the misrecognition of someone whom he thought of as a friend, Rank has no choice but to set the record straight. In many ways the stories of Rank and Larry articulate tensions between the ethical demand of responsibility and the desire for autonomy in relation to literary sousveillance. Both Larry and Rank go through what Rorty might call the process of redescription in that they desire to have agency over the way they are perceived. While Larry begrudgingly takes on aspects of responsibility, Rank eventually learns to embrace the perspective of others in a way that resembles Ruti's cultivation of the self.

In *Mean Boy*, Larry often struggles between maintaining his relationship with his family and becoming closer to his hero, Jim Arsenault. Larry's home life fails to offer him access to what Marcus Boon in *The Road to Excess: A History of Writers on Drugs* calls imaginal realms, which include "animal states of consciousness … vectors of desire, intoxication, death, and truth" (221). In contrast to his family, Arsenault appears to have the potential to help Larry reach these realms. Therein lies the beginning of Larry's internal conflict between his home life and his artistic life. However, as the novel progresses, Arsenault – a kind of precursor to social media influencers – creates new impediments. Alongside this need to explore his imagination, Larry also desires to become known in the same way as famous dead authors and literary stars are. To achieve this dream he assumes that he needs to imitate their behaviour. His focus on renown, combined with the charismatic influence of Arsenault, distracts Larry from the pursuit of the imaginal realms. Until the young author realizes the gap between Arsenault's professional persona and home life, Larry spends more time pretending to be a poet than actually writing poetry, because the truth is that Larry does not want to be Arsenault; he wants to be his idealized version of Arsenault. Gradually Larry realizes that his heroes are human, even at times childish and pretentious. The secularization of his poetry gods grants him the agency to cultivate his own personality as a poet rather than to mimic Byron, Rimbaud, or Arsenault.

In many ways Coady uses literary sousveillance to satirize and critique self-reflexively. Larry's initial understanding of what it means to be a poet is energizing but also limiting. He expresses pleasure not just in the writing process but also in emulating the behaviour of the poets about whom he has read. Instead of being open and conversational, he decides that "[r]eal poets are careful. They are circumspect. They don't just call each other up in the afternoon to see if everything's okay [as he did to Jim]" (Coady, *Mean Boy* 35). He has an ideal of how a poet should be, and he attempts to become that person even if that means being closed off and rude to family and friends. Similarly, Larry accepts Arsenault's division of Canadian poets into the "hucksters" and the "real thing." He dreads so deeply being classified as a "huckster" that he is willing to conform to Arsenault's arbitrary whims. Not only does he model his behaviour after Arsenault's shifting definition of the "real thing," but he reads his actions in relation to the lives of famous authors: "Dylan Thomas was a drinker. Ezra Pound. Eliot. Good old Anse Surette is, from what I hear coming out of Fredericton. Too many of them to count. Acorn. Oh, all of them are – were. All the greats, they were all drunks for some reason. That derangement of the senses thing" (19). From his selective history Larry posits a connection between great poets and alcoholism to justify his hangover. Just as Rimbaud used hallucinogens to help him write poetry, the student poets in *Mean Boy* experiment with magic mushrooms. Importantly, they are not simply avoiding the work of writing; they are using hallucinogens in an attempt to free their minds and to enhance their creativity. There is, as Boon argues, a long history of creative writers using psychedelics to gain access to imaginal realms. He argues that "the history of what we now call the psychedelics is intimately linked to the evolution of literature in the West, insofar as literature provided a set of maps or blueprints for the imaginary, and a place to situate and explore the imaginal realms, when this was impossible elsewhere" (Boon 223). This history quickly becomes satirized in *Mean Boy*. Ever the ironist, Larry quickly realizes that Rimbaud's method of deranging the senses does not prove fruitful for himself or his classmate, Todd Smiley. He writes: "Todd … is paralyzed with self-consciousness about how high he is. This strikes me as an appalling repudiation of everything I've ever heard regarding drug use" (Coady, *Mean Boy* 179). Instead of opening their minds to imaginal realms, experimenting with mushrooms actually stifles their perception, making them unable to move or think clearly. The discourse of great authors influences Larry's behaviour, but it does not necessarily improve his poetry. Ultimately, through sousveillance of artist mythologies and of his hero, Larry finds a path to redescription and autonomy.

Larry grows from his interaction with other poets, but he remains stifled as a writer until he becomes aware of the gap between the literary reputations of his heroes as writers and their imperfections as human beings. When Larry begins to humanize Arsenault, he understands that the mythology of great authors is misleading. Before Larry meets the author of his favourite text, *Blinding White,* his experiences of Arsenault are mediated through a newspaper interview and through Arsenault's poetry. He knows Arsenault's carefully cultivated persona only as an exciting and fiery voice in Canadian literature. Larry, however, gradually becomes aware of the gap between Arsenault's construction of reality in *Blinding White* and Arsenault's actual life. He writes: "Jim describes her [Moira] as having a face like the Madonna, a moonface, radiating bliss and wisdom like you see in paintings. Similarly, I seem to recall, he describes her as silent. That's also how the virgin is depicted – smiling, close-mouthed like the Mona Lisa. Soft and round. The other thing is, Moira's talk is crazy talk. *Tree died. Dragon blade*" (Coady, *Mean Boy* 82). Arsenault's poem uses religious mythology to express the persona's adoration of his beloved. From Larry's point of view, however, Moira is the rough and harsh antithesis to Arsenault's poetry. Observing the disparity between literature and reality allows Larry to realize that individuals do not always live up to their own mythology or to the lore that others cultivate around them. Larry gradually escapes the shadow of Arsenault, but he must first face his disillusionment during a dream in which he declares to Jim, "'You're not fooling anyone'" (306). This dream, for Larry, "sets off a mini-cascade – it's as if a dammed-up part of my brain," he writes, "has broken through. I write sixteen ghazals in the course of one marathon afternoon at Carl's [tea shop]" (309). Larry learns to disentangle himself from the discourse of great authors when he accepts that Arsenault is also trying to play the role of the great literary genius. Rather than mimicking famous poets, Larry chooses self-analysis and sincerity in cultivating his own identity as a writer.

Unlike early Canadian writers discussed by Margaret Atwood in *Survival* whom she believed were "deprived of audience and cultural tradition" (184), not to mention like-minded artists, Larry is stifled by his literary community in an altogether different way. He has an audience, he has the beginnings of a cultural tradition, and he has friends who are also writers. Larry's output as a poet is hindered by the discourse of great literature and great authors. Until he realizes the duality, perhaps even the inauthenticity, of his idol, his craft suffers. His interactions with Arsenault, whom he initially believes to be "the greatest living poet of our time," allow him to understand that his hero also strives to embody mythologies (Coady, *Mean Boy* 3). Larry interrupts the discourse of great authors and tragic geniuses in part through a careful analysis of the gap between Arsenault's real life and the life Arsenault constructs through writing. In certain ways the arc of Larry and Arsenault's story is summarized by Northrop Frye in *The Bush Garden*: "[O]nce society, along with physical nature, becomes external to the writer, what does he then feel a part of? For the rhetorical or assertive writers [like Arsenault] it is generally a smaller society, the group that agrees with them. But the imaginative writer [like Larry], though he often begins as a member of a school or group, normally pulls away from it as he develops" (237). Arsenault remains stuck in his posture as the poet who opposes the establishment, believing that "'[t]he philistines don't grow miraculously enlightened, the hucksters never see the light and walk the straight and true path. *What is Grand is necessarily obscure to WEAK MEN*'" (Coady, *Mean Boy* 235; italics in the original). In contrast to Arsenault, once Larry has humanized his hero and secularized poetry, he is able to move beyond the influence of the artist as hero motif. He still interacts with Arsenault because he has a great deal to learn, but he has far more agency in his own education. Larry continues to engage with his classmates and friends, but he learns to view his peers and his heroes with a sense of irony. He knows that no matter how they might present themselves, there will be something unsaid. He still seeks imaginal realms, but he does so on his own terms, with a cup of tea rather than a handful of mushrooms. Coady consistently reminds readers that mythologies are motivating, but they can also result in a type of arrested development as exemplified by Arsenault. In this way Coady's *Mean Boy* combines sincere representations of the ineffable power of art with satirical observations about the pretentiousness of the writing world.

For both Larry and Rank, change is aided through writing. Whereas Larry employs literary sousveillance, Rank uses a blend of literary sousveillance and digital sousveillance. The modes they use and the way in which they describe their processes imply that Larry views himself as a recorder of profound realizations, and that Rank is an active creator of knowledge. Larry pushes for redescription through the poetic form of the ghazal; Rank seeks a combination of autonomy and responsibility through his e-confessional. Once Larry has escaped the shadow of Arsenault, he writes that "it's as if a dammed-up part of my brain has broken through. I write sixteen ghazals in the course of one marathon afternoon" (Coady, *Mean Boy* 309). The ghazal is introduced to Larry by Arsenault, and this may hint that what Larry describes is a partial autonomy mixed with a begrudging responsibility. To explain this point, it might prove helpful to consider briefly Arthur Rimbaud and his "derangement of the senses."[2] In *Altered Reading: Levinas and Literature* Jill Robbins writes that Rimbaud's understanding of the poet is as a "receptacle rather than an initiator, an instrument rather than an intention, in Rimbaud's phrase 'like the wood which finds itself a violin'" (123). Similarly Larry views writing as a type of release or a recording as opposed to a creative knowledge-making process. He describes the dammed-up part of his brain as though the ghazals are a liquid waiting to be poured out. Like Rimbaud, he is a recorder of imaginal realms. In this sense his search for autonomy incorporates some level of responsibility in that Arsenault and Rimbaud remain connected to him through his choice of form and through his understanding of how to write poetry.

Much like Larry, Rank finds himself seeking out imaginal realms. After all, he describes writing as "dreamy fun" (Coady, *The Antagonist* 58), but the key distinction is that Larry's transitory growth through the ghazal seems to rely on a release of energy, whereas Rank comes to view writing as the creation of new experience. The e-confessional – whether or not Grix actually reads these emails – becomes an embrace of responsibility and a path to autonomy. Before Rank can reach this state, he must overcome a host of assumptions about writers and writing. Larry needs to redescribe and demystify the writing life, and Rank begins to understand how literary artists blur fact and fiction. Despite his realization that authors often lose themselves in the process, Rank experiences anxiety and frustration about being observed and judged. His response to Grix's novel, however, is partially influenced by his perception of authors as being profoundly insightful cultural heroes. He reads

2 Boon writes: "Rimbaud sought to break down conventional semiotic systems through derangement of the senses and experimented with a synaesthetic alchemy of words that aimed at finding the truth that lurked behind signs. The use of hashish encouraged such ideas" (147).

Grix's novel narcissistically, and he overemphasizes his friend's literary celebrity. Nevertheless, Rank highlights specific aesthetic components of literary sousveillance, such as indirect social commentary and quasi-biographical details, that can prove to be frustrating and deceitful.

In short, Rank feels violated by literary sousveillance. Grix has used private details that Rank shared with his friend at a particularly vulnerable time. When Rank first reads Grix's novel, he believes he has been unfairly characterized. Adding to his frustration, Rank cannot return the gaze of judgment. Through digital sousveillance he finds a way of looking back and observing Grix by writing his own version of their past. Rank feels that Grix has committed something akin to espionage, that the novelist has been a type of spy who posed as a friend only to observe and record private information that could be used at a later date. The way in which this information is delivered makes Rank feel that Grix has unfairly acted as a judge of Rank's life. His secret worries have been revealed in a public document. A complication of his sense of humiliation and anger is that Grix tended to be guarded. Rank writes: "You kept your own counsel most of the time. You never turned to me in the midst of one of our drunk-stoned hazes to implore: Help me, man! I'm all fucked up!" (Coady, *The Antagonist* 4). Grix's apparently withholding nature suggests to Rank that Grix observes people for personal gain, that he has taken Rank's confessions and used them to develop a minor character. To achieve a petty and childish revenge, Rank reveals one of Grix's admissions – that he was afraid of getting fat – to an imaginary audience: "And look at you, now, say it together everybody: chubby; pompous" (6). Despite the absurdity of this initial interaction and the vagueness of Rank's "everybody," his response reveals one way in which biographical detail can be cruel. Whether the audience knows or connects the real-life person to the character in the novel is not necessarily the issue. Biographical information, particularly about the author's friends and family, can publicize private shame.

In its indirect commentary, literary sousveillance creates a power dynamic between Rank and Grix. Judgment in novels tends to be far less direct than judgment in conversation, and Rank finds this element of fiction to be infuriating. Echoing the similarities between Thompson and Arsenault, Grix uses a character who is like Rank but not an exact duplicate. In this way Grix avoids a direct confrontation with Rank: "If you said something … to my face, you know, like one man would to another – then I could say to you … that's a whole buttload of assumptions you just made" (Coady, *The Antagonist* 11–12). The apparent critique of Rank's personality and behaviour is not directly of Rank but of someone who is recognizably like him and who has a similar past. Rank's only chance of actually communicating with the author about his representation of the Rank-like character is to write to Grix online. Rank writes, "[W]hat you've done is a lot more complicated than simply giving utterance" (11). Thus, literary sousveillance in its indirect connection to real life contributes to what Rank would describe as Grix's trespassing. This betrayal is worsened by the fact that Rank feels as though the novel is akin to a monologue in which Grix frames and dictates how readers should understand their past. Since the representation of the Rank-like character exists in a world created by Grix, the novelist becomes the overarching, all-powerful voice communicating to the reader, choosing the metaphors, and controlling the implied ethical framework. Rank feels powerless to respond until he begins practising digital sousveillance through his emails to Grix. Reading his friend's novel proves infuriating and bewildering for Rank, particularly since he perceives Grix as an all-powerful author.

Even though Grix's observations have more cultural capital in a novel than they would in an email or a conversation, Rank's initial anger at Grix is exacerbated by his preconceptions about writers, writing, and books. He needs to find a way to interrupt the artist as hero motif on his own terms. Part of the reason that he feels so powerless upon his first reading of Grix's novel is that he has an unrealistic perception of Grix's fame and success. He writes: "I don't know why but for months after I first read the thing I felt as if you were the most famous man on the planet ... it seemed to me like you had taken over the world" (Coady, The Antagonist 294). Rank perceives Grix, an average novelist, as a wildly successful and famous writer. He expects to see Grix "hitting the talk show circuit, yukking it up with Oprah" (294). This inflated expectation for the success of a first novel highlights Rank's misconception of the power that literary artists possess. Despite the fact that Grix's novel may have been read by only a handful of people, Rank feels that an old friend has become an overnight celebrity and that he is using that celebrity unjustly. Far from having taken over the world, however, Grix's novel is largely ignored and treated with indifference. Beforehand Rank assumes that authors are legitimate judges of moral and ethical standards, not imaginative people who exist on a cultural fringe. His guilt and his desire to escape the past create a heightened sense of anxiety about being observed. Novelists, for Rank, are perceptive and articulate judges of character. As a result, Grix's work is a source of intimidation and humiliation. Rank writes: "This is where I, the all-powerful author, get to explore my exciting new character ... what kind of narrator would I be if I didn't ruthlessly delve into what makes good old Adam tick, warts and all" (121). The choice of the phrase all-powerful situates the author as a god in the world he creates, and Rank's revenge involves attempting to subject Grix to the same powerlessness of feeling trapped in someone else's language.

In the novelist's defence, authors do not need personal information about their readers to make them feel they are being observed and judged through literary sousveillance. Sometimes we recognize ourselves in unexpected places, and we are confronted by our past. As a young man, Rank punches the town troublemaker, Mick Croft, giving him incapacitating brain damage. Before the punch Croft quoted a line from T.S. Eliot's "The Love Song of J. Alfred Prufrock." When Rank stumbled across this poem in the library, he assumed it was an otherworldly intervention. He writes: "So there they were glaring up from the page, Croft's famous last words, emanating wave after wave of uncanny terror at me. Not to mention the creepshow pertinence of the lines that followed, as if someone – some malignant entity – had affixed a psychic spigot directly into my past and let it drip, one word at a time, into the book" (Coady, *The Antagonist* 107). Rank imbues T.S. Eliot's language with private significance. He reads the poem in such a way that it makes him feel intensely self-conscious and judged by an unseen force. One of the great strengths of fiction and poetry, as Michael Winter states in his caveat to *This All Happened*, is that literature allows readers to evaluate their own lives (xii). It helps them understand themselves better through association with characters and events. Therefore, judgment in literature comes in a variety of forms, and it is not exclusively intentional or malicious. Nevertheless, there remain specific uses of biographical information that come across as shifty, provocative, or manipulative.

Before Rank witnesses the mediocre reviews of Grix's novel, he experiences what it means to practise literary sousveillance, and he realizes that writing involves indeterminate and intuitive processes. He begins to understand that Grix could not have been in complete control over everything that he wrote. Rank admits: "I kind of imagined you sitting around rubbing your hands together and cackling to yourself as you plotted out your miserable theft ... The interesting thing about the whole process is that I find myself realizing what I think about everything at the exact moment I'm typing it out. Then I sit back and read it over and go: Huh" (Coady, *The Antagonist* 35). Understanding the development of a novel as exploratory helps Rank to be more accepting of Grix. Rather than seeing the author as an evil genius who chose to represent the Rank-like character as a cliché, Rank understands that it is easy for writers to lose themselves in the process. The gap between the theoretical goals that writers set out for themselves and the difficulty of attempting to achieve them becomes far clearer. As he progresses through his e-confessional, he realizes that the "weird, dreamy fun" of writing occasionally diverts him from his original goal of showing Grix where his novel had lied or misrepresented the past (58). He writes: "To take your bullshit version of me, flush it like the steaming turd of half-truths and oversights it was, and replace it with the glorious, terrible, complex, astonishing truth of Reality … But recently I've been getting lost in it … I spent about a half-hour trying to figure out the best way to describe your Adam's apple, how it seemed to glow, enormous in the shadows" (208). Rank's noble purpose begins with an attempt to accurately describe reality, but he has to rely on descriptive practices that highlight the subjectivity of his experience. Tinkering with sentences becomes an obsession, and he realizes that his perception of reality is created by language. This subjectivity temporarily transforms his narration into a site of play: "You let it distract you from your noble purpose. Suddenly people in the story are doing and saying things you never meant for them to do or say – and you're letting it happen, because it's fun" (209). Despite the fact that the composition of the e-confessional is enlightening for Rank, he still condemns Grix for the way in which he used biographical detail. He comes to understand the complexities of literary sousveillance, but Grix's novel still amounts to a transgression of their friendship.

Rank's anger at Grix is borne out of more than narcissism and a sense of betrayal. He feels that Grix attempts to claim ownership over Rank's past and that he has done so through stylistic and descriptive choices. Before Rank comes to see the past as a landscape, he writes: "[I]t's my story and it exists and has existed in a very specific way, despite what you have done. It is a thing that hangs in the air around me at all times" (Coady, *The Antagonist* 8). Early in the novel Rank's descriptions of his own identity sound extremely similar to the way in which Ruti describes the tyrannical self: "We may even end up with a tyrannical self that never allows competing versions have their say. Such a tyrannical self displays a false coherence that diminishes our capacity for existential versatility even as it gives us the (mistaken) impression that we are in complete control of our destinies" (Ruti 31). Grix's descriptions offer a competing version of Rank and his past. Although Rank might not be willing to accept it, Grix's literary sousveillance actually helps Rank view himself with open-mindedness. It is only in considering how other people feel about him that he begins to break free from this tyrannical self. This unintentional benefit does not negate the fact, however, that Grix wrote Rank as a cliché. As Rank writes, "The biggest pisser? The fact that the cliché of me was all you really took, you boiled an entire life, an entire human being into his most basic, boneheaded elements" (Coady, *The Antagonist* 9). Important moments in Rank's life are reduced to background information for a minor character in Grix's novel. The insult of cliché is that it indicates an indifference to attempting fully to understand the thoughts and feelings of another human being; it obliterates their individuality and reduces them to a type. Grix's descriptive choices hurt Rank because he thought they had shared meaningful experiences. The willingness to see someone as a cliché implies a lack of affection and an inattentiveness to the qualities that make a person unique. Rank is humiliated by the fact that although he believed that he and Grix shared important memories, Grix refers to him offhandedly. Rank writes, "And it was hard enough when I discovered you shared it [their past], when I found it immortalized in your book – immortalized but in such a freakily offhand sort of way. Somehow enshrined and chucked aside all at once" (131). Rank is grateful that he was included, but he also feels dismissed. One of the nuances that Rank wants Grix to be aware of is that Rank's behaviour as a stereotypical jock was occasionally self-conscious and performative: "I think I felt the weight of those million universes, those billion clichés ... You: geek; me: jock" (55). Rank does not want to be easily defined as a simple copy of a type. He chooses to fight the weight of cliché by consciously accepting his role as a jock. Grix's descriptive choices fail to represent that complexity, and Rank is infuriated to the point where he feels he must redescribe what has been implied about his past.

Rank gradually understands that each person's history is a competing discourse, and fiction is a tool that can alter the way in which the past is understood. Despite his realization that writing is an indeterminate process, he remains offended that Grix attempted to impose his will onto their past. He writes: "I used to see my past as a book ... But now I'm starting to see it as something more like a frontier – a landscape I have spent my life cultivating, fortifying ... But the landscape is alive ... [it] consists of multiple things, multiple wills that shift and change and occasionally assert themselves in force" (Coady, *The Antagonist* 235). Once a text is out in the world, it can enter this landscape of competing discourses. For Rank, Grix's descriptive choices possess a detached, judgmental violence. He complains of "the half-assed way you told my story. Your approach, I'm noticing as I go over your book for the fourth time, was practically not to tell it at all ... to preserve the twenty-year-old me in my misery like a bug someone had closed the pages on" (293). Rank feels his past has been defined and trapped in someone else's book. He writes: "What you've killed is yours forever – a trophy picked off from the landscape and hung up on your wall" (235). The only way that Rank can escape from this metaphorical death is to create on his own terms, to reanimate, that version of himself as a fragile and vulnerable young man. In doing so, he attempts to destroy Grix's past self in a similar way, but he also grants his friend more centrality and depth. This consistent attempt to communicate and to grow distinguishes Rank's e-confessional as an embrace of responsibility to a person who he feels has betrayed his trust.

Grix's novel and biographical details disturb Rank, but Rank's misunderstanding of Grix as an all-seeing and all-powerful novelist exacerbates the pain and the anxiety he feels. It is not until Rank begins to write that he understands Grix as a novelist. The creative act of threading sentences distracts authors from their noble purpose. Grix becomes less of an all-powerful judge and more of an artist at play, albeit self-involved and unknowingly cruel. Rank cannot forgive Grix for his betrayal and for his indifference, but he does, at the very least, understand the impulse and the joy of writing. He demonstrates that fiction can affect readers in unexpected and powerful ways. Ultimately, Rank is better for having read Grix's representation of their past even though it causes him intense inner turmoil. Sometimes the way that a reader chooses to understand literary sousveillance, however, can be as cruel as the way in which an author chooses to observe. The power that creative writers have might be ambiguous and unwieldy, but it exists. Readers, in turn, have their own will in the interpretive process. They project their metaphors onto the novel, and this interaction is where the power of story lies (Booth, *The Company We Keep* 364). Rank's narrative elucidates how digital sousveillance gives one person a sense of agency and control in describing the past and in cultivating their own identity.

One of the major distinctions between Rank and Larry is the direction of their energies near the end of their accounts, both of which can be read – at the very least – as a stilted growth. Larry strives and fails to break away from the attachments that formed him, whereas Rank stubbornly tries to redescribe the past and to live with his attachments. This might be most clearly expressed in lines near the close of each narrative. Larry writes: "I stood there so long that the red of the kitchen had started to mellow and shift … and finally sat back down in the chair … It was bad enough to be leaving a fire unattended while people slept. I tried not to think of what my father would say" (Coady, *Mean Boy* 382). On the one hand, Coady shows the young poet caught awkwardly between two impulses, not embracing responsibility but also not being able to free himself. On the other hand, Rank narrates the damage that this search for autonomy can inflict, and he identifies his own metaphorical violence as a storyteller. He writes: "Whatever I did to you …

I struck a match, I flicked a switch, I'm sorry. And thank you for not putting it in your book. And fuck you for not putting it in your book. Your friend, Gordon Rankin" (Coady, *The Antagonist* 337). Rank wants to live with a sense of responsibility to and friendship with other people despite the contentiousness he feels. Even though *The Antagonist* is a reworking of the transitional growth typically seen in the Künstlerroman, it is not necessarily an ethical prescription to the shortcomings of *Mean Boy*. These two texts are best thought of as interconnected expressions about creative writing, both of which grant these idiosyncratic narrators different opportunities. After all, if the desperate poem at the conclusion of Mean Boy is Arsenault's, then an interruption of the narrator already exists.[3] Ultimately the changes in these narrators can be typified as an initial push for autonomy that leads to responsibility in some form. Larry needs to make his heroes a little more human in order to gain agency in his own life, whereas Rank is able to forgive a friend while still remembering the metaphorical trespassing that took place.

The ethics of using real people as models for fictional characters is a contentious subject. However, Coady's *Mean Boy* and *The Antagonist* demonstrate how the use of real people is seldom a cold, calculated process. Fredric Jameson argues in *Postmodernism or the Cultural Logic of Late Capitalism* that modernists revered the great work, the misunderstood genius, and the artist as cultural hero; postmodern theorists tend to see such writers as shrewd rhetoricians: "[T]he once-famous names [are] no longer [understood] as characters larger than life or great souls of one kind or another, but rather … as careers, that is to say as objective situations in which an ambitious young artist around the turn of the century could see the objective possibility of turning himself into the 'greatest painter' (or poet or novelist or composer) 'of the age'" (306). Jameson's description anticipates the way in which Rank sees his novelist ex-friend Grix at the beginning of *The Antagonist*. As the narrative progresses, however, it is evident that the word shrewd is inaccurate. Rank often finds himself lost in his own creative experience, making up details amid the fun of writing a story. In becoming more open-minded about his past and whom he would like to be in the future, he escapes what Ruti would describe as a tyrannical self.

The Antagonist and *Mean Boy* work through a complex ethics of literary sousveillance, specifically in relation to the use of biographical and autobiographical information. Taking another person's life and

3 Here is an excerpt from the poem that concludes *Mean Boy*: "things are sooooooooo fucked/rightnow im deqad man. Ii hiding/fromit" (Coady 384–5).

reworking details to develop a character who appears extremely similar can clearly be understood as an indirect way of spreading gossip, and it can be unnecessarily hurtful. After being scolded for developing a character who was like Thompson but also not like him, Coady responded through *The Antagonist*. As a Künstlerroman, *Mean Boy* already has qualities that highlight the grasping, cruel undercurrent to the world of creative writing (even the title seems to be directing our attention to this point). Coady narrates how in Larry's desire to be an idealized self, he loses sight of his creative pursuits. In order to become the person he wants to be, he needs to seek autonomy from his past. He also needs to redescribe his literary heroes, one of whom is Arsenault, and this is where the people who knew Thompson took offence. *The Antagonist* presents a series of demands to readers. Coady reveals the blind spots of insular literary artists fully immersed in the world of writers and writing. She asks us to think about how easily we categorize other people as minor characters in the grand narrative of our own lives, and she suggests that authors have a responsibility to think deeply about the people who care about them. Yet *The Antagonist* also implies that the so-called theft of Rank's biographical details helps him understand his past in a new way. Wrestling with Grix's novel might prove to be frustrating, but it also seems incredibly helpful. Perhaps all of this is to say that authors are not moral authorities; they have their own flaws and blind spots. Writing well often requires turning away from one's community in order to write about it. Some of the greatest authors are anti-social snobs – not people from whom to take life advice. Perhaps that is part of the appeal of a character like Arsenault. He is not a moral exemplum; he is charismatic in the profound passion he feels and articulates. The imperfect, often hedonistic gaze of the author figure needs to be kept in mind as a subtext for the entirety of this book. We should closely observe each one of these writers. Otherwise we risk mistaking them for prophets.

The Antagonist suggests that one way in which non-writers can observe authors is through digital sousveillance. As someone who grew up in a rural area, Coady appreciates the potential benefits of the online world. She is no luddite and no technophobe. In *Who Needs Books?* she writes:

> I don't like to think about all the books and films and art and theatre and music I would not have had exposure to without the mere thirteen channels of network television I accessed growing up. Those stations provided a psychic bridge, however rickety, out of my small town on Cape Breton Island and out into the larger world. If I had had access to the internet

> back then? It makes me dizzy to think how I might have feasted on the culture, literature and art that I so craved. But since I grew up in the pre-digital era, very little of it crossed my transom. Such was not my world. (Coady, *Who Needs Books?* 19)

For people living in rural areas – who might not have direct access to higher education or to literary communities – the internet is their link to the rest of the world. She even sounds hopeful for learned future generations: "[W]ith all our entertainments rolled up into a single device, isn't it at least possible that books could reach an audience they've never reached before?" (Coady, *Who Needs Books?* 24). Despite her optimism Coady is starkly aware of the tensions created by digital sousveillance. For all of the potential benefits there are just as many drawbacks.

In her short story "Someone Is Recording" Coady narrates a series of emails from a professor, Gary Weiland, to an online columnist, Erica Shaffner. Whereas digital sousveillance allows Rank to defend himself, in this short story it leads to a dangerous, gendered, group polarization. The problem derives from Shaffner and Weiland becoming influencers of echo chambers. Much like between Grix and Rank, the central conflict between Shaffner and Weiland involves how they understand their shared past. Shaffner's articles and interviews about Weiland result in a dramatic shift in their relationship dynamic. He feels observed and cornered by the same internet mob by which she is empowered. One of the key distinctions between this text and the other texts in this chapter is that there is little to no focus on a shared physical community. The conflict occurs online, and as the narrative progresses, Weiland and Shaffner represent two increasingly polarized groups. As a result, people within these groups do not have a chance to humanize the influencer of their group. In contrast, Larry had an extended period of time to witness the gap between Arsenault's curated public persona and his private self. The followers of Shaffner and Weiland do not have this same opportunity. Coady's narrative of digital sousveillance is incredibly timely in its representation of the trenchant online world. In "Why Social Media Makes Us More Polarized and How to Fix It," Damon Centola explains how influencers have power over networks of people: "In social media, networks tend to be centralized: a small number of people, or perhaps just one person, at the 'center' of the network is connected to lots of other people in the 'periphery.' The multitudes in the periphery of the social network have only a modest number of connections, while the few – the so-called 'influencers' – at the center of the network are connected to nearly everyone. This puts these people into the powerful position of being able to exert a disproportionate level of 'influence' over the group." Coady's narrative tracks the path that two characters take to find themselves at the centre of opposing, vitriolic networks. Initially Shaffner wields influence over an echo chamber of like-minded people, but as the narrative progresses, Weiland lords over his own mob of internet trolls. Although readers only hear about Shaffner through Weiland, Shaffner's efforts appear to be designed to give her some autonomy from her past with him. However, both figures by the end of the narrative exhibit a version of responsibility that feels distorted, more about power than about embracing interconnectivity.

In this story digital sousveillance, much like community sousveillance in Strange Heaven, creates a strict gender binary: Weiland becomes the influencer of an echo chamber for men, and Shaffner becomes the influencer of an echo chamber for women. Weiland condescendingly questions the venue in which Shaffner's first article appears. He writes: "My wife tells me thepinkghetto.soy is sort of a DIY, Millennial-centric version of Gwyneth Paltrow's website – *Goo?* – with a sprinkling of personal essays. But I suppose a Millennial audience is the only one that matters these days, at least when it comes to those all-important 'clicks'" (Coady, "Someone Is Recording"). He attempts to characterize Shaffner as overly emotional and attention seeking, contrasting it with his own writing, which he believes is more measured, reserved, and intellectual: "I tend to be a little more circumspect in my own work, more about ideas than feelings, but maybe that's why your stuff is striking a chord with the kids on thepinkghetto.soy while mine remains a favourite of today's hottest academic journals, ha ha" (Coady). Even though Weiland might initially try to be detached and rational, he also gives in to the temptation to wield influence over an echo chamber. He stumbles across his own version of thepinkghetto.soy in the Randovians, who are even more extreme in their online harassment. Weiland writes: "Anyway, I hope your mom is ok. Andrea tells me this swatting thing is a pretty common tactic of the 'Randovians', but I promise you I had no idea. I read she was taken to the hospital after the incident but released a few hours later, which hopefully means she wasn't injured? And I dearly hope the damage to the house was minimal" (Coady). The ways in which the echo chambers are divided by gender share similarities to community sousveillance in *Strange Heaven* in that the masculine group enacts physical violence, and the feminine group is characterized – by Weiland, at least – as histrionic and dogmatic. The contrast, however, between community and digital sousveillance is that women have more freedom and power in the online world. They have greater opportunity to form groups with like-minded people, and they can look back at individuals who have abused their power in the past.

Weiland desires to break down the distance between the observer and the observed in order to reconcile. Shaffner, however, refuses to engage in dialogue. He writes: "You know, Erica, everything you said in that interview on YouTube, you could have said to my face. Is it that you think I won't hear the things you have to say? Is that why you don't bother? Because I'm telling you, I will. I have been. Can we actually talk?" (Coady, "Someone Is Recording"). But throughout the story Shaffner never directly responds to Weiland. In this way she avoids whatever manipulative rhetoric he might use to try and level their power dynamic. If she remains the detached observer, then he stays prisoner inside her panopticon. Instead of engaging in discourse with him, Shaffner posts excerpts from Weiland's email to thepinkghetto.soy and mocks them. Weiland is offended because the first letter was meant to be a private conversation, and from Weiland's perspective Shaffner manipulates what he wrote: "It's clear you're not interested in hearing my side of things, and you're welcome to post whatever you like, but I think it was a little offside to cherry pick the excerpts of my letter that you did and then embellish them with your own disparaging commentary" (Coady, "Someone Is Recording"). Privacy and communication are two concepts that could have helped Bridget Murphy in *Strange Heaven*. In "Someone Is Recording," Weiland's expectation for privacy and communication is wielded against him to shift the balance of the power he once had over Shaffner. One can only imagine how this reckoning from the past would be understood if enacted in the world of *Strange Heaven*. Shaffner would not have like-minded people to support her, and she would not have been able to keep her distance from Weiland. Therefore, digital sousveillance enables her to fight back in a way that community sousveillance could not.

Digital sousveillance taken to its extreme has serious consequences professionally and privately. Not only is Shaffner's mother swatted, but Weiland might lose both his job and his family. He writes: "I'm off work for the remainder of the semester thanks to all this. Students have started boycotting my classes en masse. The administration would dearly love to get rid of me at this point" (Coady, "Someone Is Recording"). Near the end of the narrative his wife and daughter leave to escape the chaos created by his online battle with Shaffner: "I have lots of time on my hands right now, especially with Andrea and Kenz taking a break down in Florida with Andrea's parents" (Coady, "Someone Is Recording"). In *Strange Heaven*, *Mean Boy*, and *The Antagonist* there are complex, textured ethical responses developed to counter the dilemmas faced by the characters. In contrast, with "Someone Is Recording," we are asked to witness a digital version of the sublime in that a great force of energy is manifested through people and increasingly divided through group polarization. Weiland tries to downplay the power that he and Shaffner accumulate: "I guess I was just feeling frustrated after your appearance on *Good Morning America* as I honestly assumed you would have gotten all this out of your system by now. Plus, I was floored that any respectable news organization would hold up our personal internet dust-up as something 'emblematic' of the 'cultural moment'" (Coady, "Someone Is Recording"). But even he confesses that "[t]he culture is going through some kind of catharsis right now I guess, and catharsis isn't always a logical or intellectual process – sometimes it just involves venting. Society needs its whipping boys and when I consider how easy I've had it up to this point as white, male etc., I realize there are worse things than being made the butt of a joke – even a joke that's gone viral" (Coady, "Someone Is Recording"). A culture can have a long memory, but a culture can also be intensely reactionary. The first wave of essays and interviews by Shaffner is a reckoning for past behaviour, but Weiland and his followers have their own response. Eventually, from Weiland's perspective, Shaffner's online persona backfires. He writes: "I don't suppose you've noted all the renewed interest in Hollister? A former classmate sent me a link – apparently some publisher is reissuing Psalms of Kanata. So congrats! It would seem the 'great male author' is ascendant once more, all thanks to your efforts" (Coady, "Someone Is Recording"). The group polarization escalates until the two sides are insular, extreme, and aggressive. He writes: "The level of support has been really staggering, not to mention clarifying. To know I have so many people on my side in this. You're just one person, Erica. One person who interpreted my actions a certain way, many years ago. I remember things differently. And I have as many people on my side in this as you do on yours. Maybe more, I'm starting to realize" (Coady, "Someone Is Recording"). From community to literary to digital sousveillance, the power dynamic between men and women has shifted. People still feel closely observed and misrecognized, but in Coady's first novel, Shaffner would have been ignored, ridiculed, or sent to a mental institution. In this story, at least she is heard.

In a world where bad behaviour can be documented and posted online for all to see, Coady probes the fallout between two influencers. Weiland writes: "The administration would dearly love to get rid of me at this point, especially after my impromptu speech in the quad – maybe you caught it on Facebook Live? (I had no idea someone was recording me, by the way – but then again someone's always recording these days, aren't they?) I was actually pretty impressed it got so many views" (Coady, "Someone Is Recording"). Unsurprisingly the internet mob does not observe events in a detached, measured way; instead, through the influence of Shaffner and Weiland, they move towards an increasing group polarization. Shaffner's desire to seek autonomy and redescribe her past with Weiland brings her into contact with a group of like-minded people. Her influence over this group and her rejection of dialogue with Weiland contribute to his own seeking out of autonomy. He, in turn, also becomes an influencer of an echo chamber. In the world of digital sousveillance, responsibility manifests quite differently – if it is responsibility at all. Shaffner's and Weiland's interactions with their groups is a way of harnessing power and wielding it against others. They quickly become what Ruti might describe as tyrannical selves.

Those who watch and feel watched find themselves in this complicated oscillation between autonomy and responsibility. Bridget lives in a town with polarized, repressive gender roles between men and women. She does not meet the expectations imposed on her by community sousveillance and she seeks autonomy. In her desire to resist the gaze of others she forms a distinct identity despite the pressures she faces. Larry leaves his community but trades in one set of eyes for another. The literary gaze also inhibits identity formation, funnelling would-be writers into distinct, reductive categories such as the artist as hero or the artist as cultural rebel or the artist as experimental drug user. Rank, however, employs digital sousveillance to highlight the ways in which he has been misrecognized. Building on these various representations of sousveillance, "Someone Is Recording" narrates the intoxicating power available to influencers. The concepts of autonomy and responsibility are skewed in the world of digital sousveillance. Seeking autonomy leads Weiland and Shaffner to become tyrannical selves. Their versions of responsibility are more about wielding power than about giving themselves over to others. The satirical, parodic, and subversive qualities of Coady's work encourage readers to see the flaws and ironies within each mode of sousveillance. In many ways she is the opposite of an influencer. She is what might be called a great ironizer, always showing her readers why they should observe closely, why they should scrutinize those who impose themselves onto the world, and why they should form their identity on their own terms, in their own landscape of language.

PART TWO

Vulnerable People and the Damage of Surveillance

4 David Chariandy's *Brother*: Systemic Racism, Post-Traumatic Stress Disorder, and Urban Policing

In the previous section a philosophical framework was developed in relation to surveillance and literature. In this chapter I observe how a young, Black man is misrecognized by the state and how David Chariandy highlights the need for spaces in which people like Michael, the narrator of *Brother*, can resist containment. Much like the texts in Barrett's *Blackening*, this novel depicts "both the exclusionary and racist practices of the Canadian state, alongside the strategies for coping and surviving practised by black people in Canada" (7). Michael is a visible minority living with the fallout of a traumatic incident with police services. His brother, Francis, was killed by a police officer, and both he and his mother, Ruth, are stifled by complicated grief.[1] Chariandy's first novel, *Soucouyant*, published in 2007, traces the complex relationship between immigrant families and memory; *I've Been Meaning to Tell You*,

1 In *Complicated Grief: Scientific Foundations for Health Care Professionals*, Margaret Stroebe, Henk Schut, and Jan van den Bout write, "In general terms, complicated grief (CG) can be understood as something like a 'derailing' of the normal, usually painful process of adapting to the loss of a significant person" (3). For those interested in other scholarly discussions of complicated grief in literature, Barrett highlights how *Thirsty* by Dionne Brand is about, among other things, profound loss, inflicted on a family by the state. Barrett writes: "The poem begins long after Alan has been shot by the Toronto police and traces how the women in his family remain haunted by his absence. The unnamed narrator intervenes in the historical silence that has erased Alan's presence from the nation and silenced the women in the poem. The speaker is able to articulate that which remains inexpressible for the three women and render present what she detects in their gestures of longing and yearning for the recovery of an unspoken loss. As such, she recomposes Alan's history and provides a language for his absence and for the lives of the women many years after his death" (37). The literary voice then is designed to articulate pain and absence. The state violence inflicted on a family might be ignored or forgotten, but Brand's work calls our attention back to it, demands our observation, and frames the discussion on her terms.

published in 2018, is an autobiographical work framed as a letter to his daughter that details experiences of racism in Canada. *Brother* focuses on both themes, and yet, in demonstrating that a police presence is desired by people within Michael's community, Chariandy resists a simplified view of the world in his representations of racism and state surveillance. Acts of violence within the neighbourhood necessitate a reaction from police services in order to instil calm. However, the state and media responses are racist, classist, and xenophobic. Michael seems to desire some kind of escape from the constant barrage of forces that attempt to impose an identity upon him, but he is also in a difficult position of needing to look after Ruth. Surveillance in *Brother* is visceral. It is in the narrator's face day to day. Resistance is not some aesthetic that he might enjoy in a book or on a screen. Michael needs to find spaces to which he can escape and cultivate his own identity away from the all-encompassing gaze of the state and his community.

Chariandy's representation of the police and policing is mirrored by real-life events in Toronto, a city whose police services have a history of systemic racism. Walcott discusses the fight by the Black community in Toronto to be heard and to be believed that they were being treated unfairly:

> The denial of racial profiling by the police and by politicians in Toronto points to the illegitimacy of black claims for social justice in the city. While black communities have long made claims that pointed to racial profiling, such claims and the evidence that pointed to those claims were often denied by those in authority as lacking validity. This time the claims are being taken somewhat seriously. The *Toronto Star* reports that included evidence of widespread racial profiling of black and some Asian people, have made creditable the claims that many black people have consistently been making for years. By and large, in both the city and the nation, black appeals for social justice remain unheard by those in authority, and this is largely due to the continuing ambivalent place of black peoples in the national imagination. Do we belong or do we not belong? And if we belong, when does the nation begin to acknowledge black arrivals – recently or going back to before Confederation? (Walcott, *Black Like Who?* 11–12).

As Walcott highlights, this is not only an issue in the city of Toronto but also a national problem. In "Disproportionate Minority Contact in Canada: Police and Visible Minority Youth," Robin T. Fitzgerald and Peter J. Carrington argue that disproportionate minority contact in Canada "is due to racially discriminatory policing" (473). While Fitzgerald and

Carrington are tentative in their conclusions, their study demonstrates the need for deeper consideration of the pain and lingering trauma that arise from systemic racism. In *Brother*, Francis's bewilderment and rage towards the officers when he feels unfairly targeted cry out for attention. In this sense, Chariandy's novel makes abstract data come to life. Part of the real-life policing strategy in Toronto has involved targeting young, male minorities. A 2014 documentary produced by the Policing Literacy Initiative titled *Crisis of Distrust: Police and Community in Toronto* demonstrates complex issues around carding. Even though certain members of the police services are against it, they work within a larger bureaucracy. Then deputy chief, Peter Sloly says, "As a person who's lived in the city of Toronto for almost forty years and growing up in Scarborough as a young person of colour I was very much aware of this issue" (Crisis of Distrust). Ultimately he calls for systemic changes, including greater community involvement and oversight. In "Toronto and the 'Paris Problem': Community Policing in 'Immigrant Neighbourhoods,'" Parastou Saberi details issues with racial profiling arising from strategies implemented by the Toronto Police Service: "Carding refers to an increasingly common practice whereby officers, on stopping an individual, fill out contact cards to record personal information for intelligence purposes. Carding is an updated version of the police 'stop and chats' of the late 1990s, and is similar to the police practice of stop-and-frisk in the United States. Carding has intensified racial profiling, the criminalisation of non-White youth, and the racialised security ideology around 'immigrant neighbourhoods' in Toronto. Public housing complexes soon became a major site for the police targeting of non-White youth" (58). Saberi highlights how young males of colour feel targeted and harassed by such strategies. In his development of Michael and Francis, Chariandy reflects the resulting anger and anxiety. Michael avoids violence at the hands of a flawed system, but when Francis questions it, he is punished. In this sense the fictional world of *Brother* mirrors a history of systemic racism in Toronto. Furthermore, *Brother* adds nuance to this discussion by showing that even in such an environment there are still police officers who stand out as being good and decent human beings despite the system within which they are working.

It is essential to point out that Chariandy provides clear purposes for surveillance and for a police presence in Michael's community. The city can be an intimidating and violent place, assaulting the senses and heightening whatever stress Michael already feels. When he meets Aisha, the pair are almost immediately hit with "spraying slush" as a "truck blasts suddenly past" (Chariandy, *Brother* 5). Even after they go into Michael's apartment, the assault continues: "Bullets of slush smattering upon the bedroom window. Another truck that has passed too close to the curb outside" (7). The impression gathered is one of being under siege by an urban sprawl of machinery and concrete. There are a variety of stressors that set people on edge, and some people inevitably act out. Chariandy writes: "A dispute among some young men ... had amplified into a beating. Not a showy brag of a beating, a bit of roughing up with loud threats thrown in, maybe the flash of a weapon, fake or not, but a real beating. Some guy getting whaled on hard by a group of boys" (27). Francis and Michael see this violence first hand, and they develop strategies to avoid feeling intimidated by other young males. Importantly, some members of the community observe this violent behaviour and threaten to call the police: "[A]s my brother and I returned to our block, we sharpened when we saw a bunch of guys we didn't recognize hanging out in the roundabout of our complex. They were shouting at one another ... Someone shouted from a balcony, 'We've called the cops already. The cops are coming,' but the shouting only grew louder and more threatening" (27). As this violence escalates, Francis and Michael unfortunately become associated with it because they are young, racialized males. The response of people who are worried or disturbed or frightened by this violence is to seek safety and calm through the police. Unfortunately for the young males in this novel, the police are more frightening than the groups who enact both verbal and physical violence to one another.

Chariandy consistently creates profound, complex moments of indeterminacy. He develops a situation in which a tragic incident occurs, and the state has no choice but to respond through a police presence. Community members fear the threat of gun violence for a variety of reasons, but the nightmarish extreme of this anxiety is realized when a stray bullet wounds a child. After a shooting witnessed by the brothers the police become a persistent presence in the neighbourhood. Chariandy writes: "[T]hen from around the corner of our building footsteps running towards us. He had just turned into our view when there was another shot, and a sound like a pumpkin dropped from a balcony at Halloween, and the runner fell. It was Anton [a young man whom both brothers know]" (*Brother* 28). When Michael and Francis are on the street after the shooting incident, they feel unfairly observed and reprimanded by the police. They are frightened although they have done nothing wrong but go for a walk. The parallel that Chariandy highlights is that people in their apartments feel unfairly threatened by gun violence when they too have also done nothing wrong: "The cops were explaining to Mother what had happened and why they had stopped us. There had been an altercation, perhaps a business deal gone bad. Guns were drawn. Two young men were hit but managed to stumble away. There was one fatality, someone known to the police, but there were other casualties too, the cops informed us. Bullets had flown through glass doors and windows. A bystander was shot in his arm. A stray bullet had pierced the thin wall of a unit and struck a sleeping seven-year-old-girl" (Chariandy, *Brother* 46). It seems inevitable that the various acts of violence are weighed against one another. Each act is traumatic and should not happen, but the innocent, sleeping girl functions as an exclamation to the rest of the violence, framing the young males as potential child killers. The police are not demeaning and humiliating young males because they want to; they have no choice; a child has been shot, and they need to protect the community. This indeterminacy created by Chariandy does not condone or justify the behaviour of officers in *Brother*, but it does highlight the complexity of issues related to safety, policing, and surveillance in Canada.

As the narrator, Michael concedes that a response to this violence is necessary, but he is disturbed by the xenophobia and racism that he witnesses. The shooting of the girl, Goose, ultimately leads to public outcry and greater tension within Michael's community. Michael writes: "I sat quietly for a good length of time, combing through the newspaper coverage of the shooting. There were updates, columns, letters to the editor. A lot of people were angry about the way Goose had suffered. Some called for a crackdown on crime, others for much more. One columnist wrote in that old and ready-made language about 'immigrants' and 'ethnic neighbourhoods' and 'sending people back where they came from,' even though most in the Park knew that the suspects had all been raised in the surrounding city" (Chariandy, *Brother* 73). For Michael, such a response is frustrating because it is racist and xenophobic, but it is even worse for its underlying stupidity and ignorance. The immigrants in that community are the people who had to fear those shooters the most. Furthermore, if the columnist took the time to study what had happened, then they would have known that the people involved in the crime were Canadian. What the piece amounts to is hijacking the shooting of a young innocent girl to disseminate a politics that excludes rather than embraces, that hates rather than loves.

Part of Chariandy's overall project in this story is to take the way in which news media surveils a community and to insert layers of ethical complexity underneath. Michael observes that news media distorts images of people to fit a particular narrative. After the shooting, he reads about the incident in the newspaper, and he is shocked by the image of Anton that he sees: "It was one of those high school photos that for so many of us always seem to go wrong. The photographer didn't choose the right background or adjust the light settings, and so the outlines of Anton's face and hair bled into the navy behind him. His eyes steeled, his mouth screwed tight upon his face" (Chariandy, *Brother* 73). The complexities of Anton's life are reduced to one image of a tough-looking young man. Michael does not feel like he knew Anton well, but he is aware that his life is not adequately or fairly represented by the photograph chosen to accompany the news story. For example, Michael remembers Anton being beaten by a group of males, and he goes to check on him afterwards. He sees Anton crying, but Anton pretends that he is laughing: "[H]e started pretending that he'd been laughing, his sobs turning to chuckles, the laughter becoming almost real" (74). Where most people reading the news only see the picture, Michael knows that there is so much more texture and nuance to Anton's life. Yes, he did something criminal and, yes, he put people's lives in danger, but he also grew up in a difficult situation that severely limited the types of choices that he could make.

The xenophobic and racist response to the shootings results not only in an increased police presence but also in a community whose members begin to scrutinize one another, closely demarcating between the normal and the deviant as in Foucault's discussions of the panopticon. After the shooting of Anton, Michael walks back to his apartment, and he describes how people in the neighbourhood feel seen: "I knew their faces and family names. The Cumberbatches and Rampersands and Nowaks. They had blank expressions on their faces. Maybe from the intensity of the light, maybe because they wanted to give nothing away of themselves to others. But most looked the way you do when you're being studied unfavourably. When you're being watched by also trying to see" (Chariandy, *Brother* 32). As though they are inside Foucault's panopticon, they sense they are being observed by the state, and although they want to observe back, they are not completely sure where to look. Importantly, in Michael's world, it is not just the young males on the street who feel they are being watched; it is everyone living in the neighbourhood. After a traumatic event, people talk, and the subjects of this gossip rightly feel scrutinized. Chariandy writes: "For these newer neighbors, there is always a story connected to Mother and me, a story made all the more frightening through each inventive retelling among neighbours. It is a story, effectively vague, of a young man deeply 'trouble,' and of a younger brother carrying 'history,' and of a mother showing now the creep of 'madness'" (36). For certain members of the community, Francis represents the deviant figure who has been punished. This community sousveillance is troubling because it risks simplifying and categorizing Michael, Francis, and Ruth. They would prefer to define their own identities and describe their own stories instead of allowing others to define and describe these things for them. Michael at least seems to know how he is being described and can speak against those descriptions. The same might not be true for Ruth. In a moment where surveillance and sousveillance coincide, she feels not only observed by the police but also like she has to fit into a specific performance of motherhood for others to see: "'Ma'am?' asked the cop. 'Are you the mother?' She nodded and listened but looked beyond the cops to the audience of staring neighbours. The combination of sweat and glare made her face shine like a mask, and she looked a bit like an actor who'd stumbled accidentally onto a stage and who now, too late, had to figure out her role" (Chariandy, *Brother* 32). Thus, the world created in *Brother* is one in which everyone is affected by violence and by the state's response. Although the state can be cold and distant, the community sousveillance that civilians impose on other civilians can be humiliating, cruel, and inescapable. Chariandy writes: "I do not blame my neighbours for avoiding Mother and me. They carry their own histories and their own hopes of genuine arrival. They are marked by language and religion and skin, and their jobs are often temporary and fragile" (*Brother* 38). Although the community is flawed and fraught with tension, Michael shares a solidarity and an understanding with them. In contrast, the state offers little to no opportunity for connection, only integration and containment.

As *Brother* progresses, it becomes clear that Michael lives in a state of almost constant anxiety in which he feels surveilled, sousveilled, and categorized for incidents that happened in his past. At his place of work Michael has to endure unfair scrutiny from his boss, Manny, who "has contacts in the Park, though, perhaps family or friends, because he is somehow able to track my daily movements. He knows that I 'lurk' around the neighbourhood on walks for no good reason, and that on certain days, if I don't have a shift, I can be found 'idling' in the public library" (Chariandy, *Brother* 42). There is no escape for Michael to be somewhere where he does not feel surveilled or sousveilled, where his behaviour is not defined by someone else. Even worse, Michael's boss, Manny, "conducts surprise searches of our lockers for drugs and minor thefts, searches that never result in any finds, and which may or may not be legal in the first place, and which we seem to have no choice but to tolerate" (42). Not only is this presumptuous and demeaning, but also it humiliates the workers and keeps them in a state of anxiety. Manny uses the mantra of so many people who unfairly conduct surveillance or sousveillance on others: if you are not doing anything wrong, then you have nothing to worry about. He says, "'No worries if you're not doing anything, right?'" (42). However, as simple as this sounds from Manny, he clearly uses it to hold power over others. For example, he finds a book in Michael's locker and uses this discovery to humiliate him. Chariandy writes: "Once he found a library copy of Giovanni's Room in my locker … then joked loudly about skids of coconuts and Oreo cookies waiting to be unpacked in the storeroom. 'You know,' he explained to one of the newer workers, slapping him on the chest, 'coloured on the outside, white on the in?'" (42). Clearly, Michael is not doing anything wrong, but the contents of his locker are used to mock him in front of others. In this sense, workplace surveillance is used to demean and control employees. In contrast to Manny's claim, if you are not doing anything wrong, and someone is still scrutinizing you, that is when you should be most worried.

In *Brother*, young people need an escape from being watched; they need a place where they can cultivate their own identities without fear of being categorized as deviant and punished by the community or the state. For Michael and Francis, that place is a barbershop. In "'A Different Economy': Postcolonial Clearings in David Chariandy's *Brother*," Gugu D. Hlongwane writes:

> [T]he postcolonial clearings I analyze in Chariandy's novel are spaces of refuge, self-care, and resistance. These spaces allow Black men, who have been relegated to second-class citizenship, to temporarily escape scrutiny, microaggressions, and policing in an anti-Black Canada and, indeed, in the Black diaspora as a whole. Because the political economy of racism objectifies and devalues the capabilities of Black people in general, it conceals their intrinsic value as human beings. The clearings of barbershops, historically regarded as sanctuaries in Black discourses in the West, help restore the humanity of Black men. These small businesses accomplish that restoration by enabling Black men to exercise and cultivate their creativity; such is the function of Desirea's, the barbershop in *Brother*. (Hlongwane 173)

Surveillance and sousveillance can feel stifling for a young man like Michael. After Anton is killed, Michael begins to feel as though everyone is watching him. Chariandy writes: "Every day, neighbourhood kids were stopped by the cops, the questions about their actions and whereabouts more probing. We were being watched by everyone, shopkeepers, neighbours, passersby" (*Brother* 99). When Michael escapes to the barbershop, he describes a far different form of observation, in contrast to the community at large. It is not simply positive or affirming, but it is friendly. In these moments characters are able to experience something closer to the ideal of sousveillance in that they become more than their categories: "[T]he shop seemed to run on a different economy. In the thick light filtered and refracted through those untidy storefront windows, in the spell of Jelly's music, lives and names emerged. I watched a young man get a shave … who after … spent at least five minutes admiring the work in the mirror" (Chariandy, *Brother* 99–100). As the scene in the barbershop is developed, it becomes clear that the young people in this space have more control over developing their own identities. They get nicknames and personas. They are known for their individual skills and abilities. They become more than their age, their gender, or their race, and they have complicated ways of critiquing one another's identities. For example, Michael talks about Raj who poses as a lady's man but once women start coming into the barbershop, he clams up and struggles to speak. Chariandy writes: "Everyone laughed at Raj. Everyone laughed at each other. In Desirea's, you postured but you also played. You showed up every one of your dictated roles and fates … in Desirea's, different styles and kinships were possible. You found new language, you caught the gestures, you kept the meanings as close as skin" (101). These experiences are so much of what Michael craves. This is just one example of a contrast between white and Black bodies in Canadian urban spaces; Gabriel English moves freely throughout an entire city to experience these moments, but for Michael these moments are confined to specific locations. The restricting categories are not solely racial but also geographic and economic. He says: "Our parents had come from Trinidad and Jamaica and Barbados, from Sri Lanka and Poland and Somalia and Vietnam. They worked shit jobs, struggled with rent, were chronically tired, and often pushed just as chronically tired notions about identity and respectability" (101). The past defines certain groups, which results in the attempt to seek autonomy. The barbershop is about more than young people being able to create their own identities and being able to resist the way in which Canadian society tries to define them. It is also about trying to avoid living the same lives as those of their parents and trying to create a future in which people do not have to work themselves into a stupor. One problem with these types of spaces is that they can be targeted by the state as sites of deviancy. Hlongwane argues: "While spaces like Desirea's are sanctuaries, they simultaneously become targets of oppressive acts" (185). Chariandy asks his readers to pay close attention to this detail through the fact that Francis is killed in the same barbershop in which he can develop his identity. As Hlongwane writes, "Desirea's is a sacred ground, and when the police converge there for a drug search, they violate this space. The violation manifests physically in the Black men's bodies as exemplified by Francis's exhaustion, impatience, and rage" (184). Thus, one of the central problems presented by *Brother* seems not only in identifying free spaces but also in cultivating state and policing services that allow such spaces to flourish.

The anxiety that Francis and Michael face towards the police is exacerbated by their ethnicity and their geography. They are not simply afraid of the police on a visceral level. They are afraid of being categorized by the police and the media owing to their appearance and family history. Chariandy writes: "What scares two boys aged ten and eleven? Sometimes, in the midst of our play, a siren would cut the air and cars with flashing lights would brake screeching down the avenue, a neighbourhood kid soon cuffed on the sidewalk, his face turned away from us in shame" (*Brother* 16). Their anxiety comes in part from being publicly humiliated for breaking the law, but also in the news about crimes being committed they hear about kids who look and sound like them. Chariandy writes: "I peered with Francis into a newspaper box to read a headline about the latest terror and caught in the glass the reflection of our own faces" (16). They grow up with an anxiety that they will be viewed as part of this larger group of young people. The world around them presents its own anxieties, but the media heightens it by categorizing them as part of this apparently dangerous group of young males. The resulting disproportionate minority contact by the police humiliates and intimidates them, negatively influencing their perception of the state. For Michael, the police presence in the neighbourhood increases tension. He might not like it, but he tolerates it and on some level understands why the police are there. He is startled and intrigued, however, by Aisha's more extreme response to the police. The two are hugging and

> [t]here was a long pause, a moment in which all sorts of things suddenly became possible, but then a siren wailed, and just as suddenly all was lost. A cop car pulled up beside a group of young men who had been walking down the sidewalk ... She looked down and spotted a broken chunk of asphalt that she loosened further with the heel of her sneaker. She picked it up, stepped back for balance, and hurled. It hit a window of the empty police car, making a sharp sound like the breaking of hard candy in your mouth, spider-webbing the glass into a pattern of pale blue without breaking. (Chariandy, *Brother* 60)

Whereas Michael tolerates the police, Aisha is starkly aware of the injustice and tension created by their presence. They take away the possibilities that these two young people might experience. She refuses to accept it and lashes out. In this scene the police presence itself is the spark for criminal activity.

Under normal circumstances Michael is not frightened of the police. Most of the cops are just doing their jobs, and for Michael, interacting with police officers is part of living in the Park – something to be tolerated. However, when violence occurs, Michael witnesses how quickly and how frighteningly the system can shift: "We had been stopped by the cops before. There was a routine to it all: we knew that if you carefully played along you'd eventually be released, if not with your dignity, then at least with your skin. But that night we sense an urgency we hadn't experienced before" (Chariandy, *Brother* 29). Michael is overwhelmed by the moment in which the force of the police comes alive. He sees the speed with which an officer can shift into part of the larger machinery of the state that swoops in to neutralize the situation. Even though Michael and Francis have nothing to do with the violence that occurred, they are treated as criminals: "I felt a cop grab my shoulder and yank. I heard Francis say 'hey' as he reached instinctively for me. I was a poor witness to what happened next. My face was pressed down and away from Francis right from the beginning, but I could hear beside me the struggle, a sharp slap, the hollow sound of something heavy on flesh" (29). To be treated this way when one is completely innocent creates a sense of outrage in Francis, one that he cannot forgive. It is not just the physical violence that troubles him but also the feeling of being treated without dignity.

Ideally a police presence in a moment of violence and chaos should neutralize the danger and make people feel safe. In the scene in which Anton is shot, Chariandy narrates how the presence of the police creates chaos and controversy. Clearly, this is a moment in which the police are needed: a young man has been shot, and the police have been called to the scene. Unfortunately for the young males in this novel, the police in the Park are more than an organized group who serve and protect. For Michael, they are terrifying, when they should help him feel safe. Chariandy writes: "[A] cop car raced past us … Booted feet upon the sidewalk running towards us, and now a second feeling of terror, as if welling up from some old dark dream" (*Brother* 29). In this moment of extreme violence after Anton has been shot, he is not comforted or calmed by the presence of the police; he is overwhelmed and frightened. And yet Chariandy balances his representation of the police through an older officer who treats the boys with decency and respect: "The older cop listened to the two who had cuffed us, and as he did he drew out a first and then a second stick of gum from the packet as he chewed. He looked completely uninterested in Francis and me … [he] used his bare hand to very gently coax Francis's head towards the street light so he could look at the scrape on his cheekbone. My brother jerked his face away. The cop stood and chewed for a second longer. 'Okay,' he said, 'We're taking you home'" (30–1). The more experienced officer knows to show care and concern. He is also respectful to the two boys even though they are in the wrong place at the wrong time. In this sense Michael suggests that part of the systemic issue of policing is one of experience and training. If officers knew how to behave as this older officer did, they might actually be able to help young males even when they are in a traumatic situation. They may in fact be able to neutralize danger and make people feel safe.

One of the strengths of *Brother* is that Chariandy develops a nuanced representation of police officers. His narrator, Michael, is careful to distinguish the good officers from the bad. He says of one officer, "I actually know her. She's a regular face in the Park. I've seen her talk down a drunk man when a confrontation could have easily escalated into violence. I've seen her chat casually with teenagers in the neighbourhood, really talk with them, not fish for information. She gets things, I know" (94). This officer is a positive representation of community policing.[2] She is interested in being a part of the neighbourhood and in being known to the people inside of it. Rather than solely being an enforcer, she is also able to demonstrate care and concern for those with whom she interacts. Even though she is one of the positive examples of policing, she is not able to smooth over every situation. She is still a police officer, and for Michael this causes anxiety. He says, "She's a good cop, but none of this helps me right now. Every nerve in my body is alert" (94). Once she sees Michael, however, she is able to handle the situation with a level of calm. Since Chariandy develops nuance in his representation of police officers, the subtleties of one citizen's interactions with law enforcement can be traced, and for Michael the strategies implemented by a specific version of community policing appear to be

2 At one point Canada was known as a nation that successfully practised community policing. Writing in 1994, Dennis P. Rosenbaum, in *The Challenge of Community Policing: Testing the Promises*, says: "Whatever the reason that community policing has gained ground in Canada, it is consistent with trends in other public service institutions in which total quality management and other innovations are flourishing" (212). However, perhaps owing to a top-down approach, community policing no longer holds the same standing. Thirty years later, in *Rethinking Community Policing*, John Ray writes that community policing only functions properly when paired with deliberative democracy, stating that "through deliberative democratic processes community policing's community engagement component can become the very definition of democratic policing" (5).

what most reduces fear and anxiety even if both emotions are inevitable when traumatic incidents occur.

Many characters are haunted by conflict with the police and with state violence, but none more so than Francis and Ruth. In *Policing Black Lives: State Violence in Canada from Slavery to the Present*, Robyn Maynard critiques, in relation to policing and surveillance, the focus that is solely on young Black males: "It is common in discussions surrounding anti-Black racism to focus on the Black male body as the state's primary target. Most literature and research focus on the means by which Black heterosexual males have been demonized by popular culture and the criminal justice system. This has frequently allowed state violence against Black individuals who are not young Black men to go unseen and unchallenged" (12–13). Ruth's character brings Maynard's argument to life in that her mental health is shattered by the death of Francis; she almost loses the will to keep going. Chariandy writes: "When Francis was first gone, Mother was unable to work or move. But in the past couple years she's grown increasingly independent" (*Brother* 33–4). In one sense Michael and his family want to forget the past: "In truth, none of us, not me, Francis, or Mother, had much interest in the grey pasts of photographs. We had more than enough to explore right here and now, and most of all we had the running challenge of what our mother called 'opportunity'" (10). However, their family memories are inherently connected to PTSD.[3] Michael has to live with the trauma of the past for a long time afterwards: "[N]ow at the edge of sleep, the shootings return to me with an attack of panic and wild vertigo. The living room drapes pulsing with coloured emergency lights. It takes a few seconds to recognise that these lights are from snowplow and road salter making their way down the avenue" (39). Despite the desire to escape the past, Michael understands that memory is essential to his survival. One important aspect of memory in *Brother* is that it helps a person to live more intelligently in the moment. Chariandy writes: "Memory's got nothing to do with the old and grey and faraway gone. Memory's the muscle sting of now … 'And if you can't memory right,' he said, 'you lose'" (*Brother* 1). Not only is memory about living in the present, a kind of call to appreciate the visceral, but also it is about

3 According to the UK's National Institute for Health and Care Excellence, symptoms of PTSD include re-experiencing, avoidance, hyperarousal (including hypervigilance, anger and irritability), negative alterations in mood and thinking, emotional numbing, dissociation, emotional dysregulation, interpersonal difficulties or problems in relationships, and negative self-perception (including feeling diminished, defeated or worthless).

survival. The narrator lives in a place that he perceives to be dangerous, and so he needs to remember the mistakes that others have made in the past so that he does not repeat them.

Furthermore, memory is not solely about survival on a visceral level; it is also inherent to identity formation. Michael understands that even though he wants to be able to return to the past and understand how it has shaped him, he cannot think of his memory as accurate: "I have one flickering memory of our father, and of music and dance … When I got older, I wondered if I really could have remembered this scene. I would have been just a bit more than a year old. How could I remember the peeled wallpaper but not remember Dad's face? Why the dancing when I'd never, ever, for years after, seen Mother do that?" (Chariandy, *Brother* 85). Despite the irony with which he views these memories, Michael still needs them in order to come to terms with his own identity. If he is going to combat the relentless attempts of his society to define him, then he needs his memories as a counterpoint to surveillance and to gossip. He needs these images of his family to maintain his self-respect and dignity. Music plays a key role in trying to remember the past. As Walcott writes, "music in Canada provides an outlet that allows us to chart the ways in which black Canadian cultures can be understood and engaged" (145). In *Brother*, music helps to create spaces for people to escape containment and get back what has been lost or taken. Hlongwane writes, "Time seems to stand still at Desirea's, a place where music plays an important role in cultural recovery, where all the stolen things are, for a moment, 'stole[n] back' (103)" (185–6). Jelly's Walkman is repeatedly mocked by Michael, but once Michael actually hears what Jelly keeps on it, Michael is transported to a time when his brother was still alive: "I pick it up. I press play, listen to the whine of the machine, the slight sound of a voice, perhaps a man's, before putting on the headphones. I recognize the music from a barbershop a decade ago. Nina Simone, her opening to 'Feeling Good.' But changed, remixed, so that the band never arrives, the lonely voice forever looping back" (Chariandy, *Brother* 97). Despite the fact that Michael is able to remember the place where his brother spent so much time, he does not want to be trapped in memory, forever returning to it like Simone. Ruth, however, when she has the headphones on and is listening to the music on Jelly's Walkman, appears to be momentarily happy in the past. Michael takes the headphones from her, and she responds by slapping him in the face. She says: "'These are my friends, Michael. They've heard the story and they want to know more. They want to show their respect'" (96). On the one hand, Ruth wants to make the past right or at least to have some power over it. On the other hand, Michael still wants to escape it until he goes through the process of narrating the story of his brother's passing, which works in many ways like his own remix.

In the complicated ethical world of *Brother* there are no easy answers or solutions. There is a sincere need for policing services in the Park, particularly after a tragic incident in which a young man lost his life, two more young males were shot, and a young girl was hit by a stray bullet in her bedroom. Despite this need for surveillance and for policing services, Chariandy asks readers to rivet their attention on the racist, xenophobic, and classist response of the state, which ends up inflicting more harm and more trauma on the community. Readers are not shown the "clichéd image of the innocent police officer within the homogeneous empty time of the Canadian national meanwhile" (Barrett 54). Instead, *Brother* generously narrates a variety of police officers, implying that well-trained, caring officers are vital to a community. Even if they do good work, they still intimidate Michael owing to the troubled history of policing in the Park. Hlongwane highlights the importance of specific spaces or post-colonial clearings for individuals like Michael and Ruth. For those of us who have not lived through the barrage of surveillance and community sousveillance that Michael has experienced, reading about his life hopefully opens our eyes to radical difference. In this way *Brother* demands the consideration of lives who remain traumatized long after the gory newspaper headlines of a police shooting have faded from the public consciousness. Chariandy situates one Black family at the centre of the conversation on the Canadian imaginary – so much more than an interruption.

5 Sharon Bala's *The Boat People*: Bureaucracy and Two Faces of Canadian Immigration

In *Brother*, Chariandy emphasizes the importance of spaces in which Michael and Francis can be creative and cultivate their own senses of identity. By contrast, Sharon Bala's debut novel, *The Boat People*, narrates a situation where there is no escape from state surveillance for Poonambalam Mahindan, a migrant trying to escape civil war in Sri Lanka.[1] Mahindan must perform an identity if he and his son are going to be granted entry into Canada. Although he has a dream of the great, white north's being a safe haven for all people, he is greeted by a cold, bureaucratic system that assumes the worst about him and his fellow migrants. The novel directs the gaze of the reader to the way in which specific systems within the Canadian government are manipulated by bad actors. Individuals, such as the politician Fred Blair, implement a rhetoric of fear and xenophobia to manipulate others into seeing the migrants as a threat to the safety of average Canadians. Bala's narrative not only calls into question the way in which bad actors can take

1 As they are the terms used in the novel, I am going to use *migrant*, *immigrant*, and *refugee* throughout this chapter, but I would also like to reference Vinh Nguyen's concept of refugee subjects. As Nguyen points out in *Lived Refuge: Gratitude, Resentment, Resilience*, some people are refugees before they become legally defined as such. In place of the current legal terminology he offers the phrase *refugee subject*: "refugee subjects can be a more capacious concept, encompassing those who are legal refugees; those who were at one point in time refugees; those who sought, or are seeking, refuge; those who have been persecuted and forcibly displaced from their homes but did not (or could not) acquire official refugee status; those who are culturally understood as refugees even though they were never legally refugees; and those who are at the threshold of resident and refugee, living with the imminent threat of being 'refugeed' by the forces of war, capitalism, and globalization" (108). This term encompasses not only the migrants in the novel but also some of the characters who have been living in Canada for many years.

advantage of systemic flaws within specific bureaucratic structures, but also highlights a hypocrisy in the national imaginary. Sunera Thobani argues that the national subject is exalted against a lawless Other who needs to be contained and controlled (5). This ironizes our supposedly welcoming national image. Readers are able to observe these flaws within the national imaginary and to critique the way in which migrants are surveilled and sousveilled.

Much like Chariandy, Bala takes a contentious moment from Canada's national news cycle and narrates the inner worlds of people who are profoundly affected. In 2010 the CBC published an article "Tamil Migrant Ship Boarded: Military Sources," which frames the event from the perspective of Public Safety Minister Vic Toews:

> Toews said there are 490 migrants aboard the ship, and the vessel's operator has declared them to be refugees – but Toews said some of the people on the ship are "suspected human smugglers and terrorists" … Toews said human smuggling is a despicable crime and such criminals elsewhere in the world are watching Canada's response to this incident. He said the government will send a message "loud and clear" that human smugglers will be prosecuted. The "terrorists" Toews referred to are believed to be members of the Liberation Tigers of Tamil Eelam, which have been outlawed in Canada as a terrorist group since 2006. (CBC, "Tamil Migrant Ship")

Importantly, Toews wants to categorize the migrants as potential criminals and a threat to Canadians. This framing of their character will allow the government to scrutinize their intentions and to keep them incarcerated for as long as necessary. However, in "Sun Sea Anniversary Highlights Canada's Treatment of Refugees," Sunny Dhillon writes, "[F]or all the worries that the migrants were somehow illegitimate or 'bogus' refugees, of those who have had their cases decided, nearly two-thirds were approved as refugees." Vulnerable people suffered because the Canadian government wanted to make a statement to the international community. Domestically the response to the MV Sun Sea migrants has had long-standing effects. Roughly five years later, in "MV Sun Sea 5 Year Anniversary Reflected upon by Refugees' Lawyer," the CBC interviewed Gabriel Chand, the lawyer who defended some of the migrants: "According to Chand, Canada's treatment of refugees has only become more restrictive since then. He says that the government's focus has been on preventing refugees from making it to Canada in the first place, and then making it more difficult for them to make claims, leaving them in danger of deportation." This means that certain migrants choose to remain hidden and become even more vulnerable as a result.

Two recent essays investigate how *The Boat People* offers insight into the Canadian government's surveillance of migrants. In "The Other Side of Citizenship? Narrating Flight and Refugeeism in Sharon Bala's *The Boat People*," Katja Sarkowsky's description of the interplay between real life and a fictionalized world reinforces a reading of the novel as a form of literary sousveillance: "[*The Boat People*] centers on an event in the recent past, namely, the arrival of the rusty merchant vessel Sun Sea, carrying 492 Sri Lankan Tamil asylum seekers, in Vancouver in 2010. The arrival sparked a controversy that plays out strongly in the novel: The Conservative Harper-government suspected a significant number of members of the LTTE (Liberation Tigers of Tamil Eelam) on board the vessel. Public opinion appeared to be strongly pitted against the refugees" (164). Intriguingly, Sarkowsky argues that this fictional account of the event in *The Boat People* is a vital part of the national discourse because it focuses our gaze on specific narratives. Describing the main characters as focalizers, she writes: "Bala fictionalises this event by way of three focalizers, the Tamil widower Poonambalam Mahindan, travelling with his young son Sellian; the law intern Priya Rajasekaran, a second-generation Tamil Canadian assigned to assist a lawyer in his pro bono support for some of the refugees; and Grace Nakamura, a Japanese Canadian adjudicator for the Immigration and Refugee Board" (Sarkowsky 164). Thus, for Sarkowsky, Bala has constructed characters that encourage a specific gaze back at the state. From spending time with Mahindan, Priya, and Grace, readers will hopefully come to appreciate some of the difficulties and the complexities of their lives. In "Trembling Strength: Migrating Vulnerabilities in Fiction by Sharon Bala, Yasmin Ladha, and Denise Chong," Aritha van Herk argues that Canadians tend to expect migrants to perform in specific ways, namely that they be innocent and vulnerable, in order to gain entry to the country. She writes: "Accountable here is certainly the extent to which the need for an 'audience' to watch migrants 'perform' their precarity imbues both historical, fictional, and legal rituals. These texts explore the instability of being untethered from fixed relationality by requiring the telling and re-telling of the migrant's past, arrival, motivation, and genealogy. Vulnerability then becomes a role that must be both inhabited and acted" (355–6). Canadians, in welcoming vulnerable people, can uphold their own identity as exalted rather than fortunate. The individuals who are granted entry into the country are then expected to conform and integrate. To escape a life-threatening situation, migrants who reach Canadian shores must keep in mind that they are always being watched and that there could be serious consequences for performing in the wrong way. To add nuance to the expectations for migrants to be vulnerable and grateful, Bala narrates a range of varied emotions, thoughts, and experiences of her characters. In spending time with a fictional character such as Mahindan, readers are challenged to observe their own assumptions about refugees and to feel sympathy for those who find themselves in situations in which they do not have the ability to choose between right and wrong in desperate situations.

In the world of *The Boat People*, Canada is initially presented as a safe haven for refugees. The dream of Canada is one in which the state observes the weak and needy with care and compassion. Mahindan expresses this beautiful conception of Canada: "Here was a place for all people" (Bala 14). The reality proves less idealistic. Upon arrival, the migrants come into contact with the weight of Canadian bureaucracy and are scrutinized closely by every eyeball that the government pokes in their direction. Various bureaucratic organizations are at the mercy of powerful government figures who know how to manipulate them. For no matter how Canada might be perceived or how kind Canadians might aspire to be, any organization is at the mercy of charismatic individuals such as Fred Blair, whom Bala appears to have named after the infamous Frederick Blair who ran Canada's immigration branch during the Holocaust. When asked how many Jewish people Canada should allow within its borders, Blair is purported to have said "none ... is too many" (Abella and Troper xix). Blair places Grace Nakamura as an adjudicator within the Immigration and Refugee Board so that he can manipulate the proceedings through her. She often feels out of place in her new position because she was once the operations director for the Ministry of Transportation and Infrastructure. Bala writes: "[S]he remembered the call from Fred, how flattered she'd been when her old mentor – now elected to the federal government and in a cabinet post – offered her a new opportunity. And anyway, it was only temporary. After her three-year term was up here, she'd be on to bigger and better" (Bala 46). Thus, those who are employed to surveil migrants are not necessarily doing so because they care. Fred Blair frames the migrants' stories as though Canada is being used by refugees, and he manipulates Grace Nakamura through a rhetoric of fear. He says: "Half the people on board had ties to the LTTE, the separatist group better known as the Tamil Tigers, who had been waging war against the Sri Lankan government for more than twenty years. Terrorists. Losers in an overseas war who had fled to Canada to lick their wounds and regroup. Canada has a reputation for being a soft touch ... We must disabuse the world of that notion" (47). Thus, whatever the dream of Canada may be, its bureaucracies can be manipulated through charismatic figures. This has dire consequences for the people who end up being observed by the various arms and eyes of the Canadian government.

If this novel is understood as a critique of the Canadian government, one of Bala's main targets is the manipulation of the Immigration and Refugee Board. It results in a system that observes migrants in a decidedly unfair way. Bala writes that the "Immigration and Refugee Board was independent. It was not the government. The IRB acted within the framework of the law, and its adjudicators were the ones who made the decisions" (58). Priya is constructed – among other things – as a focalizer to encourage the reader to witness the drawbacks of the in-between nature of the IRB. Observing Grace Nakamura, Priya thinks: "Even without an elevated bench, robes, or a gavel, there was a stern aura of judgment in her demeanour. But she was not a judge and this was not a court ... This was an administrative hearing. It existed in the fuzzy boundary between bureaucracy and the law" (62). The problem with Grace as an adjudicator, however, is not solely that she is stern or judgmental but that she is not ready for the complexity of the position. Early on in the text, Mitchell Hurst, a former lawyer and current colleague of Grace Nakamura, criticizes the bureaucracy of the Immigration and Refugee Board. He says, "I saw how arbitrary the process was, how much depended on the adjudicators, and how many were totally unqualified and unprepared for the job" (46). Not only has Grace been thrown into a difficult position but she has powerful people, such as Fred Blair, who are observing her and trying to manipulate her decisions. Blair wants to use the case of the boat people to send a message to Canadians that particular migrants are potentially dangerous and that the Canadian government needs to demonstrate its power. One of Priya's colleagues, Gigovaz, knows that the work of the IRB is heavily influenced by politics. He says, "[T]hey also know that by killing time, letting people rot in jail for as long as possible, they are sending a message. Joe Public is tricked into thinking he's being protected" (119). In this way Bala emphasizes that one eye of the Canadian government has a point that can be manipulated and by which vulnerable people can be treated unfairly.

Not only does Bala narrate how bad actors manipulate the system, but she also critiques Canadians for their inhospitality. There are positive moments in the text where Bala is careful to distinguish Canadians from Canadian bureaucracy: "Priya felt chastened by this, the goodwill and camaraderie of so many people willing to take strangers in" (59). For some, the dream of a welcoming country is alive and well, but there is also another side and another history to Canada that does make its way into patriotic speeches. Bala writes: "They have taken a poll, Prasad [a former journalist back in Sri Lanka] said. He read in English, slowly so they could understand: Three out of five Canadians believe the vessel should have been turned away. Half of those polled think all passengers should be deported, even if their refugee claims are valid" (170). It is this version of Canada with which Mahindan, Prasad, and the other Sri Lankan migrants come into contact. It is a shocking counterpoint to their perceptions of the country as a safe haven full of welcoming, kind-hearted people. They are observed by a cold and xenophobic state that assumes the worst and expects them to perform the role of desperate victim.

Perceptions of migrants tend to be negatively influenced by the Canadian media.[2] In his ideal of the panopticon Bentham hopes for a community with caring eyes, but this is hardly the case in *The Boat People*. Bala narrates how the stories of the Sri Lankan migrants are used by the media and the government to manipulate public opinion: "There was a colour photo of a ship and people being led off its gangplank, their faces shielded by large umbrellas. The headline screamed in a thunderous font: PM TAKES HARD LINE ON MIGRANTS" (44). The average person is encouraged to fear the migrants and be thankful to be protected from them by the government. The persuasive power of the news does not work exclusively on people outside the system of surveillance; it also influences the people who surveil and who make decisions on the migrant's future. Bala highlights how Grace Nakamura's home life and professional life are affected by the news media. Grace is not only indoctrinated with fear by the news; she is inundated with stories about immigrants who have turned violent, and she desires to protect her children from this threat. In this way noble desires turn into ignoble behaviour. Bala writes: "Today the big story was the turf war in the

---

2 Bala is astute in her reflection of the actual framing of migrants in Canada. Andrea Lawlor, in "Framing Immigration in the Canadian and British News Media," writes that Canadian media frames immigration within five themes:

- *Refugee and asylum*: Including discussion of human smuggling, refugee claims/status, deportation and human rights
- *Illegality and security*: Including discussion of law enforcement, terrorism, organized crime and illegal migration
- *Economic and labour considerations*: Including discussion of employment, foreign credentials, demographic changes and the labour force more broadly
- *Social services*: Including discussion of health care, social assistance, language training and settlement services
- *Diversity*: Including discussion of visible minority status. (Lawlor 350)

These five themes are represented in *The Boat People.*

suburbs between the Somalis and Sikhs. One crime lord had kidnapped another one's daughter and was demanding ransom. The girl was fifteen. Grace shuddered to think what was being done to her. See? Grace told the girls, This is why I worry about you" (105). In *The Boat People* the press exerts power through the stories they tell and in the way they observe. The mere presence of journalists and reporters influences how people feel seen and how they behave. Bala writes: "The reporters had surrendered their smartphones to a box beside the guard. All eyes were on Mahindan as they scribbled in their notepads" (62). When Mahindan senses these various people watching him, he feels the need to perform. Enacting its own power through surveillance, the media seems to have a direct influence on the proceedings in that they have the power to sway public opinion. Priya's brother, Rat, has a minor argument with her about whether the migrants are legal or illegal. He says, "Hey, I'm just repeating what they said on the news" (81). She replies, "Yeah, and reporters just parrot every false claim the government makes" (81). In *The Boat People* the press tends to operate as an apparatus of the state, easily manipulated by the government and often to the detriment of the migrants. However, once Prasad learns how to manipulate Canadian media, he begins to use it to his favour. When he writes a piece on his experience, a major shift in public opinion occurs. Bala describes how Priya's family understands this piece: "I read the article your people wrote, her father said. It took Priya a moment to realize he meant the open letter Prasad had penned on behalf of the refugees. It had run on page three of the *Globe and Mail*, surrounded by holiday fluff pieces. Priya hoped its publication on Christmas Eve would inspire generosity" (220). In the case of Prasad, at least, she is correct. A shift occurs in public opinion as a result of this story, and he is granted entry into the country. Priya later thinks, "Language was a superpower" (263). For Prasad, his gift with words is a massive strength that he uses to enter Canada, legally defined as a refugee. In this way Prasad is an example of what Vinh Nguyen would describe as refugeetude, which "turns away from readily available discourses of victimhood and commonplace knowledge of refugees to highlight how refugee subjects gain awareness, create meaning, and imagine futures. It signifies critical impulses to see, know, and act – ways of being political, even when politics varies in degree and form" (Nguyen 104). Prasad has an active voice and agency in his future. He is not simply a victim or a suffering, abject Other. He demonstrates resilience through the ability to articulate his own story. As Vinh Nguyen argues, "A story indicates resilience because there is someone there to tell it, someone who believes that the story should have a life in the world. A story can also persist beyond the immediacy of our lives, and acts of storytelling such as recovery, recounting, and recording are the actions of resilience" (81). Despite the impossibility of his situation Prasad creates his own narrative, and people listen. Those who do not have the same ability with language suffer. The other event that sways public opinion is an act of desperation that functions as a spectacle in the public eye: the suicide of the migrant known as Ranga.[3] This death demonstrates the struggles of the migrants, and Fred Blair's popularity plummets. Bala writes: "Fred scowled at the headlines. A terrorist decides to kill himself and now we're being crucified for it. It had been two weeks since the suicide and the media were having a field day" (339). Thus, in this text, even though the press tends to operate as yet another eye of the state, the media can be manipulated by those who are being observed. Therefore, Prasad enacts sousveillance at the press and the government when he alters the nature of the gaze that has been directed at him. Language is indeed a super power.

Bala highlights a binary of fear of the stranger and love of the vulnerable Other. This consistent contrast between a concern for safety and a goodwill towards other human beings inevitably influences the way people observe the migrants. One of the draws of Canada for the migrants, however, is that it will be safe. Bala writes: "Hard-shelled and sturdy with brass locks and snaps, it and the meagre trinkets inside – a wedding album, Chitra's death certificate, the keys to his house and garage – were all that remained of his worldly possessions. But he reminded himself he had something more precious. Safety. Here [in Canada], it was possible to breathe" (13). Mahindan believes that the sacrifices he makes in travelling to Canada are worth it to avoid greater danger in Sri Lanka. A lesser novelist might downplay one side or the other of the binary of fear and love. Bala, however, validates the fear that Grace experiences, writing, "Grace thought about the Prince Regent Hotel shooting, how the terror hadn't left her until the girls walked safely in the door" (89). This feels like a fear that should be respected and taken into consideration. But Fred Blair takes such

3 It is debatable whether or not this death is also an example of refugeetude. Vinh Nguyen writes: "Refugeetude is a coming into consciousness of the social, political, and historical forces that situate refugee subjects, and the acts that attempt to know, impact, and transcend this situation. It can be grasped, for example, when refugee subjects participate in hunger strikes and practice 'self-mutilation' – the stitching together of lips, eyes, and ears – in order to make state violence visible and protest inhumane detention and deportation policies" (111). I would argue that the migrant known as Ranga lacks the agency and awareness that Nguyen highlights. I do not understand his suicide as a transcendent act. In my reading, he is a figure of desperation and pity.

anxieties and exploits them. He says: "These people get a foot in the door, put down some roots, and then they're impossible to turf. Informants, wiretaps – if you only knew how much this Russian mobster is costing the taxpayer. But the RCMP and Border Services – those are the true heroes. They are on the front lines every day" (89). This discourse between safety and freedom influences the way in which the state observes migrants. Whereas Grace tends to be indoctrinated by Blair, Mitchell Hurst, whom Blair describes as the "King of the bleeding hearts" (89), tells Grace, "The vast, vast majority of us want the same things … Don't lose sight of that" (306). Representing the opposing side of this debate, Grace retorts, "And a tiny minority want other things … To attack our way of life. Don't lose sight of *that*" (306). When a character focuses on the potential of an obscure future threat, they become fearful of migrants. By contrast, if characters see past their anxiety and focus on love for the Other, then the observer tends to look with care. The narrative seems to accept the inevitable push and pull between self and Other: "If it was a choice between a stranger and her family, Grace would always choose her family" (376). Readers are encouraged to observe Grace's character development in relation to this discourse. She moves from being Fred Blair's disciple early on to becoming a far more independent thinker by the conclusion. For Grace, the binary of fear and love becomes an oscillation. She becomes more open minded towards the migrants, but she still fiercely desires to protect her children.

Bala offers hope in the way an individual within a system can change. However, when the full scope of international and state surveillance is considered, *The Boat People* appears far less optimistic. The far-reaching technological gaze of surveillance is misunderstood by Mahindan: "The interpreter explained that Canada had known about the ship and had been expecting them for weeks. Their arrival had been foretold. To Mahindan, it felt auspicious. A deity paving the way, all these unknown Tamils coming to their aid in a foreign land" (Bala 29). The interpreter quickly shuts this possibility down: "No, she said. The government had seen the ship with its satellite systems" (29). International surveillance surfaces perhaps most pointedly in the text through the way in which the United Nations ineffectively observes the Sri Lankan government's internally displaced persons (IDP) camps. According to Singh, "After the war, the Sri Lankan government set up temporary IDP camps. A UN report found the conditions to be satisfactory. In fact, there was no reason for this woman and her daughters to leave" (Bala 154). Readers know that this information is not true, based on Mahindan's experience. Furthermore, Gigovaz, one of Priya's colleagues, argues: "People were going missing from a government run refugee camp. Not only did the state fail to perform its duty, it in fact participated in the persecution of its own nationals" (155). Another migrant woman, whose case is also being heard, is forced to explain after great distress that soldiers had raped her daughter in one of these camps. As Razack writes, "[G]ender persecution, as it is deployed in refugee discourse, can function as a deeply racialized concept in that it requires that Third World women speak of their realities of sexual violence outside of, and at the expense of, their realities as colonized peoples" (90). Case in point: the mother does not want this information known but feels the need to tell the IRB so that she and her family can stay in Canada. The incident makes it falsely appear as though Western society is superior even though this situation results from the failure of the UN. Readers are encouraged to see that the faulty surveillance by the UN results in intrusive observation by the IRB. If the UN report had properly highlighted what was happening in these IDP camps, then this woman would not have to talk about the trauma inflicted upon her family. Thus, while individuals within these systems of surveillance might change, the systems make migrants vulnerable in new and unexpected ways.

One of the major failings of these systems of surveillance, for Bala, is that they attempt to sort the migrants into simplified categories. Like so many other aspects of Bala's novel, fiction closely resembles real life. In "'Promising Victimhood': Contrasting Deservingness Requirements in Refugee Resettlement" Natalie Welfens astutely demonstrates how governments accept migrants based on vulnerability and assimilability.[4] These categories are defined through Western eyes from a distance to the danger. Migrants then need to perform certain traits in the hopes of getting refugee status. Their actual experience in their home country, however, tends to be far more complicated than the categories allow. Sarkowsky highlights Bala's ability to communicate the ambiguities of right and wrong from the migrant's perspective: "Establishing 'innocence' – meaning not being guilty of war crimes, but also meaning

4 In "'Promising Victimhood'" Natalie Welfens writes: "In principle, refugees' access to protection and membership in another state should depend on their protection needs and human rights, or be assessed based on humanitarian grounds in a non-discriminatory fashion. However, as recent refugee movements powerfully illustrate, perceptions of who is 'most deserving' of protection in Europe do not only hinge on refugees' protection needs but also on their supposed 'integration potential'. Where these humanitarian and assimilability requirements come together a tension emerges: in order to be seen as deserving of protection – by law or societal standards – refugees have to demonstrate that they are at risk in their countries of origin or first countries of refuge, yet willing and able to 'overcome' their vulnerability to become law-abiding, self-sufficient and culturally malleable future members of their host societies" (2).

to tell the truth about one's past in the hearing and thereby establish authenticity – is a crucial element of what the refugee needs to accomplish by their narrative before a committee. In contrast, fiction can produce the ambivalences that often shape a refugee's past and that are not easily categorised in terms of innocence or guilt, as complex ethical choices are often involved" (167). In trying to survive, the migrants are forced into morally ambiguous situations. Mahindan and many others remember that surveillance by the LTTE in Sri Lanka would have limited their ability to make choices. Bala writes: "Did she not know what it was like to have so little agency? To be faced with such cruel options it was as if there was not choice at all? These Canadians, with all their creature comforts, had such meagre imaginations" (Bala 194). *The Boat People*, among other things, appears to be designed to help with this process of imagining, to help readers do as Serpell asks us and take the great leap towards empathy. In thinking with all of our strength about the Other, we get a little closer to the dream of Canada.

Although international systems of surveillance are clearly valuable in that they allow authorities to be vigilant towards criminal activity, they also sort vulnerable people into strict binaries. Bala writes: "It was a marvel to him – the power of Canadian police. Their ability to reach back in time and riffle through the minute details of his long-ago life … That authorities here could … come up with this one bus [he fixed for the LTTE] was terrifying" (197). Although the ability to gather information, particularly from such a great distance is valuable, that data is manipulated to unfairly implicate Mahindan in the criminal activity of the LTTE. Mahindan had repaired the brakes on a bus that would eventually be used to kill seventeen civilians, and Singh uses this information to argue that "[i]n repairing an LTTE-owned bus, he was party to a war crime" (199). The problem with how this data is interpreted by Singh is that she implies that Mahindan had a choice in whether or not he would repair the bus. Bala writes: "He [Mahindan] was flustered by the injustice. Do work for the Tigers or be crushed by them. Give the Canadians a reason to deport him or tell a pack of lies. There was never a good option" (198). He does not have the luxury of choice that wealthy, comfortable, safe Canadians take for granted. In contrast, Grace, as an instrument of state surveillance, has choices. She is the adjudicator and one of the final observers of the migrants. The problem is that the information available to Grace is flawed. International surveillance proves faulty, and the migrants are forced to perform innocence and vulnerability if they are going to be granted entry into the country. As Van Herk writes, "Living bodies cannot necessarily demonstrate innocence or guilt, although each person is expected to stage transparently the circumstances of their education, language, and clothing. Most important of all, the story of why they are refugees, and why they wish asylum must strike a balance between visibility and believability, a concoction marking the subject as pitiable" (355–6). Adept at creating ethically complex situations, Bala develops a sympathetic representation of the adjudicators who are asked to observe migrants. Grace is in an incredibly challenging situation. Encouraging a thoughtfulness towards the underprepared adjudicator, Bala writes: "I'm not a mind reader, Grace thought. And yet this job was all about being one, trying to guess at true motivations, to separate the deserving refugees from the ones who planned to use Canada as a ground zero for a proxy war" (Bala 200). Thus, even if Grace might change as the narrative progresses, her sources of information will not necessarily improve. If she observes the Other with care and indeterminacy instead of fear and certainty, then she might be less cruel. However, Grace would counter that such a shift in perspective puts her children at risk. In her artful construction of this character, Bala offers no easy answers.

In *The Boat People*, documentation without the texture of narrative, cultural knowledge, or experience results in reductive surveillance practices. The information or lack of information from identification papers is framed by the prejudices of whoever is discussing them. When "[d]ocuments for five people, none of them on board," are found on the ship (Bala 115), even the incredibly compassionate Gigovaz, who works with the migrants, asks, "Someone went to the trouble of destroying these papers. Why leave them behind?" (116). Priya fires back, "You're assuming it's nefarious" (116). Even worse than false assumptions is the abuse of this information by people who want to remove the migrants. Gigovaz and Priya both assume that Amarjit Singh, who functions as a type of prosecutor, will employ this information to argue that the migrants "have trashed the evidence of their old lives and adopted fake names" (116). Furthermore, there is confusion about how to read the documents. Gigovaz, for example, does not know that "[n]ames are reversed in Tamil … Tamil boys get their fathers' last names as their first names" (117). Priya, who is explaining this to him, adds, "[N]ames won't tell you much. You can't use them to trace family trees" (117). This cultural confusion highlights the limited gaze of those who are tasked with observing the migrants. The scope and depth of information required is reliant on experience that most do not possess. Not only do the lawyers and adjudicators need to be able to review documents, but they also need to understand the cultural significance of certain objects. For example, one of the migrants, Savitri Kumuran, has a necklace that Singh claims, "We have now confirmed it is a Tamil tah-li, an item of jewelry only given to LTTE wives" (130). However, this object has been misread and falsely used to identify Savitri Kumuran as being connected to the LTTE. Priya argues, "I'm Tamil and I'm telling you there is no such thing as a Tiger thali" (132). The use of objects to define identity is flawed, especially when there is misinformation about the culture of the particular group. In the difficult position of being the adjudicator, Grace thinks, "What to make of this conflicting soup of information?" (133). Thus, Bala emphasizes how observations can be distorted by prejudices and misinformation. Narrative might lie and narrative might manipulate, but in *The Boat People* literary moments contribute a necessary texture to elucidate how much is missing from the interpretation of documents and objects.

Mahindan's character, in particular, allows Bala to narrate the contrast between documentation and narrative. As a widower who wants to take care of his son, Mahindan is developed as a complicated but ultimately sympathetic figure. His main interest in Canada is to find a place where he and his family might feel safe; ultimately he wants what Grace wants. Early in the novel Gigovaz highlights the fact that Mahindan's son, Sellian, is in prison. He says: "His six-year-old son is living among strangers. It is important to consider the psychological toll, on the child in particular, or separation and detention" (Bala 66). This sympathetic understanding of Mahindan's situation is undercut with a different type of language, one that situates Mahindan within a tense geopolitical struggle for power. Singh replies, "The claimant is a foreign national from a country where known terrorists have spent the past three decades waging a civil war" (66). These uses of language clearly influence the way in which Mahindan will be categorized and processed. In one set of language choices he is a gentle, wounded man who only desires to take care of a child. In the second set of language choices he threatens to bring the violence of a foreign conflict onto Canadian soil. The full narrative of Mahindan reveals a far more complex understanding of his character when it is revealed that he steals identification cards. Bala writes: "He caught sight of a five-hundred-rupee note before stuffing the money away. There was something else. An identity card, slimy but intact. He pocketed that too without glancing at the name, then stood, picked up the handles of the barrow, and walked forward with purpose out into the sunshine" (302). Mahindan stole the card that would be used by the migrant known as Ranga; the actual owner of the ID was connected to the LTTE, which framed the migrant known as Ranga and led to the suicide. When framing Mahindan's actions, Bala implies a moral and ethical uncertainty. Even though his behaviour is criminal, he does so in a desperate moment when the lines between right and wrong blur. Sarkowsky writes, "[F]iction can produce the ambivalences that often shape a refugee's past and that are not easily categorised in terms of innocence or guilt, as complex ethical choices are often involved" (167). We are left with the necessary cliché of literature as the great creator of indeterminacy. Readers are encouraged to withhold judgment. Perhaps part of Bala's project is to ask certain Canadians to reconsider the way in which they sousveil migrants. Fighting against the certainty produced by fear-based politics is a strong place to start.

One of the great powers of fiction is that it grants readers particular ways of seeing. To use Sarkowsky's phrasing, it focalizes. Bala narrates a complex situation, ultimately asking readers to sousveil the way in which our country welcomes or does not welcome migrants. The construction of Mahindan encourages indeterminacy about his character in that he is not simply good or bad; he is placed in a series of impossible situations that remove his ability to make choices, thus challenging a simple moralistic world view. Although there is indeterminacy in relation to judgment of many of the characters, there are pockets of certainty. Fred Blair is clearly the antagonist. He manipulates others through fear-based politics, and he is willing to turn away vulnerable people, thus exposing them to precarious situations. There is also a type of moral certainty in Bala's critique of Canada and of Canadians. Our wealth, comfort, and safety allow us to operate with a particular set of ethics and to exalt ourselves as compassionate and welcoming nationals. After closely considering Mahindan's story, however, we should consider how we might wake up from a dream that is someone else's nightmare.

6 Justin Ling's *Missing from the Village*: The Failure to See the Vulnerable Other

While Sharon Bala narrates complexities related to how the state and nationals observe migrants, investigative journalist Justin Ling asks, Why – when it comes to certain groups – does the Canadian government over-police but under-protect (248)?[1] When it becomes clear that a serial killer is operating in Toronto, members of a vulnerable community are rightfully afraid. They need the police and the state to help identify and apprehend the murderer. However, this task proves to be incredibly challenging in a sprawling city such as Toronto. Once police officers have access to the right information, the tools used to categorize and sort prove to be not only necessary but highly effective. In *Missing from the Village*, this discourse shifts from fictionalized accounts of real events to a work of true crime. The stakes are different. Chariandy's novel critiqued systemic racism in Toronto, and Bala questioned Canada's kind and welcoming national image. Ling, however, discusses actual victims, survivors, and police officers, all of whom have friends and families. He focuses his attention on the victims, ideally bringing their stories to life and encouraging readers to observe them thoughtfully. The critique of policing services in *Missing from the Village* is tough but fair; Ling highlights shortcomings of the Toronto Police Service, but he also demonstrates the necessity of strong policing and of accurate surveillance mechanisms.

1 It might seem difficult to categorize Ling's gaze as either surveillance or sousveillance. In the previous chapter it was argued that the gaze of the media operates as part of state surveillance in *The Boat People*. However, in the spectrum between surveillance and sousveillance, Ling operates closer to sousveillance. He works as a journalist, but he is a freelancer and has more independence from particular publishers who may or may not be linked to corporate and state interests. Furthermore, he directs his gaze at surveillance structures. For these reasons, Ling sousveils more than surveils.

True crime fits into this study in an uncomfortable but essential way. Fiction, on the one hand, often allows writers and critics to speak indirectly about social issues, institutions, and people. This ability to critique in an indirect way has a host of benefits. An author or a critic might be able to express a complaint and avoid being persecuted for their beliefs. Furthermore, through escaping reality, readers might learn something important about themselves or people they know.[2] True crime, on the other hand, offers a different set of opportunities and problems in relation to surveillance. In "A Guarantee of Safety, a Cautionary Tale or a Celebration?," Joanna Antoniak provides a comprehensive overview of issues related to the true-crime genre. She argues that true crime is, among other things, about the attempt to gain control over social anomalies through observing them in a controlled environment; as an "unthreatening source of entertainment," it creates an opportunity "to purge and cleanse … negative impulses"; furthermore, this genre serves as "a moral warning, functioning as contemporary fairy tales – they control anomalies through discouraging others from violating the rules" (Antoniak 92–3). Focusing solely on theoretical discussions of genre feels inhumane and impersonal when living people might be profoundly affected by the retelling of traumatic events. Antoniak references an article in the *Guardian* by Lauren Bradford titled "My Family Was Traumatised First by a Murder, Then by the TV Serialisation," in which Bradford describes the reawakened trauma when loved ones are the subjects of true-crime narratives:

> What it comes down to is the powerlessness of families in this situation to have any sort of control over events that shape their lives. The culture we live in and its fascination with crime means that someone can write a book or film a drama to make money from someone else's life and be applauded for it. In the midst of trying to come to terms with the imminent release of the drama, our family endured the PR and social media build-up with sleepless nights and tearful days, while those responsible were being congratulated for a "brilliant" production. We have been left trembling in the wake of it. The insensitivity of this intrusion is in direct proportion to the trauma that it causes. (Bradford)

2 In "Opening the Closed Mind: The Effect of Exposure to Literature on the Need for Closure," Maja Djikic, Keith Oatley, and Mihnea C. Moldoveanu write: "When reading about fictional characters, one does not feel the need … to defend one's own perspective. One can simulate the workings of other minds without the fear of undermining one's own" (153).

Bradford's pain at being forced to relive traumatic events reveals the cruel nature of this genre, particularly when it is consumed as entertainment. For its consumption to be justified, viewers who desire to feel ethical require a rationale for how society might benefit from true crime. Antoniak is relatively convincing in this respect when she argues, "True crime stories are used to shield and protect oneself from anomalies as well as to control and label them" (93). Thus, true crime gives viewers a sense of agency in a world of chaos. In this study the inclusion of a true-crime narrative demonstrates the shaky ethical ground on which all these texts operate. Although I believe in the ability of books to help us be more thoughtful and humane, I cannot deny that I generally read to be entertained, fascinated, and even – I know this is strange – disturbed. This aesthetic joy in the midst of the suffering Other is not an ethical conflict that can be easily resolved. A critic might simply need to accept that the binary of education and entertainment creates an impasse, that there is no way of proceeding without it being problematic.

Nevertheless, it is clear that some ways of narrating crime, be it fiction or non-fiction, are more ethical than others. One key distinction in the way that authors observe stories of serial murderers is between victim-centred and killer-centred narratives. In "Reconsidering Television True Crime and Gendered Authority in Allen v. Farrow," Tanya Horeck and Diane Negra argue that true crime focused on victims has far more potential to encourage care and to avoid sensationalism. They discuss "documentaries [that] function as victim advocacy pieces, privileging and corroborating victim-survivor testimonies and showing critical awareness of the structural underpinnings of gendered violence" (2). Thus, while the trauma caused to friends and families of victims needs to be kept top of mind, there are specific choices that can increase or decrease the potential pain that a text might inflict. Furthermore, as discussed in the chapter on Coady's work, even if a writer goes through the effort of turning biography and autobiography into fiction, such work is still related to lived experience in complex ways. Those who feel written about will make their own connections between truth and fiction. For friends and family members of a victim who has a relatively similar fictional counterpart, the violence in crime fiction can be traumatic in its own way, not only when one knows that others are using it as a source of enjoyment but also when the criminal or criminals are portrayed as charismatic, gifted, and clever. Katie Jones highlights the aestheticization of violent crime in fictionalized accounts of serial killers in "Returning to the Scene: Seriality and the Serial Killer." She writes: "In many of the best known depictions of serial murder in fiction and film, the crimes are highly aestheticized; there is a perverse genius lurking behind the criminal acts" (9). Presenting the criminal as a disturbed genius who effortlessly manipulates both their victims and the police might intrigue readers and viewers, but it presents a perverse misrepresentation of reality that aggrandizes the violent criminals who take advantage of vulnerable people. While the serial killer as super-villain trope is questionable and problematic in fictional representations, it would be a profoundly disturbing choice in true crime. Jones hypothesizes what true crime should aspire to be in relation to victims: "[T]he generic constraints of 'true crime' products should be transgressed to unearth the victim's experience – but not just the experience of victimisation ... few narratives ... explore the subjectivity of the person before they become entrapped in the perpetrator's narrative" (11–12). To his credit, Ling encourages readers to think at length about the victim's lives. In this sense, *Missing from the Village* is a strong example of literary sousveillance. One of the vital aspects of Ling's book is that he provides extended character descriptions of each of the victims. He strives to ensure that they will be seen by the readers as distinct human beings who tragically crossed paths with the wrong person. Of Skandaraj Navaratnam, known by friends as Skanda, Ling goes into great detail about his life in Sri Lanka and his personality of having a charm that "wasn't aggressive or cloying, it was earnest and genuine" (Ling 9). He also provides more quotidian details such as "Skanda was a master of Scrabble and a pool shark. He had an interest in tropical fish and gardening" (12). Demonstrating how Skanda would be identified and categorized as a person of colour and as an immigrant by the state, he also shows how Skanda is so much more, how he is unique through his personality, his quirks, and his interests. In various ways Ling avoids aggrandizing the serial killer, Bruce McArthur, and relates this traumatic series of events from a victim-centred perspective.

Yet, even if the text is victim centred, there are new ethical issues that might arise in relation to the author's emphasis on gender, sexuality, race, class, religion, ethnicity, or geographical location. In "'Missing' Racialized Violence, Disturbing Continuities: Countertopographies of Violence in the Bruce McArthur Murders," David K. Seitz hopes that his essay "will inspire respectful curiosity about, and meaningful solidarity with, the lives and geographies of the men lost in this case as well as with similarly positioned people whose untimely deaths are rarely marked as exceptional or newsworthy" (467). Seitz argues that while sexuality was one aspect that increased the marginalization of the majority of the victims, they were not targeted by McArthur solely because they were part of the LGBTQ+ community. Desiring to focus the discourse of the victims around Canada's immigration policies and the state's involvement in conflicts around the world, Seitz argues that the victims were part of "complex geographies of racial, colonial, imperial, and capitalist violence at play in Canada's relationships with Afghanistan, Sri Lanka, and their diasporas" (466). Focusing solely on sexuality would ignore broader, more complicated realities of Canada as a nation state. Even though the police services come into direct contact with migrants, there are other institutions that influence their displacement. Sousveilling the Toronto Police Service then would paint an incomplete picture of the Canadian nation state and the way in which it influenced the lives of people who became McArthur's victims. Seitz criticizes how the response to these crimes has tended to focus on the victims' sexual identity: "[A]lthough much has been made of the fact that McArthur dated or had sex with a number of the men he later killed, less has been said about the fact that he also employed several of them, including Navaratnam and perhaps Kanagaratnam, at his landscaping business. [Ling 2019]. McArthur's sexual exploitation of his victims, and the often racialized character of that exploitation, is clear. But this sexual exploitation was also intimately connected to his exploitation of their often racialized, often precarious labour." (Seitz 473). Therefore, simply being victim centred does not ensure an ethical approach. There will always be some kind of limitations to one's perspective. When one offers a critique, it is likely best to do so from a position of humility and an openness to one's own faults.

One text that Seitz analyses closely is a CBC documentary about the murders titled *Village of the Missing* (2019), which also presents an argument about Canada's immigration policies in relation to the LGBTQ+ community and SOGI (sexual orientation and gender identity) refugees. Even though the documentary is victim centred, it ignores broader geopolitical implications. Seitz pointedly asks: "What kinds of transformative reckoning could result if journalism and documentary films about the McArthur case connected his violence against Afghan men to Canada's broader violence toward Afghans in the global war on terror, instead of troping the Middle East as a hopelessly backward region whose queers need Canadian salvation?" (470). Seitz questions are vital in considering the intersections of otherness that connect these victims. One cannot focus solely on sexuality when considering how they were observed or ignored.[3]

3 To be fair, even though Canada is an imperfect country, its government has been a leader in legalizing gay marriage and has also strived to help LGBTQ+ people globally. Under the heading "The Human Rights of Lesbian, Gay, Bisexual, Transgender, Queer, 2-Spirit and Intersex Persons," the Government of Canada website states:

While Ling focuses on the LGBTQ+ community, he also considers the victims as migrants who were often forced into precarious positions as a result of the complex geographies that Seitz highlights. One of Ling's strengths in *Missing from the Village* is his describing of how the community members felt and how they practised sousveillance. For Ling, not only do vulnerable people need help from the state, but there are also moments in which those at risk form a network to look after one another. For example, he writes: "So there's Mita [someone Ling sees at a coffee shop] and her German shepherd bumping into Skanda [one of the victims] and his husky, outside a scarf stall. We all know each other and recognize each other and watch out for each other" (Ling 12). However, some of the victims had wider circles than others did. This resulted in a stronger response to their absence: "Basir, Hamid, Selim, Soroush were all reported missing, but they simply didn't have the organized support needed to pressure the cops into taking those cases seriously. Dean and Kirushnakumar were marginalized onto the frayed edges of society" (245). There is an unsettling truth that many of the victims who were persons of colour received less attention from the media and from policing services. However, Ling cautions against casting judgment: "To conclude that police forces are racist, and conclude that is an answer in and of itself, misses the more pernicious problem: that to be prioritized as a missing person, you need social capital" (245). Although Ling is striving for nuance and precision, he does offer this thoughtful point afterwards: "Queer people of privilege have, generally, not stood up for others in the community who have faced oppression or violence. The community should not have been a place where men disappeared with little notice or panic, especially from the bars that were supposed to be safe havens" (245). The main contrast is between Basir, Hamid, Salim, Soroush, and Kirushnakumar, who were all persons of colour, and Andrew Kinsman, who was white. Ling argues that when Andrew went missing, his "constellation of friends, co-workers, and neighbours turned into an organizing committee … When it came to the police, his friends were unrelenting" (70). One significant difference between Andrew and the other victims is that Andrew had a bigger network of people: "Unlike some of the other missing men, there were a huge number of friends and acquaintances ready to speak to

---

"In February 2019, Canada announced its new LGBTQ2I international assistance program. This program helps the country achieve the aims of its Feminist International Assistance Policy. The program consists of $30 million in dedicated funding over 5 years and $10 million every year after. These funds promote human rights and improve socio-economic outcomes for LGBTQ2I people in developing countries."

police" (111). Thus, even within the world of the vulnerable, there is a hierarchy among those who have a strong network and those who do not. Ling questions whether the lack of response among Canadians to the three initial disappearances implied an inherent bias related to an intersection of class, gender, race, and sexuality. He ponders, "If three white women had vanished from the wealthy neighbourhood of Rosedale, just adjacent to the Village, their disappearance would have been national news" (25–6).[4] Although Ling is cautious about solely blaming racism within policing services, it is undeniable that complex geographies and community connections influence the way in which one is surveilled and sousveilled.

There are troubling connections between this text and *The Boat People* in that the MV *Sun Sea* incident is also an important part of *Missing from the Village*. Ling writes that "Vic Toews, then Canada's public safety minister, announced that migrants would be detained to 'ensure that our refugee system is not hijacked by criminals and terrorists'" (203). Toews sounds unnervingly close to Fred Blair, which highlights how well Bala has fictionalized real events in order to focus her reader's attention on the painful consequences of such rhetoric. We do not need the world of fiction, however, to see the continued trauma caused by Canada's response to the MV Sun Sea incident. Ling writes: "One of those 116 who had their claims denied [to enter Canada as a refugee] was Kirushnakumar Kanagaratnam. He was ordered removed from the country. But, unlike many of the others, Kanagaratnam was never deported" (204). He became one of McArthur's victims. Ling writes, "Police believe he was killed just two years after his refugee claim was denied" (210). Disturbingly, Kanagaratnam was part of a trend in the people whom McArthur targeted: "[S]ix of McArthur's seven known

4 Although Ling's point is speculative, it feels as though it carries an important truth. Seitz is more expansive and damning in his critique: "Taking the lived experiences of McArthur's victims seriously, and reckoning with the racialized and classed, as well as the sexualized, character of his violence, necessarily implicates white supremacy and capitalism in Canada" (466–7). It is difficult to disagree, but I worry about describing a nation – one that currently has a strong record for resettlement of refugees – in a way that simplifies and sorts. According to the UN Refugee Agency, "Canada is a world leader in finding lasting and durable solutions for refugees, including through the resettlement of refugees – ranking first among 26 countries. In 2019, Canada provided 30,082 refugees with the chance to build a new life for themselves and their families," There are institutions within Canada that have implemented specific practices, such as carding by the Toronto Police Service, that can be clearly defined as racist. In this study I am striving for specificity and a focus on provable claims.

victims were immigrants or refugees, it would have fit well within his victimology to target a man new to Canada, with little family or social connections in the country" (205). A refugee whose claim had been denied would have every reason to avoid state surveillance, which would make him extremely vulnerable to McArthur and make it impossible for the police to know that anything had happened. This is just one moment to highlight complex geographies as opposed to failing police services. Ling writes: "When his family stopped hearing from Kirushnakumar, they suspected he had gone deeper into hiding to avoid being sent back home. They worried, they waited to hear from him, but filing a missing persons report was out of the question – alerting the police to his presence in the country would only be a license to find and deport him" (208). Throughout this tragedy it seems essential to highlight that there exists an inverse problem to that discussed in *Brother*, in which certain groups were categorized and scrutinized too closely. In *Missing from the Village* many of the victims were not observed closely enough.

Surveillance structures struggle in relation to missing-persons cases. In "Policing the Lost: The Emergence of Missing Persons and the Classification of Deviant Absence," Mathew Wolfe argues that governments have historically avoided helping with missing-persons cases and have placed the responsibility on families and friends. Owing to the high number of those who go missing,[5] it becomes an incredibly difficult task to actually find people. Ling writes, "Frontline officers have felt the squeeze – they don't have the time, the resources, the capacity to dedicate teams for every missing person" (243). Issues related to online missing-persons databases make it difficult for average people to practise sousveillance and search for missing persons in their free time. Information about some missing persons is not loaded onto the databases, and so it is not clear that they are officially missing. One of the more complicated subtexts of missing persons is that the available search categories might not fit their identity: "On multiple occasions, I sifted through missing persons databases, both official and volunteer. I plugged in the pertinent variables. Gender: Male. City: Toronto. On the RCMP database, there's a category for 'bio group' – that means race, I gathered – but the options are limited. I try 'Asian' 'east Indian,' and 'other.' There's no search field for 'lifestyle,' and no category on any of these sites for 'gay'" (Ling 57). Even if categories and identities are synchronized, for some of the victims there was not enough evidence

5 "In any given year, between 70,000 and 80,000 people are reported missing to police in Canada. While most are found within seven days, missing persons cases can be extremely stressful for family and loved ones" (RCMP).

to warrant shifting resources in an already overwhelmed system. Others were situated between different bureaucracies and, either through faulty technology or failed communication, became lost in the system. Although these vast bureaucracies might be confusing and frustrating to one gathering information, they proved to be tragic for the families and friends of McArthur's victims. While these structural issues are kept in mind for Toronto and surrounding areas, surveilling or sousveilling missing persons becomes even more complicated when considering the entire country. Ling writes: "As I go case by case, something hits me hard: it is not easy to find open missing persons cases in Canada. When I plug in my search to the RCMP database … Skanda's name does pop up. Trouble is, Basir's and Hamid's don't. I'm puzzled by that … there are so many people who aren't listed" (58). Ling pulls no punches: "[T]he Royal Canadian Mounted Police set up a missing persons database and linked it to a public-facing website. To this day, that website is virtually useless, hosting just a tiny fraction of active missing persons cases in the country … It is a platform that serves to marginalize [vulnerable people] … all over again" (248). Thus, despite it only being fair to bring up structural complexities in the way that missing persons are surveilled – or not surveilled – it is difficult not to sympathize with Ling in his criticism of these structures.

To his credit, Ling maintains a delicate balance between respectful sousveillance of police officers and condemnation of the structural faults of the Toronto Police Service: "The system of policing itself is desperately in need of repair, and we shouldn't blink in the face of that challenge. While it is critical we hold the police, as an institution, accountable for the failures that led to this story, it is also important we recognize the hard work and dedication of the officers assigned to these cases" (ix). As a reporter and observer of the police, Ling has a sense of how difficult the work of policing can be. In fact, he tried to solve the case himself, and when he did so, he began to understand some of the challenges: "I've spent two years poking the cops, asking for accountability for their decision to move this investigation to 'open, but suspended.' But here I am, stuck at the foot of the same stone wall they were in front of. And I can understand some of what they must have felt" (66). While Ling has an idea of the difficulties officers face, he also is distanced from the institutional pressures of policing. Officers and administrators are being pulled in many different directions. While the Toronto Police Service was struggling to adapt to the needs of the LGBTQ+ community, the service itself was also under close scrutiny. Ling writes: "On an operational level [in 2015], the force was facing a budget crunch. On a political level, it was facing intense scrutiny over practices and programs that can only be described as racial profiling" (166). The kindest way to describe these issues might be to say that the Toronto Police Service has been going through a period of change; it is identifying problems and hopefully evolving. For massive bureaucratic structures these transitionary periods are challenging, to say the least. So much of the blame and responsibility is placed on officers. Ling, however, repeatedly sticks up for the individuals who are placed in these precarious and complex positions: "Police officers are not Swiss Army Knives. They cannot fix every problem. The core jobs of police are to keep the peace, collect evidence, and lay charges. Missing persons cases sit uneasily outside of that triangle" (254). What results from Ling's sousveillance of the Toronto Police Service is a thoughtful but decidedly critical evaluation of the system that surveils the public.

No matter what one says about the Toronto Police Service, once it had the necessary information in place and the proper warrants to move forward, the response was swift, decisive, and impressive. Ultimately McArthur's arrest relied on strong surveillance practices. The case remained open for as long as it did, in part, because of a failure of data gathering through Versadex, which is "the database of 'all general occurrences, known offenders, street checks, radio calls for the Toronto Police Service and any other data by the service'" (Ling 113). As vital as this data-collection service could be, it needs to work 100 per cent of the time. If it fails to operate with complete fluency and accuracy, officers will be misled by omission of whomever they are searching. Ling writes:

> The one thing that would have fundamentally changed the outcome of that night [that McArthur was arrested and released for a 2016 assault] would have been if Bruce McArthur's name had popped up in Versadex. The system should have indicated that McArthur was interviewed as part of a murder probe in 2013, and that he was arrested and charged for an unprovoked assault fifteen years before, in 2001 … McArthur's name, the officer told me, wasn't in the system at all … Dueling databases may be part of the problem. Versadex was supposed to centralize various other record management programs used by the service, although fusing them together was not seamless. (Ling 251)

Ling justifiably wishes for accurate, comprehensive recording of data that is properly shared.[6] Whatever happened with the Versadex seems

6 People are working to respond to this problem. In a study titled "Police 'Empires' and Information Technologies" Carrie Sanders and Samantha Henderson write: "For police technologies to address the problem of information sharing and integrated

to be a tragic failure of that particular program. Nevertheless, it remains undeniable that being able to sort through massive amounts of information is essential. Through video surveillance and databases, officers are eventually able to identify the murderer. Ling writes: "[I]nvestigators started tracking down security footage from around the neighbourhood. One camera, in particular, pointed at the street just in front of Andrew's building … Police widened the search. They sifted through more footage and caught the van driving away from Kinsman's address a couple of blocks away. But frustratingly, the cameras failed to capture the license plates" (112). When the search for the killer begins to narrow, Ling details how officers found the vehicle he was driving. He writes, "There are thousands of vans in Toronto that, roughly, match that description: 6,181 vans to be exact" (113). From the vehicle they were able to narrow their search even further: "How many, Detective Dickinson wondered, were registered to a Bruce? … There were five Bruces who owned that model of van, as it turns out. Only one Bruce owned a 2004 Dodge Caravan 20th Anniversary Edition. That Bruce also had a record in Versadex, the Toronto Police records management software'" (113). Ultimately, sifting and sorting pointed the officers to Bruce McArthur, granting them justification to observe him more closely. As Ling writes, "Police had ample evidence McArthur had killed Andrew, which gave them enough to go to a judge" (119). They were able to search McArthur's house without his knowledge, and eventually they applied for an arrest warrant. In this circumstance, surveillance and policing services identified and categorized a deviant criminal. Although flaws were revealed, the system ultimately worked.

The tragedies of these victims demand a hard look at our country and its bureaucracies. For Seitz, McArthur was a monster who was brought to life through the machinations of the state. Whatever Canada is or is not, we should all hope that McArthur is a disgusting aberration, and whatever we might want to believe, the behaviour of our government has made connections between McArthur and his victims a possibility. Improving the means of observing and protecting the people who fall into these vulnerable categories is a humane response. The lives of Abdulbasir "Basir" Faizi, Majeed "Hamid" Kayhan, Skandaraj "Skanda" Navaratnam, Soroush Mahmudi, Andrew Kinsman, Selim

---

policing we must address the situational, cultural and organisational elements embedded within their very use … policy must not simply focus on the implementation of IT, but instead be directed at establishing standardised protocols for technological integration in the hopes of breaking down the digital divides operating throughout police services within Canada and abroad" (258).

Esen, Dean Lisowick, and Kirushna Kumar Kanagaratnam were all taken. Systems designed to protect these individuals failed. Undoubtedly many have to live with a regret and a grief that I cannot understand but only have partial access to in the pages of this book. At the same time, *Missing from the Village* is a strangely and disturbingly pleasurable text. Reading a book is not a unified, rational experience. Some of the best books produce a variety of contradictory thoughts and feelings. In one moment we might feel responsibility to the victims. In another moment we might be fascinated or intrigued by the thrill of a sensational case. The play of desire and its restraint, the acceptance of a wide range of responses, and the simple willingness to be altered – no matter how slightly – for better or for worse are all part of the experience. More might be asked of us from *Missing from the Village*, but in the end all we can do is take Serpell's leap and see where we land.

PART THREE

How Should We Look at Those Who Surveil?

7 Principles to Sort By: Surveillance and Policing in David Adams Richards's *Principles to Live By*

Just as creative writers observe others, literary scholars enact their own kind of sousveillance. One author to whom the revered scholar Herb Wyile continually returned was David Adams Richards. Wyile's evaluations of Richards's later novels were not always positive, but Wyile clearly respected Richards and saw immense value in his work. In *Anne of Tim Hortons: Globalization and the Reshaping of Atlantic-Canadian Literature*, Wyile laments that Richards, "has been vocal in emphasizing the primacy of moral and spiritual concerns in his writing, and, indeed, his work does not fit that readily with the kinds of political, social, and economic considerations driving this study, nor is Richards particularly receptive to the interpretation of his work in these terms" (6). Wyile's disenchantment with Richards's writing was complicated. Essentially, however, "Firing the Regional Can(n)on: Liberal Pluralism, Social Agency, and David Adams Richards's Miramichi Trilogy," which Wyile wrote with Chris Armstrong, criticizes Richards for turning to a didacticism that puts him "in danger of being lumped in with the contemporary neo-conservatives clamoring for the dismantling of the welfare state and generating a backlash against a demonized, progressive political correctness" (Armstrong and Wyile 15). Indeed, Armstrong and Wyile's critique of Richards's later novels sparked one of the liveliest debates in Canadian scholarship.[1] It is unfortunate that Wyile did not have the chance to turn his critical gaze on *Principles to Live By*, because Richards's text is concerned with how forces outside the region have social and political consequences within it.

1 For further reading on this debate see *David Adams Richards: Essays on His Works*, edited by Tony Tremblay.

In "Making a Mess of Things: Postcolonialism, Canadian Literature, and the Ethical Turn," Wyile argues that literary fiction is rich territory for ethical considerations as a counterpoint to the transcendental truths traditionally sought by philosophy (821–2). However, he warns that, even though novels offer "a more nuanced and ambivalent exploration of the ethical complexities of cultural politics in Canada … [and] that literature can cultivate ethical engagement without positioning itself in the role of 'moral ideology for the modern age'" (Wyile, "Making a Mess" 825), critics cannot simply prescribe how novels should be understood; rather, literary novels "exhibit a resistance to moral prescription that has the significant effect of placing the responsibility for ethical judgment squarely in the hands of readers" (836). One of the many lessons to be taken from Wyile's reading of ethical criticism is that, even though *Principles to Live By* offers a powerfully imagined world, readers will not simply accept the author's perspective. However, the narration of John Delano's inner world might still benefit the discourse on surveillance and policing in granting readers the opportunity to consider those who surveil as a dominant Other. This term contrasts with earlier usages of the *vulnerable Other* in highlighting the power of individuals while also recognizing their difference. In directing our gaze towards the dominant Other, we might observe a fuller range of tensions and complexities within this discourse. In one of his final essays, on Lisa Moore's *Caught*, Wyile considers surveillance from the perspective of those who enforce the law and from the perspective of those who break it.[2] Elucidating how government institutions affect personal identity and limit the autonomy of citizens, Wyile also elaborates on the human qualities of both criminals and police officers. To carry on with his scholarship,[3] a close reading of *Principles to Live By* will demonstrate how surveillance influences the personal identities and the autonomy of police officers in the novel. Wyile's critique of *Caught* contributes an important element to the discourse on surveillance and policing, by focusing on the intersections of surveillance and genre. Where Wyile considers the thriller, I take a closer look at detective fiction in order to probe the thoughts and feelings of those tasked to observe and protect the public. John, the protagonist of *Principles to Live By*, is an RCMP officer nearing retirement who consistently expresses anxiety about the ways in which others observe him

2 In *Principles to Live By*, the lines between surveillance and sousveillance feel blurred.

3 It should also be noted that although my approach differs slightly, the scholarship of Tony Tremblay is extremely informative here, particularly in *David Adams Richards of the Miramichi*. As well, "'Learning about the Crucifixion'" by J. Russell Perkin considers the focus on the ethics of Richards's work.

and characterize his behaviour. Like many of Richards's protagonists, John maintains an inner goodness despite being profoundly misunderstood. As he investigates a cold case of a missing boy from Rwanda, John feels unfairly surveilled and sousveilled by co-workers, reporters, and ex-convicts. The weight of constant and often misplaced scrutiny damages his mental and physical health. In *Principles to Live By*, the police tend to feel closely monitored by their society and by other police. This surveillance and sousveillance contributes to the perception that John is being pressured to resolve complex issues too quickly. In Richards's world, those tasked with surveillance, traditionally the metaphorical guards in the tower gazing down on society, seem to be glancing over their shoulders inside their own panopticon.

John's character arc highlights aesthetic shifts in Richards's writing. When John is first introduced in *The Coming of Winter*, he has just received news that a close friend has died in an accident. Richards presents a troubled, afflicted young man, one more likely to break the law than to enforce it. John is full of uncertainty and doubt, traumatized by the present and worried about the future. In *David Adams Richards of the Miramichi*, Tony Tremblay aptly describes this early characterization of Delano: "John is a character in a moral crisis whose delinquency on the outside refracts a spiritual anguish within … [H]e is trying to come to terms with himself in late adolescence, a messy prospect at best" (172). Even though the behaviour of John is often upsetting and disturbing, Richards never presents him as a one-dimensional villain in either novel. In *The Coming of Winter* and *Blood Ties*, John is not simply good or bad; he is a complex human being afflicted by grief. Richards's consistency in portraying the humanity of even the most unlikeable characters is often praised. As Tremblay writes of *Blood Ties*, it is "most fully alive when rife with the small negotiations and compromises that people constantly make with themselves" (184). John resurfaces in *Hope in the Desperate Hour* and *Mercy among the Children* as a police officer. In many ways he becomes a character who represents a force for human decency through his work for the RCMP. These different permutations of John make up an important way to contextualize the criticism of Richards's career as an author. Even though a character might prove to be one-dimensional in a particular text, he or she often returns in other texts. Depending on the aesthetic strategies and the narrative structure, that character might be more fully developed depending on his or her role in the particular novel.[4]

4 John also appears in *Mary Cyr*, published in 2018.

These different permutations of John are particularly notable in consideration of criticism of Richards's career. Changes in John from *The Coming of Winter* and *Blood Ties* to *Hope in the Desperate Hour* and *Mercy among the Children* elucidate key shifts in Richards's aesthetic strategies. Armstrong and Wyile regret "a decline in the subtlety of characterization and narrative conflict in Richards's work" (13). This shift in Richards's aesthetic can be seen in his characterization of John in *Hope in the Desperate Hour*: "Sergeant Delano, with his reddish hands and his dark eyes, wanted to learn. He had spent his entire life wanting to know" (195). Although Richards's description of John here might not prove to be as subtle as in *The Coming of Winter* and *Blood Ties*, it is economical and intriguing in that it provides a glimpse of a minor character's inner world. David Creelman, in *Setting in the East: Maritime Realist Fiction*, observes that Richards's aesthetic moves away from realism and towards the genre of moral romance, which also explains such a shift in characterization (168). In this genre the differences between right and wrong are easier to separate. J. Russell Perkin, who focuses mainly on *For Those Who Hunt the Wounded Down*, argues that Richards's "characters inhabit a fictional world in which there are identifiable ethical categories of right and wrong, good and evil, and the characters are seen to make meaningful choices in that world" (121). In *Mercy among the Children*, John operates as a moral centre, righting the wrongs and failings of other characters. Standing near the narrator's bookshelves, picking out certain books, and musing on them, John says: "'I promise if I have a breath in my body, your father will never be an outcast again ... The truth does matter. There was a time I did not think it. All of a sudden falsehood just goes away'" (335). Not only is John an important character to observe in the trajectory of literary criticism of Richards's work, but also he is a compelling figure to consider in relation to ethics and its focus on ambiguity. As a police officer, John often operates on hunches, complex blends of certainty and uncertainty. He does not claim to know the truth. However, he has instinct, and he has the conviction to do what he believes is right, which will lead him to certainty and to truth.

Principles to Live By offers a powerfully imagined world in which to consider how both watching and being watched affect the world of policing. Some might argue that police should be closely monitored and scrutinized, considering their power and influence in society. That point is vital, but it also makes sense to consider the effect of this public scrutiny. In *The Vigilant Eye: Policing Canada from 1867 to 9/11*, Greg Marquis details how "[f]or decades the dominant narrative in Canada was that its justice system, including its police, was tough but fair ...

[However,] a national poll [in 2012] suggested that confidence in the RCMP had fallen to a historic low, and attitudes toward the municipal police were almost as negative" (2). Criticism from the public does not necessarily contribute to positive change within police culture; in some cases it results in more negative behaviour among police officers (Nix and Wolfe 100–1). One of the biggest concerns in the discourse on surveillance is not just how the public watches the police but also how the police watch their own. Unfortunately, at least in Canada, there does not appear to be a benevolent professional gaze. In fact, there appears to be a significant problem in the RCMP with workplace harassment, and this professional tension can affect how officers watch the public. *The Report into Workplace Harassment in the RCMP* conducted by the Civilian Review and Complaints Commission for the RCMP offers this warning in its conclusion: "Workplace harassment, bullying, intimidation and sexual harassment can cause significant harm to individual RCMP members and employees, in some cases damaging careers and causing serious emotional and physical harm … [S]uch problems are also eroding the trust of the Canadian public, who are asking whether the RCMP's internal problems have 'filtered outside' and affected the treatment of members of the public" (4). Observing the public is a tough task. A weakening of public trust and a troublesome workplace environment can only make the job tougher. As part of a larger effort to restore the relationship between the public and the RCMP, thoughtful considerations of policing and police culture might help. In this sense it is important to consider the perspective of those who surveil, as Richards does in *Principles to Live By*. John manages to do good work despite the pressures that he feels in watching and being watched. However, the same pressures clearly influence Sergeant Melonson, who seems to operate as John's insidious foil, to intimidate others and to behave in ways that he himself does not respect.

In Richards's novel, social sorting is enacted on the poor. Melon Thibodeau, a vulnerable loner who has information on one of the central crimes in the text, is followed by Officer Melonson: "He noticed the man, and thought nothing of it as he was going home … [H]e saw the man straddle the wrought iron fence and approached … He beckoned, but Melon pretended not to notice. He turned again and went back the way he had come, always looking over his shoulder" (Richards, *Principles* 89). Officer Melonson asks Melon for a light, and when Melon produces matches, Melonson teases the ex-convict: "'[Y]ou broke your parole. You have matches on you'" (90). Melon has information on Melonson that would reflect poorly on the officer, so Melonson seeks to control the ex-convict through threats. Melonson is a clear example of an officer who abuses his power. Through surveillance and threats he seeks to keep his own name clear of blame even though he behaves unethically. This is not behaviour that Melonson himself would condone, but he feels trapped in this course of action: "Melonson was in fact enraged at having to act like this" (91). One can surmise that he feels threatened by the way in which he would be surveilled if Melon's story were heard by others. As this example demonstrates, there are basic problems with social sorting in terms of equality and fairness in that those already struggling are observed more closely than others. Unfortunately there are circumstances in which it is necessary to categorize people. *Missing from the Village* certainly demonstrates the need for accurate surveillance and sorting. The problem is that while some treat their power as a sacred trust, others abuse it to further their own interests.

Discussions of surveillance often focus on the absence of privacy, but it is not just the lack of privacy that is worrisome in the surveillance state; surveillance itself is a form of power. In "Totalitarian Paranoia in the Post-Orwellian Surveillance State," Henry Giroux writes: "Under the surveillance state, the greatest threat one faces is not simply the violation of one's right to privacy, but the fact that the public is subject to the dictates of arbitrary power – and a power it no longer seems interested in contesting. It is not simply the existence of unchecked power, but the wider culture of political indifference that puts at risk the broader principles of liberty and freedom which are fundamental to democracy itself" (127). Melonson, the bad cop to John's good cop, exhibits the kind of behaviour about which someone like Giroux might worry. He uses his position to advance his own interests rather than the interests of the public, and he does so in a way that humiliates others. Richards writes that Melonson "loved to gloat over catching people in lies – it was part of the forte of being a bully" (*Principles* 132). Such bullying tactics are used not only against the public but also against other officers. Melonson begins to observe John and even tries to have him end his investigation of the missing boy. The narrator writes that "Melonson told him not to bother 87 Shelf Street [the address of the foster home] again – for no boy was ever reported missing from that house; and no one they knew of ever resembled anyone from Rwanda. That the McCrease family [the foster family who took in the missing boy] certainly had a right to privacy from the police or anyone else" (137). Rather than shy away from issues of privacy, Melonson actually uses the right to privacy to advance his own interests. In truth, he is trying to cover up an error that he made years ago on the case that John is now investigating.

One way in which literary criticism can contribute to the discourses on surveillance and policing is through the observation of telling intersections of real-life police and fictional representations of police. For example, the classic detective hero, embodied by John, upholds societal values despite an unappreciative public, and a similar storyline can be found in the real-life world of policing; it is known as having an "exaggerated sense of mission" (Cummins and King 3). These intersections do not necessarily reveal anything about actual police officers, but they might be helpful in discussions of the cultural politics of Canada in that they contribute to viewing with either empathy or alterity the difficult work of policing. One strength of Wyile's essay on Moore's *Caught* is the way it connects the politics of surveillance to genre. Wyile details how the thriller genre "is characteristically preoccupied with hermeneutic questions, particularly the importance of reading appearances and evaluating the veracity of both people and situations" ("'Best Stories'" 273). Although distinct, the thriller genre and detective fiction are closely aligned. John Scaggs points out in *Crime Fiction*: "Perhaps more than any genre, detective fiction foregrounds the related view of reading as a quest for meaning, or a form of detection, and the relationship is an important one for various ideological reasons. Primary among these is that the first-person narrator of the private eye story is easily identifiable with the private 'I' of the solitary reader …, making the hard-boiled novel a powerful ideological tool" (74). John's attention to detail during crime-scene investigations is closely connected with his love of reading. The narrator of *Principles to Live By* frequently comments that John is well read, even that there are "writers he had got to know from Newfoundland to Saskatchewan" (60). His ability to do a close reading contributes to his skill at analysing his surroundings and vice versa. This connection between reading and detecting encourages an alertness and an attention to detail – a way of seeing the world that is closely aligned with the discourse on surveillance. In this sense, Wyile's focus on generic concerns might prove to be an important step in articulating yet another reason that modern surveillance is troubling. Detective fiction sheds light on how those tasked with surveillance internalize and negotiate their positions as observers. Scaggs makes repeated connections between detective fiction and Foucault's understanding of the panopticon: "The difference between the Panopticon, however, and the constant surveillance of the new judicial ideology … is that the Panopticon presupposes that the prisoners open to constant visual inspection from the tower at the centre of this model prison are guilty of some crime, whereas the objects of Miss Marple's gaze are nothing more than suspects and potential criminals, and in the textual Panopticon of detective fiction, it would seem that everybody is a suspect" (45–6). From the perspective of those who detect, society needs to be observed closely; anyone and everyone could turn out to be a criminal. From the perspective of those observed, it is unsettling to be viewed as a potential criminal without having committed any crimes.

D.A. Miller argues that novels encourage readers to internalize an author's sense of right and wrong (216), but monitoring and judging should be contemplated in relation to the larger culture of books, not solely during the reading experience. In an interview with Tony Tremblay, Richards expresses anxiety about feeling unfairly judged: "The outrage over my novels comes mostly from these types – academics or intellectuals who work for the CBC. Their criticism of my work can be self-serving and hypocritical because it says that Dave Richards is not allowed to say this and that about us, but we can say anything about his characters and him" (Richards, "Interview" 40). Similarly, in *Principles to Live By*, books leave certain characters feeling closely monitored. Although Miller's argument is about the influence that books have on readers, the narrator of *Principles to Live By* is acutely aware that being written about affects one's psyche. A scholar, Professor Milk, writes a book about Gilbert, the missing child of John and his wife, Jeannie: "For Jeannie it was the only way to keep Gilbert's story alive. The only way to keep hope alive … And if enough people read her story, maybe just one would have seen him" (Richards, *Principles* 206). In this sense the book spreads important information, even potentially encouraging people to look for the missing boy. For John, however, the book changes how people observe him: "*Tragedy in the Campground* the book was called. John had a copy. In it he was a rude, backward-thinking RCMP officer with an eye on his career – and according to anonymous reports, known as a bigot, neglecting and bullying the child, who would have been better off with people like Melissa Sapp [who runs child-protective services]" (207). *Tragedy in the Campground* frames and characterizes people's observations of John's life situation. As an observer and protector of the public, John might be viewed as the man behind the panopticon, as it was imagined by Foucault, but he too has his troubling paranoia, his own fear of being watched. Books at their best, however, might help people to move past the anxiety of the surveillance state in significant ways. Fiction aids in this process by allowing people to observe or to imagine the interior of Foucault's panopticon. For Scaggs, this looking back is really about seeking comfort: "In the case of mystery and detective fiction, [the pleasure of the text for] … the home-owning bourgeois reading public … is to see the dominant social order of which they are a part maintained … and their stake in it protected" (45). Both Scaggs and Miller view fiction as a kind of ideological tool that maintains the status quo. Although comfort seeking might contribute to the appeal of the crime genre, it is reductive and dismissive in grouping all readers and viewers into one category that implies they are not sophisticated or brave enough for more complex fiction. *Principles to Live By*, for example, offers little comfort to readers. Although the central mystery is resolved, the novel focuses on missing children and genocide. Furthermore, certain texts within the crime genre and certain readings of texts, such as Wyile's interpretation of Moore's *Caught*, provide meditation and ethical groundwork that could open dialogues between citizens and their government institutions.

Principles to Live By helps readers to consider the lives of those who surveil, to openly engage with their world view, and to observe how their ways of seeing might be internalized. Richards's narrative fluctuates between understanding for and alterity to John. There are moments when he can be observed and understood, but there are also moments when his pain is beyond comprehension. In considering his various permutations, we can see that his troubles go further back than his policing career. From the moment that John is introduced in *The Coming of Winter*, he is battling some kind of trauma. In *Blood Ties* he takes part in extremely dangerous behaviour, and in both *Hope in the Desperate Hour* and *Mercy among the Children* he is involved in highly stressful situations. It becomes clear in *Principles to Live By* that John suffers from PTSD, the narrator describing him as "[a] man who asked the battered darkness about him … the one question that pertains to us all: 'Why?'" (Richards, *Principles* 170). His work experience as a police officer in various capacities, including time spent in Rwanda during the Tutsi genocide, has left him profoundly damaged. Richards does not develop John as an uncomplicated and easily understood character. His pain is wholly other. This portrayal of the psychologically damaged police officer is consistently seen throughout the genre of detective fiction. Ian Cummins and Martin King argue that the dominant representation of police in television dramas is "almost classic cases of PTSD," yet the officers and their colleagues do not "see their behaviour in these terms. While Dirty Harry … was damaged, he was in control whereas in modern-day representations the predominant model is out of control and staring into the abyss" (12–13). In *Principles to Live By*, Richards characterizes John's profession as harrowing, difficult, perhaps even heroic in how John is misunderstood: "John was unloved and did an unloveable job, and [he] exacerbated this alienation by his analytical approach to those about him" (74). His PTSD surfaces more than once as the narrative progresses. His psychiatrist asks him if he ever thinks of taking his own life. John replies, "'[N]ot so often. Four, maybe five times a day'" (171). His own son disappears, and he has several professional struggles that put him in a severe depression: "[I]t came over John in waves as he spoke to his psychiatrist about it ... [Events] had made his life so bitter that for days on end he did not get out of bed. Once, when people told him he would die if he did not eat, he replied, 'Well, why in God's name do you think I am not eating?'" (81). This consistent portrayal of officers who suffer from a host of mental and physical troubles, some resulting from the job and some not, presents questions for those who study crime fiction. Is this kind of suffering an expectation within the culture of policing, or is it an expectation of the public? What are the intersections of fiction and real life, if any? If there are any intersections, can they be employed to lessen this suffering?

Although public perception and popular media impose certain values or principles onto the policing world, police aspire to live by their own code. Cummins and King argue that "any discussion of police culture needs to explore the attitudes that officers have about their own roles but also the wider society that they live in and police. This is vital because these attitudes underpin officers' conduct. One feature of this set of attitudes that has been highlighted is the police officers' exaggerated sense of mission. As Skolnick (1966) comments, [because] ... police officers are charged with the defense of societal values (obviously, a contested concept) ... it is inevitable that they see themselves as the living embodiment of these values" (Cummins and King 3). John consistently struggles with trying to live up to an idealistic set of values. As the protagonist of *Principles to Live By*, he exhibits a selfless human decency, and he is capable of great sacrifice with little reward. As Richards writes, "it was a thankless job very well done. In fact like great men and women John had done his job heroically, without the benefit of help or hope of applause" (*Principles* 310). John's sacrifices take a toll on his mental and physical health, but his greatest anxiety and suffering occur when other people do not live up to his ideals. His relationships with those in power, embodied by a group of Canadians working at the United Nations who fail to adequately respond to the Tutsi genocide in Rwanda, are often tense and confrontational. These repeated negative interactions with others give John a bad reputation, and instead of being seen as an individual who upholds a set of principles, he becomes "the poster child of intolerance within the police" (65). However, the assumptions that people draw from their observations of John are almost always counter to his internal self as characterized by the narrator. This distinction between the complex inner world and the simplified and unfairly judged outer self is similar to social sorting except that it is enacted on a police officer.

Richards's representations of John and Melonson encourage a productive sense of uncertainty about policing and surveillance. For Wyile, the importance of literary ethics lies in producing what he describes as messiness, a kind of moral ambiguity: "Perhaps more importantly, the ethical utility of literary texts may well reside most of all in their lack of amenability to clear judgment (whether that judgment be consensus or disagreement) – that is, in their recurrent ambiguity" (Wyile, "Making a Mess" 831). Scaggs's reading of crime fiction ties nicely into Wyile's description of ethical criticism. Scaggs writes that "highlighting the impossibility of what has always been central to crime fiction [is] ... the process of interpretation itself. It is the indeterminacy of the interpretative act, and the parallels between detection and the reading process that allow postmodern crime fiction to underline this indeterminacy" (4–5). The narrator of *Principles to Live By*, despite the thematic emphasis on principles, also values a level of uncertainty. In the dichotomy developed between Melonson and John, Melonson is notable – among other things – for exhibiting false certainty and seeking the most obvious answer: "He already believed the [missing] boy was Jack Toggle [a local kid], who had run away – Jack Toggle had run away before so now he had done so again. That was the paradigm Melonson insisted upon" (Richards, *Principles* 131). John also exhibits certainty but not until he has experienced a moment of self-doubt and hesitation: "I am now thinking that he [the missing boy] came to the wrong city – there was a mix-up, and perhaps he was supposed to be in St. John's, Newfoundland. But I am uncertain" (102). The narrator develops these two competing methods of observing the world and observing an event. Melonson begins with a solution to the problem and plods along with absolute certainty to prove that it is correct. John has a hunch and, through careful observations, trial, and error, finds out if his hunch is true or false. This productive and humble sense of not knowing, which might eventually lead to certainty, is an important lesson for ethical criticism, which seems to be fixated on uncertainty. Tremblay describes Richards's moral philosophy as "his belief in the ethical superiority of spontaneous action over calculated intent, which is always more ideologically laden" (*David Adams Richards of the Miramichi*, 313). Richards has been criticized for his apparent favouring of spontaneous action over more self-conscious action. Discussing the Miramichi trilogy, Armstrong and Wyile argue that "[t]he narrative voices across the trilogy are predisposed to place under suspicion reason, causality, and larger complexes of social meaning, privileging instead spontaneity, chance, and un-self-consciousness" (7). The behaviour of John, clearly the hero of *Principles to Live By*, does not fall on either side of this dichotomy but is a strange mix of reason, causality, chance, and spontaneity. His hunches are reminiscent of Serpell's "flinging of the self" in that John accepts he does not know the truth but must act nonetheless. He must throw himself into the case, and as he sifts through the past, his hunches are his best method of acting justly within the moral ambiguity of complex moments.

Considerations of the police are not solely about developing an ethics of surveillance or sousveillance; imagining the difficulties of those tasked with surveilling the public might actually contribute to better police work. In "The Impact of Negative Publicity on Police Self-Legitimacy," Justin Nix and Scott Wolfe argue that "it is irresponsible for researchers (and the public) to ignore how … negative publicity can diminish officers' sense of self-legitimacy. This is important because research suggests that self-legitimacy is associated with a number of beneficial behaviors for law enforcement agencies and the public more generally. Officers with greater confidence in their authority are more likely to identify with their agency and its goals … support the idea of interacting with citizens in a procedurally fair manner … and – perhaps most relevant to the current debate surrounding the police – be more restrained in the decision to use force" (100–1).

Self-legitimacy is how self-perception melds with public perception, and in *Principles to Live By* public perception of the police is heavily influenced by the news media. In this sense, Richards is perceptive in that the majority of the information available to average people about surveillance and policing comes from popular media. As Kenneth Dowler and Valerie Zawilski write, "popular media [is] … of fundamental importance in the construction of attitudes toward criminal justice and criminal justice agents. The majority of public knowledge about crime and justice is derived from media consumption … As such, the perception of victims, criminals, and law enforcement officials is largely determined by their portrayal within the media" (193). In *Principles to Live By* news media obstructs policing efforts and unfairly characterizes the protagonist's motives. One of John's more infamous cases is heavily influenced by his portrayal in the media: "[H]e did not address a suspect in French when he was making an arrest. The case was overturned and the man walked free. This was a major victory for the forces of liberty and equality, one paper had said. And John was the man who had subverted liberty and equality in order to get the job done" (70). Commenting on the case, John says, "'I was looked upon as a bigot'" (70). Even though he acted reasonably, "the media and others became increasingly wary – John Delano was not the most savoury person; well, not in Canadian terms, anyway" (312). The man arrested,

Bennie Cheval (who speaks English almost exclusively), is implicated in a murder case, and he walks free in part because of the media's intervention. Richards presents an ethical dilemma in that liberty and equality are social goods, but they are used to a negative end in freeing a murderer. The case hinges on how the media influences observations of John's character, thus exemplifying the intersection of surveillance and language; the words used to describe John change how he is watched, and such scrutiny damages his mental and physical health. He is still an effective officer, but he is not able to work as much as he did in the past. In contrast, similar pressure on Melonson alters his self-legitimacy, and he does not always interact "with citizens in a procedurally fair manner" (Nix and Wolfe 101). Condemnations of those tasked with watching the public, though certainly necessary from time to time, might not be as productive as are even-toned attempts to understand their difficult jobs.

Although *Principles to Live* By offers insights into the lives of police officers, some of the characters who interact with the police are designed to be one-dimensional. In a review in *Quill and Quire* James Grainger criticizes the portrayal of Melissa Sapp: "Sapp, as Richards characterizes her, is the embodiment of everything wrong in the modern world: an intellectually arrogant hypocrite who uses left-wing pieties to mask and satisfy her will to power. She's also a feminist, a position that, for reasons never specified, infuriates Delano." This criticism seems to be well founded, and it is not a new criticism of Richards. The same critique that Armstrong and Wyile make of his antagonists could be directed at Sapp and the Lion of Justice (a UN envoy): "The majority of the antagonists in the novels have achieved a certain level of social respectability – enough, certainly, so that they are acutely conscious of others' lack of it – and come across as self-aggrandizing, hypocritical, calculating, yet insecure ... [B]ut their motivation is constructed as self-concern rather than genuine concern for others" (Armstrong and Wyile 9–10). The one-dimensionality of Sapp is particularly notable considering that Richards is adept at developing characters who feel completely alive. John and Melonson, for example, are complex, nuanced, and extremely interesting representations of police officers. Grainger adds: "She [Sapp] and other representatives of liberalism and the left – including a UN special envoy referred to as 'the Lion of Justice' – are described with hectoring sarcasm, as if Richards's contempt prevents him from elucidating their inner lives and motivations (a notable omission, given his talent for creating believable villains)." To be fair, the actions of both Sapp and the Lion of Justice deserve sarcasm. Furthermore, the Lion of Justice is clearly designed to be a satirical character in that his actions consistently play against his name. To understand better this aesthetic choice, it makes sense to go back to one of Wyile's earliest essays on Richards. In "Laughs in the Desperate Hour" Wyile argues that "Richards' fiction is much more consistently humorous than it gets credit for" (107). He adds that "if Richards' writing is humorous, most of that humour is of the dark variety" (111). The Lion of Justice is written with this "dark" sense of humour that Wyile noticed early on in Richards's career. The desire for exclusively well-rounded characters in a novel might be more reflective of expectations embedded in scholarly sousveillance rather than of a failing of *Principles to Live By*.

Nevertheless, Grainger's point still stands: Sapp and the Lion of Justice are not developed with the same complexity and nuance as is John or Melonson. What results is a kind of didacticism in which a moral lesson is implied about good behaviour and bad behaviour. Armstrong and Wyile make a similar criticism in their evaluation of the Miramichi trilogy: "[T]he trilogy often appears to be a didactic exercise, a set of modern morality tales about the dangers of progressive political correctness – to be sure, a practice that is at odds with Richards's valorizing of 'life'" (12–13). Didacticism is a problem for literary fiction because it tends to simplify complex issues.[5] Grainger's criticism is essentially that Richards sorts characters into conservatives and liberals and that the liberal characters are often examples of bad behaviour. However, looking closely at the scholarship on Richards, he is not the only one who sorts people into groups. Lawrence Mathews strongly argues that Richards has been simplified and categorized by academics: "Armstrong and Wyile suggest that Richards' philosophical position is not the result of decades of intense thinking and feeling about art and life but rather something like a reflex action" (134). Perhaps a lesson that can be taken from this discourse is that when people can be separated into groups, they begin to simplify one another in extremely complex ways. The heart of this tension between Richards and the academy is partially aesthetic, but it is also a difference of politics. Whether rightly or wrongly, he is viewed as a conservative author, and to be blunt, this conservatism has bothered some critics. To be truly pluralistic, however, means embracing authors who appear to be conservative as well

5 The same criticism does not ring true for *Principles to Live By* when it is bracketed within the crime genre, which has its roots in the cautionary tale (Scaggs 13). Crime novels are almost always didactic in the sense that, by their conclusions, at least one of the characters is generally punished; if the wrong people are punished, then their punishment also presents a moral lesson.

as those who appear to be liberal. Respectfully, this openness has not always occurred in the discourse on the work of Richards.

A similar kind of social sorting plays out in *Principles to Live By*. John feels harassed by his enemies, and they feel harassed by him. One root of harassment is a failure to consider other people's thoughts and emotions. John feels unfairly observed and criticized by Sapp, and undoubtedly she has similar feelings about him. Sapp and the Lion of Justice think of John as a one-dimensional person. He is characterized as rude and bigoted, when he is actually far more complicated than people think. The failure to appreciate the complexity of other people results in part from the false assumption that one can fully understand their thoughts and feelings, that their inner worlds can be approached with empathy alone. John and Sapp think that they know one another. However, she merely projects a simplified version of his inner world onto his behaviour; he in turn does the same to her. Each has a poor approximation of the other. In this sense, alterity is an extremely important concept for the discourse on surveillance, sousveillance, and social sorting; it discourages simplified understandings of other people's behaviour; and it encourages humility, respect, and open-mindedness. Thus, though Principles to Live By does not present a holistic understanding of the surveillance state, it offers a perspective that, when paired with ethical criticism, could be particularly informative to the cultural politics of Canada.

Wyile's scholarship deftly tracks the political and social changes that have shaped Canada's Atlantic provinces, from both a regional perspective and a global perspective. Whether positive or negative, Wyile's observations of Richards's work are passionate, well articulated, and perceptive. Principles to Live By demonstrates Richards's interest in the way in which Atlantic Canada is situated within the broader world, and, whether or not one agrees with the politics of this novel, there is undoubtedly a political undercurrent. Wyile's critical gaze informs and challenges Richards's creative work well and vice versa. Furthermore, Richards's text might add to the discourse on surveillance in narrating the interior of the panopticon. Those who enact surveillance are not necessarily secretive, unfeeling individuals concealed from the public. Sometimes they are strangers, but they are also neighbours, friends, and parents. Sometimes they revel in their role as observers, and sometimes they feel trapped in their position. Richards is careful to contrast public perceptions of police officers with their interior worlds. The public in Principles to Live By tends to view the officers as blunt, forceful, and even crude. However, the officers' inner worlds are always more complex. Marquis concludes his study with a call to action: "[I] t is imperative that academics, interest groups and ordinary citizens resist … 'police as hero' narratives and hold police organizations and their governance bodies accountable" (237). However, if this resistance is carried out in a way that increases tension between the police and the public, then both sides lose. The idea of resistance might need to be exchanged for less dramatic notions such as cooperation and mutual compromise. *Principles to Live By* is, among other things, a literary imagining of what happens when the public fails to appreciate the RCMP and when police officers fail to support one another. Introducing the concept of self-legitimacy to the discourse on surveillance might be an extremely productive step to ensure positive interactions between the police and the public. Calmly and evenly considering the perspective of those who surveil might contribute to a more realistic understanding of the complex work that police officers do, which in turn might generate more positive interactions with the public and a greater likelihood of a healthy police work culture (Nix and Wolfe 101).

Many of the officers in *Principles to Live By* who are powerful and exert force on their surroundings do not feel powerful. They tend to express – in their thoughts, at least – a sense of feeling trapped in an unjust world, suffering to make it better in some way. In this sense, thinking about policing and surveillance as informed by genre might not only help identify connections between real and imagined worlds but also be a way to develop a nuanced image of police culture within this discourse. The public in *Principles to Live By* tends to presume that officers do not have complex inner worlds. They observe police in a way that is informed more by social positions than by individual characteristics. This consistent failure to imbue the public figure with a private self might well be considered poetic justice; those who enact social sorting are also categorized and sorted in their own way. However, narratives such as *Principles to Live By* are important components of the discourse on surveillance in that they broaden the scope of the discussion to imagine the internal conflicts of those who observe; they pull back the blinds inside the watchtower to reveal another series of panopticons, a matryoshka doll with a hidden camera in each layer.

8 Broken Principles: One Police Officer's Relationship to Indigenous Identity in Katherena Vermette's *The Break*

In *Why Indigenous Literatures Matter*, Daniel Heath Justice writes: "The struggle to understand and articulate our humanity is at the heart of most literatures, customs, laws, faiths, nationalisms, identities – even our basic sense of self. All peoples have developed complicated understandings of that existential question and the ways it has fascinated, frustrated, and frightened all human cultures throughout our varied histories" (36). Although Katherena Vermette has published widely,[1] in this chapter I am going to focus on her descriptions of a young, Métis police officer named Tommy Scott who appears in *The Break* and on how he feels pulled between a responsibility to his community and a responsibility to his career. This struggle is one that involves trying to come to terms with his own identity and – to use Justice's phrase – to articulate his humanity, which proves to be incredibly challenging to a police officer caught in the middle of settler-colonial relationships. Coulthard is extremely helpful in defining the all-encompassing nature of such an experience: "A settler-colonial relationship is one characterized by a particular form of domination; that is, it is a relationship where power – in this case, interrelated discursive and nondiscursive facets of economic, gendered, racial, and state power – has been structured into a relatively secure or sedimented set of hierarchical social relations that continue to facilitate the dispossession of Indigenous peoples of their lands and self-determining authority" (6–7). This settler-colonial relationship

1 Vermette has published two works of poetry, *North End Love Songs* and *River Woman*; two children's books, *The Seven Teachings Stories* and *The Girl and the Wolf*; and a trilogy of novels, *The Break*, *The Strangers*, and *The Circle*. Truly a prolific author, Vermette published the novel *Real Ones* in 2024. I am choosing a literary analysis of Officer Tommy Scott in *The Break* as I feel this approach works well alongside *Principles to Live By*.

frames every interaction in *The Break*. Tommy's path to working against it comes by finding wholeness in his Indigenous identity. However, his position as police officer obstructs his journey to achieving fully what Coulthard describes as a resurgent politics of recognition.

As a settler scholar, I want to avoid using Vermette's novel solely to extract data. As Pauline Wakeham writes in "Outsourcing Reconciliation: The Government of Canada's #IndigenousReads Campaign and the Appropriation of Indigenous Intellectual Labor," "the extractive approach to Indigenous literatures … has strong correlates to a more longstanding Euro-Western scholarly tradition of treating texts as ready resources for critical analysis and experimentation without considering accountability to Indigenous communities" (20). I hope that this chapter, instead of extracting data, focalizes and adds nuance through a close reading and a thoughtful consideration of narrative. I want to highlight at the outset that Tommy Scott is only part of a larger story in *The Break*. Vermette's novel concentrates mainly on the domestic lives of Indigenous women dealing with a traumatic incident against a young girl, Emily Traverse. Tommy's narrative arc highlights the complex, challenging relationships negotiated by police officers within the discourse of surveillance. As Tommy's narrative progresses, he becomes more invested in his Indigenous identity. Rather than simply choosing to do the right thing, he finds himself in ethically dense situations that he must navigate, doing as little damage as possible.

This chapter is not intended to be a final or definitive statement on how one author narrates interactions between fictional police officers and a fictional Indigenous family. It would be apt to quote the way that Helen Hoy identifies herself in "How Should I Read These?": "From a position of race privilege, I feel a responsibility to combat structures of power and entitlement. Teaching or writing about texts by Native writers, from my position of privilege, may not do that politically efficacious work; my academic activity is seriously implicated in the very systems of stratification and dominance it critiques" (Hoy 18). Highlighting my own privilege and my own fraught position of working within a settler institution is essential. It frames the way in which I am able to understand this text and its contingencies. Hopefully, it also makes me more aware of potential interpretive blind spots. In "The New People: Reading for Peoplehood in Métis Literatures," Jennifer Adese articulates some of the key issues that settler scholars tend to get wrong: "[T]he majority of academic literature written about Métis peoples has been written by non-Métis. Instead of engaging with Métis worldviews, the wider body of academic literature as it pertains to Métis has been preoccupied with writing about Métis people through the lens of racial discourse, specifically through Métis people's proximity to whiteness and Indianness" (59). Although Adese's point is taken, this chapter necessarily discusses a split identity in Tommy as his police work is affected by a history of colonialism. This history undoubtedly influences his sense of self and the way in which he interacts with others. As a counterpoint to focusing on mixedness, Adese argues that scholars should instead focus on the concept of wahkootowin (aka wahkohtowin), which "provides Métis with an understanding of their relationships to one another and to all of creation across the wide range of their homeland" (63). Part of Tommy's journey in *The Break* involves recognizing his own togetherness with the Traverse and Charles families. In this sense he begins to find wholeness through his work.

Generally speaking, representations of surveillance in literature demonstrate that observing and being observed changes people,[2] but when this conversation is applied specifically to Indigenous and settler relations, the significance heightens. In "Settler Governmentality and Racializing Surveillance in Canada's North-West" Jeffrey Monaghan details the extent to which the Canadian surveillance structure has historically overseen Indigenous Peoples in Canada and how "[i]nformation gathered ... was compiled and scrutinized by the Department of Indian Affairs (DIA)" (495). *The Break* takes place in the city of Winnipeg's North End, where one of the main sources of surveillance is the police. Vermette develops a representation of a policing system that is intensely racialized both in the way police officers view each other and in the way they observe civilians. Throughout the novel, police officers draw a clear line between Indigenous and non-Indigenous, with Indigenous people often being the subject of prejudiced commentary. This reflects the way in which Monaghan views surveillance structures in Canada: "Racializing surveillance fulfils prefabricated stereotypes and prejudice held by colonial authorities and produces a social hierarchy defined by normative standards and signifiers of whiteness" (492). Unfortunately certain officers, such as Tommy's older partner, Christie, make assumptions about Indigenous people that become self-fulfilling prophecies. More often than

2 In *Transparent Lives: Surveillance in Canada* the authors write: "The increased prevalence of surveillance is important not simply because of how it might track and identify suspicious people but also because it can alter everyone's behaviours" (Bennett et al. 32). In a society where people might feel they are being watched through their medical history, their DNA, their credit card purchases, their internet search history, this sense of being watched alters their behaviour.

not, one can trace the intersections between Monaghan's criticism and Vermette's narrative world.

The existing critical work on *The Break* tends to focus on the way in which the characters connect despite a history of colonialism that still affects them to this day. In "Shifting the Narrative of Winnipeg's North End in Katherena Vermette's *The Break*," Susan Birkwood highlights the importance of Indigenous women's voices: "The voice that introduces this narrative remapping of the city belongs to the spirit of Lorraine Charles, a Métis woman whose death is the result of violence and marginalization ... Vermette illustrates the complex legacy of the historical dispossession of Indigenous peoples within Canada's borders, evident in the city's profound social divisions and in the violence against Indigenous women and girls" (18). Thus, while my essay is focused on a male police officer, it is important to pause and stress that Tommy Scott – although an important character from whom much can be learned – is only part of a much bigger story. Aubrey Jean Hanson, in "Holding Home Together: Katherena Vermette's *The Break*," emphasizes the importance of family and community as a contrast to institutionalized efforts such as those implemented by the police force. She details the social relevance of the novel and the failures of the Canadian government to support Indigenous women: "The resilience of Indigenous women in particular is not a story that is told, or heard, often enough. News and statistics tell a dire story, one that also must be heard. More than a thousand Indigenous women are missing or have been murdered in Canada: in 2017 Patty Hajdu, Canada's Minister for the Status of Women, 'pointed to research from the Native Women's Association of Canada (NWAC) that puts [the figure] at 4,000' (Tasker)" (Hanson). For Hanson, the failure of the state is exemplified by Phoenix Stranger, the young woman who commits sexual assault against Emily: "Instead of a kin web of unquestioningly supportive women, Phoenix experiences state care and institutionalization" (Hanson). Keeping these details in mind, it is clear that readers have a responsibility to rivet their attention on the diverse, complex representations of the Indigenous women that Vermette develops. Nevertheless, Jamie Paris, in "'Men Break When Things Like That Happen': On Indigenous Masculinities in Katherena Vermette's *The Break*," astutely argues that important lessons can be gleaned from the male characters in this novel as well: "Vermette combats stories of Indigenous male deficiency by demonstrating the high social, emotional, and political costs women pay when Indigenous men try to embody settler masculinities based on domination and control, while also showing that 'good men' like Peter and Tommy can lift up themselves and Indigenous women by embodying non-dominative ways of being male" (71). Tommy Scott represents a male police officer who helps other characters find togetherness. Readers are granted the opportunity to observe how one richly developed interior world, as cultivated by Vermette, persists in a particularly challenging work environment that is deeply affected by colonialism. Finally, in "Attention, Representation, and Unsettlement in Katherena Vermette's *The Break*, or, Teaching and (Re)Learning the Ethics of Reading," Cynthia Wallace demonstrates how Vermette's narrative develops an ethics of observing the Other. Wallace writes: "In the interpersonal encounters of the characters, this thematics of looking and face-to-face encounters accrues a broader significance through repetition: the refusal of responsibility that could arise from face-to-face relating is overwhelmingly coded negative in the text, whereas attentive face-to-face encounters, which register the vulnerability of the other and provoke responsibility and active caretaking, are overwhelmingly positive" (Wallace). Although Tommy is flawed and human, more often than not he is able to embody such attentive face-to-face encounters, offering sincere care and sympathy to Emily and her family. Among his peers, he is the exception rather than the rule.

The officers' behaviour and mannerisms are of deep importance to the civilian characters in *The Break*. Where Tommy is sensitive and attentive to the needs of others, Christie is suspicious and pushy. As Birkwood highlights, "Stella feels 'a familiar rage' as the older, white officer questions her perception of what she witnessed. He does not see a university-educated woman who is clearly sleep-deprived and distraught at having witnessed a violent assault; instead, he dismisses her as 'a crazy bitch ... Dime a dozen' and sees no point in pursuing the case. His Métis partner, however, works hard to ensure that the case is investigated" (Birkwood 22). Vermette's aesthetic strategy of shifting the narrative point of view effectively works to demonstrate a variety of perspectives that focalize the consequences of Christie's and Tommy's behaviour on civilians. In the section focused on Cheryl, the narrator highlights that "[o]ne is an older bearded white man, the other a very young-looking Métis. The young one looks long at Emily, still and sleeping, her eyelids pressed together like she's faking. He stands beside the bed by Paul. His body in its uniform so wide it makes Paulina look even smaller. The older one just stands off, against the wall" (Vermette 111). In the Anglo-Canadian imaginary the police officer might stand for discipline, heroism, and order, but for this family the police are symbols of colonial oppression. The presence of the officers is a source of new and unwanted confrontation. Although the family members seem to appreciate the fact that Tommy is concerned, they can feel Christie's judgment and disinterest. The narrator writes: "The other cop, the older one, Christie just leans against the back wall and keeps surveying everyone. He looks at Pete and then Louisa, who both stare back. Defiant" (Vermette 112). The energy that the officers project to the family and to suspects is often returned. Tommy's sensitivity is rewarded with breakthroughs in the case, whereas Christie's stubbornness and prejudice often stifle Tommy and alienate the Traverse and Charles families.

Tommy's behaviour is deeply informed by his own family history and the connection he feels with the Traverse and Charles families. The narrator writes: "He has light skin and hair, so young, with dark freckles across his nose but definitely Métis. In any other situation, Cheryl would ask him where he's from" (Vermette 112). Although this connection with the family helps him to advance the investigation, he does not use it in a purely utilitarian way. It also helps him to be more compassionate and to think about his own relationship with his mother. As Justice argues, this connection to a community of people is deeply important: "the status of 'human' is intimately embedded in kinship relations. It's why some version of the question 'Who's your family?' or 'Who are your people?' continues to be so important in Indigenous conversations: such questions don't just connect you to a lineage, however that may be understood – they place you in a meaningful context with your diverse relatives and the associated relationships of obligation, where you have people who claim you and who have, hopefully, trained you well in the ways of being a good human being" (41). Not only do these types of connections bring Tommy closer to the people he is trying to help, but they also serve as a reminder that he is invested in the pursuit of being good. The virtues and the values that he learned from his mother continually play on his mind. Vermette writes: "She is only looking after her daughter, with a sort of pride and sorrow. Tommy knows that look, too" (125). Tommy's relationship with his mother informs his work and helps him resolve the case. The breakthrough occurs when Tommy goes back to visit his mother, and he is once again in a place of kinship and community: "Marie knows how crazy it all really is. 'You don't want it to be this girl, hey?' 'How can it be a girl, Ma? That's insane. A girl couldn't have done that'" (297). Marie explains: "'When I was a girl, there was this girl, an older girl, two years ahead of me. Boy she was scary. I never went anywhere near her. She was skinny but mean, you know … It's a power thing. Rape is about power. She wanted power … She was probably messed with. Kids that are messed with get messed up'" (298). If Tommy is meant to function as a focalizer of policing in *The Break*, one of the key distinctions between Tommy and Christie is that Tommy listens and he respects the knowledge that others, particularly women, might offer. For the bulk of the text he is able to observe with insight, texture, and care. Vermette highlights his ability to emote compassion and humility to the people whom he is trying to help. This care and attentiveness is noticed by others and makes him a better officer in the world of the novel.

Nevertheless, Tommy's idealism for the potential to help his community quickly dissolves. Vermette repeatedly demonstrates that the difficult work of policing can change some of the officers, such as Christie. Policing does not prove to be as exciting as it is in the television and movies that Tommy watched before becoming an officer. Instead of helping his community, Tommy feels that he ends up mainly in the role of passive observer, occasional recorder: "This work isn't what he thought it'd be. He thought he'd be breaking down doors and always in the action. At the academy, he learned about community policing, which basically meant that he was supposed to be nice and make relationships with people, but he doesn't do that either. Mostly he just takes notes, makes reports and never thinks of them again" (Vermette 76). Although Tommy might dismiss the idea of building relationships with communities, he manages to connect with several characters in the novel, and even if these characters do not express their appreciation for him, they clearly view him as a more helpful officer than Christie. Nevertheless, it is easy to see how Tommy might become disenchanted with lessons from the academy when faced with the grinding reality of policing. Tommy's first call on the job sets the tone: "A fat guy drunk with puke down his once-white shirt, a wife beater ironically enough, and his woman, small and skinny, face mashed with blood and beginning to swell. She didn't want to press charges, but they had to anyway. 'Zero tolerance,' Christie bit his words, and then again in the car. 'Zero fucking tolerance.' The fat guy cried in the back seat … Tommy had no sympathy, just squared his face and drove this guy in" (76). In this moment Christie's hardened certainty is an important component to the job. A reader might very well see how a lifetime of these incidents would undoubtedly change an officer. The older officers view the series of traumatic incidents they have to deal with as routine and mundane. Tommy is consistently met with a similarly dismissive view of the people he is meant to serve and protect. For example, Officer Clark describes his night of work as "'just nates beating on nates. Same old'" (72). Worst of all, Clark is one officer who Tommy looks up to for advice. Although Tommy knows to avoid talking to Christie, he sees Clark as a "good guy, grew up poor in Elmwood so was what Christie would call 'fucking sensitive,' but Tommy liked picking the guy's brain on the hard stuff" (75). Compounding the stress of work and the failure of older officers to be positive role models, Tommy's own life has been affected by domestic violence, and such incidents force him to relive his own childhood trauma, in which his father, Tom Sr., abused his mother, Marie. The domestic abuse is both physical and verbal. Tom Sr. would make comments such as "She's a wild one ... Got her off the reservation for cheap. She was on sale'" (77). Tommy's domestic life and professional life cannot be disentangled. Not only does he have little escape from such painful memories, but also they highlight the tension between two worlds. He is both part of the colonial project and painfully affected by it. Thus, the possibility of compartmentalizing his home life from his working life is not an option for Tommy.

Not only is Tommy's domestic life intertwined with his professional life, but also his family history directly influences the way in which he is understood by his fellow officers and by civilians whom he is expected to investigate. Paris's essay tends to emphasize the importance of being a non-dominative male, but there are times when Tommy seems almost too passive. He spends plenty of time during his working hours thinking about his girlfriend, Hannah. While he is dealing with a new case, she "went out ... drinks with friends at a cowboy bar, so she will sleep in tomorrow ... tomorrow's Saturday so she'll sleep in until at least noon. That'll be nice, to stay warm in bed for a few hours. Almost perfect" (Vermette 71). Tommy's difficult work situation and his meagre desire to sleep contrast with Hannah's partying at a cowboy bar. Her evening feels extravagant in comparison. In the sections focusing on Tommy, Hannah seems to push him into situations that he might otherwise avoid. For example, when talking about declaring his Métis identity in his job application, "he should've never checked that fucking box. He only did it 'cause Hannah made him'" (73). Hannah proves to be ignorant of Métis people and issues of indigeneity, instead seeing Tommy's ancestry as an opportunity to be taken advantage of. On the one hand, Tommy is persuaded by his desire to please his partner, but, on the other, he is also deeply conflicted with his family history. In reference to gender discrimination in the Indian Act, Vermette highlights how Tommy's mother lost her status when she married his father, who Tommy remembers as a "racist prick" (74). The decision to click the box signifying "Métis" might not be one Tommy would have made – at least early on in the novel – were it not for Hannah. However, owing to her well-intentioned desire to help ensure that Tommy land a good job as a police officer, she pushes him to obtain his Métis card and use it in his application. In part, Tommy worries that his fellow police officers will wrongly assume that people only check that box in order to advance their careers. Adese highlights a common misconception of Métis identity "that people can elect to adopt for the pursuit of individual self-interest … [This misconception] obscures that although Métis as a word exists as a fact of French language, it was through a complex interplay of cultural, social, economic, and political transformations that it became the identifier of choice of a distinctive Indigenous people" (Adese 60). Not only is Tommy worried about a misconception of self-interest, but also he might have avoided the decision because of his traumatic family history, which is deeply affected by colonialism and about which he would prefer to avoid thinking. As Justice writes, "Settler colonialism isn't something one just gets over; it's woven into all aspects of our experience, and those strangling threads are too often invisible and all the more wounding as a result. What Indigenous texts do is make visible what's so often unseen, and suggest a much more complicated perspective on what is too often grossly simplified in popular culture and mainstream media" (48). Vermette asks readers to focus on Tommy's experience as an officer and how these strangling threads are slowly untangled.

Enforcing the law for the same country that enacts settler colonialism further complicates Tommy's situation in that it is more difficult for him to be a part of his community. Adese's work proves to be particularly helpful in imagining a way in which Tommy might feel less divided and more at peace with his sense of self: "That we are attuned to reading for confusion and not for racist oppression is, I believe, the product of not being taught to think of Métis as a people who have experienced the impacts of racism and colonization in ways distinct from, and yet shared with, other Indigenous peoples. We are rarely prepared to consider the most devastating ways in which colonization and race thinking have impacted and continue to impact Métis – the fracturing of perceptions of Métis identity and the attempts to divorce it from its communal roots" (Adese 68). In many ways Tommy is the fractured subject that Adese describes. Even though Tommy's domestic life and professional life are at odds, the connection he feels to his Métis identity contributes to his police work. As Hanson writes, "Marie, Tommy's mom, tells him that the women seem familiar because he is recognizing his own belonging in Métisness … Tommy shares a parallel sense of home to that of the Charles and Traverse family … Tommy recognizes home as embodied through his maternal relations" (Hanson). Thus, while Tommy's domestic life and upbringing can be a source of frustration and trauma, he is also able to feel a sense of relatedness with the Charles and the Traverse families. He is able to see elements of his own life in Emily and her family and does a better job of helping them as a result. Nevertheless, he still struggles with his identity as a young, Métis police officer, particularly in relation to his partner, Christie.

Tommy's battle for respect among his colleagues is difficult enough, but it is compounded by his partner's racism. Often their relationship involves Tommy being ambitious, and Christie mocking him as a result. From Christie's perspective, Tommy's indigeneity means that Tommy has been on an easier path than white police officers have. After refusing to shake Tommy's hand, he says, "'Well, young buck, your special treatment ends here. Got it?'" (Vermette 73). Christie is also sexist, completely dismissing Stella Rose when she attempts to communicate what she has seen to the officers. After their meeting Christie says, "'I wouldn't worry about it, May-tee. She's just a crazy bitch is all. Dime a dozen, those kind.'" (70). Tommy is in a difficult position because the most important thing to him is solving this case. He does not assume that he can lecture Christie into becoming less of a bigot. He believes he has to wait it out and pick his battles. Instead, "Tommy just cringes. She was troubled, that's for sure, disheveled and clearly emotional" (70). The beginning of Tommy's career is framed by these types of interactions with a senior officer. He has one sense of how things should be done and how people should be understood, but he has to deal with the weight of a partner who is overly certain, consistently reductive and dismissive, yet experienced and knowledgeable, and, perhaps most of all, exhausted from working an extremely challenging job. As Christie points out from a lifetime of experience, "'The worst shit happens on the late shift'" (119). Even though the older officer can teach Tommy a few things about policing, it would seem impossible for Tommy to listen with an open mind to a man who is obviously bigoted.

Christie's racist and sexist way of seeing the world inhibits his ability to do good work. He ignores the insight of female characters in the novel, and he enacts racial profiling of Indigenous people. As Paris writes, "Pete is racially profiled by Christie, a racist police officer who works in Winnipeg's North End. When Christie discovers that the crime was an assault, he assumes that it was Native gang members attacking each other" (Paris 80). He tends to make assumptions about the case and then seeks out confirmation. Christie says, "[Y]ou were so … busy trying to be sympathetic to the mom, you didn't even notice the big fucking Nate fucker sulking and staring at her in the corner … He was shifty as fuck!'" (Vermette 120). Time and time again, Christie's confirmation bias stifles the investigation, and rather than helping Tommy to improve as an officer, he ends up being an obstacle to Tommy's development. In his own way Christie attempts to compliment Tommy, but it is difficult not to view Christie's positive commentary as an attempt to diminish Tommy's indigeneity. In an attempt to be nice Christie says, "'It's not like I think of you like you're those Nates out there or anything. I don't think of you like that. You're different. I mean, you're not that different but you're some different'" (296). Essentially Christie approves of the aspects of Tommy's character that he would view as not being native. The narrative articulates how a dominative settler mentality institutionalized through policing services obstructs and diminishes Tommy's indigeneity and his ability to help others. Christie's supposedly kind words sound all too familiar when one looks at how Monaghan describes the historical practices of settler surveillance strategies to diminish Indigenous culture: "Race becomes a signifier of threat when racialized individuals do not adopt and recirculate the rewards system offered by the settler colonial state. Defiled as savage, deviant, abnormal, and backwards, expressions of indigeneity were systematically repressed by Canadian authorities as they developed reformatory strategies focused on making Indians into proper Canadians" (Monaghan 505). Tommy is aware that Christie's comment of him not being like the others is not really a compliment but a reflection of the older man's prejudice. It momentarily leaves Tommy feeling caught between two worlds, not really fitting into either. Tommy says, "'You know what Christie called me today? … He called me different … Like, you're not like me, but you're not like them Natives either … I'm not like anything. So what am I?'" (Vermette 299). Not that this is an excuse, but Christie is of a generation where there is a different code for men interacting with other men. When Tommy finally asks him to stop calling him "May-tee," Christie says, "'Settle down, kid, no need to get your panties in a bunch. I don't have to call you May-tee if you don't like it'" (295). To be fair, Christie agrees to stop using the racist nickname, but he does suggest that Tommy is being effeminate in making this request. Ultimately this moment seems to represent a shift in Tommy's behaviour in that he resists being misrecognized. He can begin to create his own sense of identity, perhaps one that is less divided. Not only does he challenge Christie's use of "May-tee," but also he tends to seek his actual Métisness more and more as the novel progresses.

The portrait that Vermette develops of Tommy is that of a young officer with few positive role models and at great risk of being altered by the job. Even though Tommy has good intentions, he also takes pleasure in the power of his position. With his uniform and squad car there comes an allure of power, one that can risk influencing the way in which he interacts with suspects and victims. Wallace argues that Tommy "serves as a double for the reader, both exemplifying the need to pay careful, minute attention to another's story and also exposing the problem of finding pleasure in piecing together the parts in order to solve the crime" (Wallace). Tommy's pleasure, however, is more complicated than that of a mystery reader solving a puzzle. He enjoys the sense of order that he feels from his status as police officer: "What cars there are fall into this same slow, careful drive, the way civilians do around police cars. Tommy always liked that, how he'd drive and the world around him seemed to straighten out, get better" (Vermette 70). He truly wants the world to be a better place; improvements are signified by order and by positive responses to his presence. This sense of what the uniform provides is inspiring to Tommy, but it also risks allowing him to feel superior to others. Vermette writes: "[W]hen he wore his uniform – everyone stood up a little taller, and some would even smile and nod at him, some even looked genuine. It has been nearly a year but the feeling still hasn't gotten old" (70). Being a young, impressionable man and seeing people's behaviour change as a result of his presence risks altering Tommy's attitude from confident to arrogant. But Tommy is a consistently intelligent, self-reflective, and perceptive observer. Despite such a risk, near the end of the novel Tommy seems to understand how pleasure and closure might not be a part of his work: "Tommy thinks of his case again and lists it all in his head. His mom's stories make him feel better, but he is still not reassured. He wants everything to be different. He wants the simplicity of finality, but it's never like it is in the movies. It always lingers on" (302). The more experience Tommy has as a police officer, the less he feels like a hero in an action movie. Vermette seems to be suggesting that power can corrupt anyone, but kinship to community can keep one grounded. As Justice writes,"If our humanity is defined in large part by the stories we tell, then the storytellers have a vital role to play in bringing us back to healthier relationships with ourselves and with one another. They remind us of who we are and where we come from, and Indigenous texts offer possible visions for who we might once again be" (60). Having a connection to his own history through his mother's stories serve not only as solace but also as a constant reminder of the virtues to which Tommy aspires.

Vermette's use of Officer Tommy Scott as a focalizer offers insight into the ways in which one group of Métis women understand policing and one Métis police officer persists despite incredibly difficult working conditions. As a young officer, not only does Tommy have to fight for respect, but he also has to fight against the pleasure he receives from feeling powerful in his uniform. The hard life of policing in *The Break* wears officers down while their position as police officers paradoxically builds them up. Tommy's sensitive approach is criticized and mocked by Christie, but it allows him to connect with Emily and her family in a way that

Christie cannot. Although Tommy's domestic life and professional life are at odds, his willingness to listen to women, particularly his mother, helps him identify Emily's assailant. Thus, Vermette's representation of police and policing in *The Break* communicates the desire of one community to be heard and respected; the inner world of Officer Tommy Scott narrates one voice amid that complex conversation. This ethics of care is vital but tenuous for police officers in *The Break*. Like all things, it has its limits. Vermette writes that when Tommy eventually arrests Phoenix, "[h]e went to cuff her with rage in his eyes, too full of hate to even say anything. His hand passed over her hard belly and he turned white. Whiter. Phoenix saw it" (319). This appears to be the moment at which the resurgent politics of recognition breaks down even for Tommy. How can he truly see or understand Phoenix? Instead, it is Phoenix who sees him.

Coulthard's resurgent politics of recognition might prove to be an important shift in rethinking Phoenix's relationship to the settler state. He writes that the present situation in Canada demands "that we begin to approach our engagements with the settler-state legal apparatus with a degree of critical self-reflection, skepticism, and caution that has to date been largely absent in our efforts. It also demands that we begin to shift our attention away from the largely rights-based/recognition orientation that has emerged as hegemonic over the last four decades, to a resurgent politics of recognition that seeks to practice decolonial, gender-emancipatory, and economically nonexploitative alternative structures of law and sovereign authority grounded on a critical refashioning of the best of Indigenous legal and political traditions" (Coulthard 179). In contrast to Tommy, readers are privileged to have access to a fuller understanding of Phoenix's life. They can see how the system will never work for her even if there are positive figures within it. As Rinaldo Walcott writes in *On Property: Policing, Prisons, and the Call for Abolition*, "We have become overwhelmed by a vague and nameless fear of the other, the sick, the mad, of the poor and unhoused; of young, unkempt men and women rattling Starbucks cups, and we have come to believe that policing is the necessary barrier between us and those who have been abandoned. Between us and those we have abandoned" (86). Phoenix is among those who have been abandoned. Policing works for some but not for all. Decolonial, gender-emancipatory, and economically non-exploitive structures might be the only path forward if the aptly named Phoenix is ever to achieve resurgence.[3]

3 In *The Circle*, Phoenix and Tommy return. Vermette's development of both characters adds many new layers to this discussion.

9 *Foreign Radical:* Watch Yourself!

Foreign Radical creates an immersive theatre experience in which the audience enters into a cruel, perverse game, asking the players to observe and cast judgment on Hesam Rahmani, an Iranian Canadian man, who is friends with an individual on a terrorist watch-list, Jamal Rahi. Thobani's discussions of the exalted self and villainized Other are incredibly relevant here: "The use of particular technologies of surveillance at airports and borders … said to be necessitated by the form of the 9/11 attacks … constitutes the Muslim traveller/immigrant as a potential suicide bomber in the national imaginary. The figure of the Muslim stranger is recast by such surveillance technologies as the archetype of the current global menace in the western imagination, the 'suicide bomber'" (242). Undoubtedly this play demands that theatregoers become dubious towards the exalted national subject and observe how they are implicated in the nastier side of maintaining a national imaginary. The creators of *Foreign Radical*, Tim Carlson, Jeremy Waller, David Mesiha, Kathleen Flaherty, Milton Lim, Aryo Khakpour, Florence Barrett, and Cande Andrade,[1] encourage the audience to consider the ways in which the state scrutinizes certain cultures, religions, and races. The host of the show and a disembodied voice deliver a series of prompts and questions that categorize not only Hesam but also themselves. Although the questions and the prompts are not arbitrary, the lack of time and consideration that audience members are allowed in their responses inevitably removes any nuance or sustained thought to their responses. They simply have to categorize and sort as quickly as possible. *Foreign Radical* does not simply ask the audience to sousveil

1 *Foreign Radical* was produced through Theatre Conspiracy, a collective of artists based in Vancouver, British Columbia.

the surveillance practices of the state, but the construction of the play also encourages a thoughtful contemplation of the dominant Other, those individuals who are placed in the profoundly difficult position of having to categorize human beings.

Foreign Radical aspires to be a didactic spectacle. However, to phrase it mildly, the ability of literature to elicit a specific response is a contested topic. In *Theaters of Justice: Judging, Staging, and Working through Arendt, Brecht, and Delbo*, Yasco Horsman questions the way in which playwrights employ trials as didactic spectacles to teach audiences a specific lesson (19–20). Dubious of a clear transference of knowledge, he asks, What is "required for a scene of public enlightenment?" (18). *Foreign Radical* situates audience members in a world in which certain people have not even been afforded a trial, and insists that viewers observe individuals who go unseen from the public eye. One potential to garner specific responses from viewers is to move them from passive observers to active participants in the performance. Therefore, if there is potential for literature to enlighten, it might very well be through gamification. In "Forced Entertainment? Gamified Surveillance in Theatre Conspiracy's *Foreign Radical*," Matt Jones argues, "As we have come to share more information about our lives on social media, those data have become increasingly subject to surveillance by both governments and private companies ... Consumers are coaxed into supplying information to marketers by playing apparently innocuous (and often mediocre) games" (52). While surveillance and sousveillance are gamified in *Foreign Radica*l, the tone of the game is decidedly unsettling, and the aesthetics encourage self-awareness and self-reflection. The games that harvest information online seem to operate in a far more unsuspecting fashion in order to obtain our data without our full understanding that we are sharing it. Shoshana Zuboff argues in *The Age of Surveillance Capitalism*: "Most research on games concludes that these structures can be effective at motivating actions, and researchers generally predict that games will increasingly be used as the methodology of choice to change individual behaviour. In practice, this has meant that the power of games to change behaviour in practice is shamelessly instrumentalized as gamification spreads to thousands of situations in which a company merely wants to tune, herd, and condition the behavior of its customers or employees toward its own objectives" (314). In *Foreign Radical*, involvement in the play works to counter the conditioning of what Zuboff calls surveillance capitalism firstly by making participants aware of it and secondly by showing them the harmful events that result from their participation.

The creators of *Foreign Radical* offer two characters, the Host and the Voice, who represent a strange blend of state surveillance and gamification. The Host is designed to be reminiscent of a typical, zany game-show presenter. However, this comfortable familiarity only lulls the audience into a false sense of security. The script indicates that "[t]he Host, can be gender and age fluid and must have excellent physical comedy and improv skills. The Host is referred to as male in this script to reflect this production. Movement is highly stylized, riffing on game show host or MC mannerisms" (Carlson et al. 58). Although the gender and age can be fluid, the master of ceremonies must possess a capacity for humour and entertainment. This should work to draw in the audience members and remind them of television in one way or another. The Host takes command of the performance but also concedes control to a disembodied Voice, which "varies between journalistic (when delivering documentary material) and bureaucratic (when giving direction)" (58). This God-like figure is authoritative and ominous. Although the Host might operate at the behest of the Voice, the two figures ultimately work together to lure the audience into this perverse game. Being the conduit for the state takes a toll on the Host, who by the end of the play begins to sound paranoid and unhinged in a distinct quasi-comedic way: "(The Host now screaming, writhing on the floor.) WOULD YOU BE WILLING TO HAVE AN ID CHIP IMPLANTED IN YOUR BRAIN SO THAT YOU COULD CROSS A BORDER?" (70). If *Foreign Radical* starts out as a game, it becomes clear by the end of the performance that it is not a particularly fun one. Instead, the so-called game is dark and didactic, insisting we are all part of a racist, xenophobic system.

Middle-class Canadians – those who, I have argued, are in a position to sousveil their own country – can be terrifying. Bentham's ideal of the caring community is replaced by prejudicial eyes. The printed version of *Foreign Radical* that appears in *Canadian Theatre Review* features an image of "[t]he audience seen through a scrim in the Calgary production" (Carlson et al. 59). The image appears as a line of silhouettes who can look onto others but, much like the panoptic gaze, cannot be seen; it brings to mind an abstract self, perhaps a darker self kept secret from our public interactions, one that hides the prejudices and desires that do not fit a public persona. The way in which the figures are positioned suggests that the viewer is offered a brief glimpse from Hesam's point of view, in which the silhouettes appear threatening. Initially the play mocks this ignorance and prejudice. As Matt Jones writes, "The play uses [Farsi and Arabic] … phrases as red herrings, giving the impression that something secret is being communicated, even though the actual content of the phrases is innocuous (in this way, the lines also function as inside jokes for audience members who do speak those languages). This is possible because surveillance culture has coded signs of Middle Eastern identity as 'abnormal,' apart from the rest of the body politic and indicative of higher risk" (56). The stage directions read: "A projection appears in Farsi, then Arabic, and finally in English. The (Projection: [In Farsi]). Take a look around. How many others can read this? Just you? And perhaps the man leaning on the table? Most everyone else assumes this is a terrorist message in Arabic" (Carlson et al. 59). There is a laughter emoji next to the word Arabic in the script, and while it is meant to be humorous, it plays upon the presumed ignorance of North Americans. The audience is then encouraged to sousveil one another. The Voice says, "Take a look around. Do others look nervous because this is in Arabic?" (59). In observing one another, the audience members have the opportunity to make assumptions about the other theatregoers and to attempt to create some kind of conformity among the group through scrutinizing one another. If these theatregoers attending an avant-garde performance in an urban centre already uphold antiracist beliefs, the authors are extremely clever here in highlighting the potential for prejudices towards rural people. The Voice says: "Anyway ... A redneck walks into a bar. And then shoots everyone because he lost his job at Walmart. What a joke" (59). In the script there is a skull emoji after the word Walmart. The joke is clearly mean-spirited and in poor taste. Thus, if one is not made uncomfortable by one's own ignorance or racism, then one might need to evaluate one's classist world view. The performers prepare the audience members to be open to the spectacle that will follow. As Baz Kershaw writes in "Curiosity or Contempt: On Spectacle, the Human, and Activism," "Spectacle seems to produce excessive reactions ... and at its most effective highly sensitive spots in the changing nature of the human psyche by dealing directly with extremities of power" (592). In *Foreign Radical* the participants are encouraged to be critically engaged with the surveillance state. However, they are also asked to see themselves as part of that state – to use Kershaw's phrase, as "extremities of power" – who support bad actors in the surveillance state through ignorance, prejudice, racism, and/or classism.

One of the central messages of *Foreign Radical* is that state surveillance enacts systemic racism in that certain people are more closely scrutinized than others. As Matt Jones writes, "the show reveals the role that racism and Islamophobia come to play in the interpretation of surveillance data. Although surveillance operates on a seemingly empirical basis, the stories it tells about people nevertheless remain fictions, assembled from statistical probability and speculation" (56). The play works to question the way in which statistical probability and speculation fail as a means of understanding human behaviour and result in cruelty by the state. One of the focal points of the play is Hesam, "an Iranian-Canadian man. The role and text, both spoken and projected, can be adapted to other commonly politically profiled identities" (Carlson et al. 58). Through Hesam the audience is asked to consider who might be scrutinized by the state's gaze. The design is malleable if a particular troupe wants to adjust Hesam from being Iranian to being another commonly profiled identity. While this malleability allows the troupe to adjust to world events, one of the issues around social sorting is that it reduces people to categories. Rather than problematic, however, it strikes me as being observant of how the political enemy shifts and changes in the news. Surveillance is racialized, and certain cultures are targeted more than others, but those targets tend to change over time. There is always an Other, and there are often deep connections between the state and those who are othered. If immigration becomes framed negatively through policy or in the media, there will be direct consequences for migrants.[2] Hesam delivers a poignant monologue about his friend Jamal and how both men have changed. He says: "Jamal used to be one of us. Out on the town partying. The women loved him. Now they avoid him. He's been defriended by all of Montreal. I don't blame them. Look at the shit he's posting. Angrier. And angrier. And angrier" (65). Jamal becomes ostracized and alienated. This pain about losing his friend affects Hesam so greatly that he too falls into a spiral of hatred: "Fill me full of hate. You want it. You want my hate. Demand my hate. You can have it. Make me sick. I will vomit my hate in your face. Spew hate upon your house. Upon your family. Barf hate all over the land. Until the future stinks of my hate. I'll give you what you want" (65). In Hesam's eyes he himself is not the one starting the fight. He believes he is in a situation where he is already hated, not only by the state but by the people in his community, and he has no choice but to return the anger in the only way he knows. In these moments, Jenn Stephenson hypothesizes in *Insecurity: Perils and Products of Theatres of the Real* that the audience also has a sense of Hesam's pain caused by unfair surveillance. She writes, "In these specific examples, it is through locating uncertain affects of realness in the aesthetic reflection on audience as audience that these works activate mimetic shimmering, and attempt to bear witness to trauma" (Stephenson 185). The involvement in the

2 See Huot et al., "Constructing Undesirables; Cheong et al., "Immigration, Social Cohesion and Social Capital"; and Feldman, "Essential Crises."

performance also highlights other types of participation of which Canadian citizens might not be aware in their relationship to new Canadians and migrants. In portraying state surveillance and sousveillance as racialized and trauma inducing, *Foreign Radical* implies that our government and our communities create terror and have a hand in developing would-be terrorists.

Sympathy for victims of state surveillance is undoubtedly one of the goals of the didactic spectacle created by *Foreign Radical*. Carlson et al. desire that the audience experience the arbitrary and unfair nature being categorized. Matt Jones hypothesizes: "This public sorting of people on the basis of their responses to banal questions mimics the creation of silos of shared values that often characterizes online communities. As participants shuffle around, they are left in physical proximity to only those they have experience in common with. But in stark contrast to online worlds, this public taking of positions occurs in front of other people and is therefore subject to a certain peer scrutiny" (55). The distance between those who are observed is removed, but the spectre of state surveillance remains detached. This peer scrutiny feels like something akin to Bentham's panopticon or community of sousveillance, in which people from small towns would watch one another from their windows. However, owing to the fact that this experience occurs during a performance, the participants might not truly feel observed. Stephenson questions whether audience members are actually revealing personal information or taking on a persona for the purposes of the game. Stephenson writes: "We are ourselves, but also not; the qualities that impel game-playing shape our behaviour … the game frame creates an ethically-rich disjunction between the morally weighty content of *Foreign Radical* – Do I endorse practices of holding potential terrorists in judicial custody without a warrant? – and the more playfully callous motivation of how my answer to that question affects my status in game" (197–8). Thus, instead of revealing how they actually think and feel, they might only perform an identity within a public space to help progress the game, or they might conceal aspects of their identity that would be viewed unfavourably. *Foreign Radical* strives for responses that are more intense than peer-to-peer scrutiny and introspection. Thus, through encouraging the audience to experience a sliver of what Hesam feels, if only briefly, the creators of the play ask even more than sympathy; they urge participants to take the leap to empathy.

Of course, this leap will inevitably fail. The Host quickly begins to identify the audience members and then categorizes them based on their responses to specific questions. The Host says: "Please answer the following questions quickly and honestly. I'll have you vote with your feet, moving into one of these four lovely quadrants as located on the ground. Now, time is of the essence, so we can't get into nuances of the questions – you just have to go with your gut" (Carlson et al. 61). The categorizing is framed as part of an active process, creating an illusion of choice. However, the lack of nuance removes the distinct reasons and individuality that a person might have for making a particular decision. It also serves a secondary purpose in showing how difficult the task of social sorting can be. As an audience member Stephenson describes this experience: "Answers are limited to yes or no, agree or disagree. It is an experience that is reminiscent of bureaucratic processing ... Moreover, when confronted with more complicated questions ... and asked to respond in seconds, these simplistic binary answers are woefully insufficient. And we are shamed by that insufficiency" (201). Those who are given the task of categorizing people in a short amount of time based on limited data will make mistakes. The processing system unfairly simplifies as it sorts. The first two questions ask about who has used a credit card online and who has looked up pornography. The first feels innocuous, but it also presents a vulnerability – one's bank account – that one would want protected, thus implicating the audience members loosely within the discourse of safety and freedom that Bala obsesses over in *The Boat People*. The second question introduces a whisper of deviance. Some people might find the consumption of pornography to be bizarre or perverse; others see it as a personal choice or as an individual's right in a free society. However the audience members respond to this question, they are in a discourse of deviance and punishment. Deviant behaviour, when identified, tends to result in public shaming or legal action, depending on the society in which it occurs. Whether or not the aesthetic strategies work as they are designed is unclear, but these questions take that which is implicit and make it explicit. Whatever the questions represent for the participants, the answers define their identity in a quasi-public forum.

Ultimately the purpose of making the audience experience the feeling of being observed becomes explicitly political when the Voice explains how people end up on the watch-list: "In 2015, US security agencies added almost half a million people to the watch list. After the nominations were reviewed, 99 percent of the names remained on the watch list. There is no requirement to prove beyond a reasonable doubt that someone IS a terrorist to be placed on the watch list" (Carlson et al. 63). This might seem detached from the national discourse in Canada. However, Stephenson succinctly explains why this is not solely an American issue: "This Watchlisting Guidance formed the basis for

Canada's controversial security law, the 2015 Anti-Terrorism Act (also known as Bill C-51 before it passed into law). Without solid parameters for this designation … 'terrorist' – can be created arbitrarily" (202). Alongside this arbitrariness is an implied fear and paranoia of the Other. Rebecca Foley, in "(Mis)representing Terrorist Threats: Media Framing of Bill C-51," highlights how the government frames the Anti-Terrorism Act as reducing threats and improving security; she argues that the "'us vs. them'" dichotomy is inherently racist in the context of 'terrorism'" (205). As the play progresses, the tensions around race and geography heighten. To further divide the groups, the Host asks participants to take a step forward if they can answer yes to the following statements:

> I have been refused entry when trying to cross a border.
> I have been strip-searched while trying to cross a border.
> I have been detained for more than 24 hours while trying to cross a border.
> *(Projection: [In Arabic.] I fear it will become impossible for me to travel in the future.*
> *Ominous industrial sound fades into spy theme.)*
> I have been cavity-searched while trying to cross a border.
> I have crossed a border illegally.
> I have fled for my life across a border.
> I have been deported. (Carlson et al. 64)

These prompts show the gap between the audience members and people who have been forced into impossible situations. Hopefully this will encourage participants to contemplate the cost of global imbalances of power. Not only do the prompts implicate audience members in the web of the state, but also they push them to question whether or not civil disobedience, protest, and even violence are sometimes necessary for the greater good:

> It's fine for democratic countries to sell military equipment to Saudi Arabia.
> Civil disobedience is sometimes necessary to preserve democracy.
> Violence is sometimes necessary to preserve democracy.
> Detention without access to a lawyer is sometimes necessary to preserve democracy.
> We'll all be safer now that US border officials can detain travellers at Canadian airports.
> Trump's travel ban is not anti-Muslim; it's anti-terrorism. (Carlson et al. 65–6).

These prompts seem to suggest to the audience members that under certain circumstances some of them – middle-class Canadians – might be labelled as terrorists as well, which is particularly loaded with significance in relation to Bill C-51. As Kent Roach points out in "Terrorist Speech under Bills C-51 and C-59 and the Othman Hamdan Case: The Continued Incoherence of Canada's Approach," the government gave "CSIS a mandate up to and including violating the Canadian Charter of Rights and Freedoms" (204). Part of the anxiety around repressive legislation is not only that it is insidiously hateful towards the vulnerable Other but also that it will limit the freedoms of all Canadians. First, people are sorted into governable categories; then limitations are placed on behaviour, speech, and movement.

Not only do the creators of *Foreign Radical* encourage the audience members to experience how it feels to be simplified and sorted, but they also want them to see how certain information is gathered and withheld from the public. Matt Jones writes: "[A]s intelligence breaches such as those revealed by Edward Snowden have shown, states often have much more sweeping access to information. These new techniques have been added to a security arsenal that includes mass data processing, individual and group profiling, and traditional spying" (53). Before the questions and prompts become more provocative, however, the Host asks participants to vote for the Most Paranoid, the Most Suspicious, and the Most Radical. Each one will be given a key to open a box that holds specific information to move the play forward.[3] Only certain people have access to this intelligence, which creates an information hierarchy and signals the reality of classified information. The reveal of such information might come as somewhat of a shocking surprise in relation to the extent that Jamal and Hesam have been observed. The creators of *Foreign Radical* use this potential surprise to encourage participants to consider how frequently they are being watched. First, they are sorted by political beliefs. The Host says, "You are the most progressive. So progressive … that you are progressing right in there" (Carlson et al. 63). All of the progressive people are divided from people who own weapons. The Host says, "Who here owns a hunting knife? Who here owns a gun? Who here owns a pressure cooker?" (63). Then

---

3 The stage directions read: "The key given to the Most Paranoid can open the box. There is a journal in the box, belonging to Jamal, a friend of Hesam, as well as another locked box. The key given to the Most Suspicious can open the box, which contains surveillance photos of Hesam and Jamal and a third metal box. The key given to the Most Radical can open this box, which contains a recording device with a wiretapped conversation between Hesam and Jamal" (Carlson et al. 62).

the progressives become the subject of observation. The stage directions read, "Surveillance camera is focused on the faces of the people in Area D" (63). The feeling of being observed becomes a part of the experience. In feeling scrutinized, the audience members will internalize the implied ethics of the play and alter their behaviour. To watch someone be labelled, sorted, and punished by the state, only to feel the eye turn in your direction, is unsettling.

To support this reading, let us focus on an audience member's reaction to *Foreign Radical*. Describing the play as immersive, Stephenson writes: "Embedded in a full-surround fictional world in which one is a participatory character, audiences experience a dual consciousness, being simultaneously both inside and outside the fictional world. We are actively engaged both in making of performance and being audience to that performance; a duality that produces a self-conscious meta-awareness of both these tasks" (169). Thus, as audience members observe and participate, they become more aware and thoughtful not only of the play but of themselves and their roles within it. Ultimately, for Stephenson, the goal of this participation is to encourage audience members to become more knowledgeable of their own government and the way in which it observes people. She writes: "A play about surveillance and the collection of online information by government intelligence agencies to create profiles in the interests of protecting Canada from homegrown terrorists, *Foreign Radical* asks, to what extent are we culpable in the actions of our elected government? What price are we willing to pay for safety?" (177–8). Stephenson's description of her experience of the play is incredibly revealing. From her own articulate, highly educated position, the play culminates in a profound experience. She writes: "I'm not sure I can adequately describe the tension and profundity of this [final] encounter. Those of us who bore silent witness to the interview were riveted. The reality-effect of the introduction of our fellow audience members as 'experts of the everyday' catapults us back to acute awareness of our real-world selves, dragging the fictional Hesam and the concerns of Foreign Radical with it" (205). Nevertheless, Stephenson is careful to insist that the meaning of the play is open ended. She acknowledges that audience members likely responded in a multiplicity of ways. Thus, with Stephenson, we can trace some key points on the aesthetics of watching and being watched. *Foreign Radical* works as a scene of public enlightenment largely in the way the text was designed; it takes middle-class audience members who have some level of education and open-mindedness and challenges them to question their own morality and the ethos of their country.

However, alongside this open-minded questioning, audience members are also asked to use state criteria to determine who should be defined as a terrorist. The responses to specific questions posed and the choices the audience members are allowed to make effectively become the game. In the second scene the Voice describes an article from *The Intercept* that "examined the content of the March 2013 Watchlisting Guidance, the rulebook shared by nineteen US security agencies ... The US Watchlisting Guidance provides the model for its allies. It's a solid foundation on which to build Trump's Muslim travel ban. In defining who is a terrorist ... these are the rules of the game" (Carlson et al. 60). Upon overhearing the word game, the Host opens scene 3, and he transforms the tone of the play into that of a faux game show. The direction reads: "As part of an energetic dance routine, he connects with individual participants, welcoming them [improv]. Music resolves into a mid-tempo spy groove playing beneath" (61). The shift in tone highlights the decadent detachment of going to a play about something as serious as surveillance. No matter how much the performers and the theatre company attempt to highlight the stakes of the topic they are discussing, they are always detached from the reality and the consequences of the so-called war on terror. The humorous, playful, ironic tone shifts quickly to possess an undercurrent of menace. The Host says: "Let's play the game! We're going to fucking play a fucking game! Goddamn play the goddamn game!" (61). The stage directions read: "Game show light fades, brightening so everyone's face can be seen. Pause" (61). The curse words highlight the intensity of the Host and that the game itself might not be a simple or an innocent one. Stephenson writes: "That semantic crossover in the repeated word 'game,' effectively mixes the rules for governmental identification of terrorists with the rules of *Foreign Radical*" (196). Even though this play gamifies surveillance, the experience of *Foreign Radical* does not necessarily feel like fun. The stage directions clearly highlight the audience members as objects of close scrutiny. The Host says, "Who wants to bag some tourists ... I mean terrorists?" (Carlson et al. 61). The word *tourists* has a dual meaning in its slippage with terrorists. Countering the supposedly welcoming face of Canadian tourism is the xenophobic and racist nature of the war on terror. One might come to see Niagara Falls and end up on a watch-list. Furthermore, the audience members are tourists strolling through the intimidating world of state surveillance. They do not experience the anxiety that vulnerable minorities might feel on a daily basis. However, for a brief period of time they can feel something akin to what Hesam might feel. In this sense, they are able to gawk at Hesam while knowing that afterwards they will return to the comfort of their homes. Thus, one has to question, as Walter Benjamin might, whether performance always turns "the depiction of human misery as well as the struggle against it into 'an object of consumption'" (Horsman 73). One could ask the same question of all literary or scholarly efforts.

Whatever the intent of the creators of *Foreign Radical*, the audience response will be complex and multiform. Stephenson's own theatre-going experience most likely aligns with the aesthetic goals of the play, and yet she herself becomes an observer of the other participants. She writes:

> Selected audience members who have "won" a previous challenge are sent into another room and tasked with searching through a suitcase to collect intelligence and determine if the suitcase's owner should be placed on the terrorist watchlist ... Some audience members dig avidly, pulling out clothes, flipping through books, searching pockets, even unwrapping gifts. Some stand back; perhaps they are unsure how they feel about this invasion of privacy or perhaps they are just reluctant game-players who prefer to observe ... For my own part, the remnants of the disemboweled suitcase, its contents tossed willy-nilly, chills me somehow; nevertheless I do assist. (Stephenson 199)

As Stephenson consumes data for her scholarly work, she reflects on various responses to the performance. There is the potential for guilt and self-reflection alongside the pleasure of being in an immersive quasi-tragic experience. Participants might leave feeling that gamified theatre is naive and foolish – that it provides a sliver of experience in a far more complex, cynical world. In its potential for a multiplicity of responses *Foreign Radical* exists as a counterpoint to the certainty that it takes to categorize people on the watch-list. It also highlights the complexity of the faceless people behind this system of surveillance. They must have nuanced responses to the type of work that is expected of them. Many must feel that the information and the time that they have is insufficient. However, they need to do what is required of them within this system. The job is the job, and our comfortable lives persist in part due to their work.

I can understand if my response to *Foreign Radical* might ruffle some feathers. In a play critiquing xenophobic surveillance practices, I am arguing that there is an implied sympathy for those who are tasked with practising surveillance. Allow me to stress that the focus of care is on Hesam and Jamal, two individuals who are unjustly scrutinized and confined by the state. This is not a version of care that allows the participants to exalt the Canadian national as a profoundly compassionate subject, however. It implicates them in the mistreatment of the vulnerable Other. Nevertheless, the play insists that state surveillance itself is flawed in the way it removes nuance from the lives of those it observes. There are human beings who operate at the behest of this system, and it only follows that some of them must have serious criticisms of the way surveillance sorts and simplifies. Ultimately the play works to immerse the audience members in a place of self-conscious observation of their government's surveillance practices. Middle-class Canadians are partially responsible – whether they know it or not – for the actions of their state. As a middle-class Canadian, however, I feel completely powerless in influencing any change in the massive web of bureaucracy that constitutes a country. In her conclusion Stephenson writes: "What theatres of the real are producing instead of reality is insecurity … Instead of being fearful, insecurity makes me hopeful" (233–4). Despite the lack of control I feel, I too am hopeful. Instead of *insecurity*, I would choose the word *indeterminacy*, but the point remains that the radically open moment of the interpretive act – the moment when a person realizes how much they do not know – remains fundamental, holy.

Conclusion: Enter the Nuance Machine

The truth is that I lied in the introduction. I lied about my neighbours in St John's. They lived with another couple, who were pregnant. The expectant teenage mother smoked like a chimney, and the expectant father was a know-it-all. I avoided him. I changed these details because I felt the story worked better with the argument and the tone I was trying to establish. This is what writers do. I also lied about their names. I do remember them, but if you are hoping I will reveal some surprising detail as I write this book, sorry, I will not. I hope they are all well, but I do not want this discourse to be mistaken for one that demands everyone watch everyone else all the time. For the most part, I like to be left alone. I would not have been able to read these books and write about them otherwise. And yet, despite my curmudgeonly pose, I would like to present a few ethical demands. We need to cultivate a healthy discourse between surveillance and sousveillance. We need narrative to perpetually complicate data. We need to appreciate the spaces where people can engage with various, contradictory desires and the spaces where people can shape their own identities.

The written word grants us the opportunity to look back at the various people, places, and things that constitute a nation. The first step in this discussion has to be to acknowledge that authors are imperfect observers. Some literary artists, as shown by Lynn Coady, observe other people from a detached position. They are only interested in extracting stories and gathering data. Once the data and stories have been recorded, they reduce the observed to a cliché. Such reductive observational practices must result in part from notions of the artist as seer, as the guiding light of the common life, as the unacknowledged legislator of the universe, as the hero of culture in a fallen world, as the upholder of tradition in a time of sudden change, as the recorder of special moments over which others gloss – in short, as whatever rhetorical position grants one person a sense of superiority over whomever they are observing. In response, authors can choose to strive for responsibility rather than autonomy; their ethical imperative becomes to give oneself over to others, which necessarily entails a humility about one's place in the world. And yet there are also moments in which autonomy is necessary. For example, Bridget Murphy has to redescribe her community and resist the way she has been misrecognized.

The ideal of sousveillance is that it offers a parodic way of observing. It starts by looking from below with a radical sense of indeterminacy. Michael Winter's *This All Happened* is one example of literature that resists the simplifying and sorting of surveillance. The literary gaze is always open to new interpretations through the slippery nature of language. Where surveillance attempts to define human beings, literature has the potential to burst through these definitions and to create spaces in which people can cultivate new identities. Importantly, Gabriel English is no artist hero but a flawed observer whose journal we scrutinize. Through the act of reading, we bring him to life and share the imaginative space that Winter has created, negotiating our own identity in this quasi-fictional world. Sousveillance grants this opportunity of looking with care and imbuing whomever is observed with sympathy and complexity, but those who aspire to practise this way of looking are imperfect, and the minute they start observing others, they open themselves up to being more closely observed, too.

One consistent issue in discussions of surveillance is the distance between the observer and the observed. Whereas Ken Babstock critiques the ability of human beings to look with care from far away or from up close, AF Moritz posits the importance of the poet to cut through time and space in order to imagine a fuller sense of the Other. One of the many innovations of Larissa Lai and Rita Wong's work is to remove the distance between themselves and the structures they observe. They strategically become part of the machines they contemplate and criticize. Particularly fascinating is the moment in Lai's *Iron Goddess of Mercy* in which she presents the head-spinning possibility of the liberal machine that breaks down the distance created by social media echo chambers. In an increasingly polarized online world (Hills and Menczer), indeterminacy and unknowingness might disrupt a dismissive certainty that seems to surface when there is so much mediocre information to fuel confirmation bias.

Yet, certainty is a necessary response to particular events. We can say with certainty that Francis from David Chariandy's *Brother* should not have been harassed and killed. We can say with certainty that David Adams Richards and Katherena Vermette represent policing as stressful work. We can say with certainty that Sharon Bala's Fred Blair uses fear to manipulate others. Certainty exists as part of the literary experience. However, one of the most powerful aspects of the novel as a form is its addition of complexity and nuance as a counterpoint to ignorance and certainty. Chariandy's *Brother* asks readers to live with the family of a victim of police violence long after a sensational headline has faded. In these moments of remembering with Michael and his mother, we might realize how little we know based on information gleaned from news stories. Thus, while certainty exists, indeterminacy is the overarching focal point of the literary gaze.

In focalizing part of her narrative on Mahindan, Sharon Bala asks readers to pay close attention to an imagined life of a migrant who hopes to live in Canada. His main goal is to provide a safe and prosperous future for his son. This is the dream of Canada for Mahindan. Canadians might hold this ideal of the country in our hearts as part of our national imaginary, but Mahindan is confronted with a different reality. He is separated from his son and incarcerated. Through her focus on one migrant and his interactions with Canadian bureaucracy, Bala adds nuance to the national imaginary. She offers readers a fictional migrant who is not simply good and guiltless but makes mistakes and is occasionally cruel. Upon finishing *The Boat People*, I felt certain about some things. For example, I felt certain that Mahindan's separation from his son was unethical. Paradoxically, reading this novel also made me certain that I could not fully appreciate the experience of migrants. I took the leap towards empathy, but I had to respect difference. Mahindan was placed in impossible situations, and I have led an extremely comfortable life. Thus, I gave my best effort, but I always return to indeterminacy and alterity. I am left with no choice but to see the many ways I have misrecognized both self and Other. The gaze of surveillance might simplify and sort, but the literary gaze breaks down the categories that are used to define people.

When one is thinking of true crime, however, an overemphasis on indeterminacy feels unethical. Justin Ling's *Missing from the Village* directs our gaze to the victims rather than the serial killer. We are challenged to know and to remember biographical details that bring the victims back to life on the page. Furthermore, there are specific criticisms that Ling offers in relation to surveillance and policing in Canada, mostly focusing on Toronto. Indeterminacy feels like an insufficient response to these aspects of *Missing from the Village*. More is asked of readers if they desire to be ethically engaged in the true-crime genre. Sousveillance needs to be victim centred and resist intrigue for the criminal or criminals. Indeed, uncertainty might seem unethical in relation to the crimes committed and the pursuit of justice that follows. Nevertheless, there are moments in which readers are encouraged to withhold judgment, particularly in relation to individuals who are tasked with surveilling and policing the public. Even though Ling critiques policing services, he repeatedly highlights the difficulty of the job. In this sense, even if indeterminacy is not the main focus of *Missing from the Village*, it remains an important component in the construction of the text.

The people who are employed to observe and protect the public often find themselves also being watched. David Adams Richards focalizes our attention on the interior world of one police officer who is consistently placed in difficult positions but always desires to do what he perceives to be the right thing. This opportunity to look at law enforcement through a sympathetic lens does not excuse police violence. It encourages the viewing of police officers with nuance rather than simplifying and sorting them. The literary gaze that Richards offers in *Principles to Live By* might be typified as conservative or right wing, but it is part of a broader literary discourse. Even if I have an issue with the implied politics of the text, I can still learn a great deal. Engaging respectfully with someone who has a different point of view from my own seems like a necessary act if I want to seriously consider how to add nuance to the Canadian national imaginary.

In Katherena Vermette's *The Break* we are asked to sousveil in a different way than in other texts in this study. Even though Larissa Lai and Rita Wong posit the importance of the hybrid self through the concept of the cyborg, Métis authors, such as Jennifer Adese, stress that a mixed identity tends to be imposed on to Indigenous groups by settler scholars. Officer Tommy Scott's narrative arc might be read best as a journey back to wholeness and to community, helping him to feel less divided between his professional and private selves. Vermette creates a complex representation of policing and of the ways in which officers enact surveillance on the people they are tasked to serve and protect. Scott has to negotiate his values alongside officers who reinforce stereotypes of Indigenous people as violent and self-destructive. This reductive lens on a community causes their police work to suffer. Thus, implied in Vermette's text is this value of observing with complexity and sympathy. Even though Scott is an admirable figure, his interactions with Phoenix near the end of the novel highlight that the current system of surveillance has severe limitations. Radical shifts, as argued by Coulthard, might be the only path forward.

Nonetheless, I remain wedded to one maxim. For better or for worse, literature changes us. Texts encourage us to observe others and to observe ourselves through multiple ways of seeing. For example,

Brother asks readers to think about life from the point of view of a man whose family has been devastated by police violence, but *Principles to Live By* reminds us of the demanding nature of police work. These experiences do not cancel each other out; they teach us that we always need to learn more. This relatively passive relationship between person and text is shifted in *Foreign Radical* to force audience members into direct participation with contemporary surveillance issues. In doing so, *Foreign Radical* insists on our complicity in the wrongs committed by our government. We might crave some kind of action in response, but such an experience still insists on nuance. When a text limits or reduces complexity, it moves away from the literary and into the world of propaganda.

In this study I have shown various ways that authors observe Canada. Ideally this book is the beginning of further studies into literary representations of surveillance and sousveillance. There are topics that I have not touched and topics that could be explored in greater detail. I hope scholars observe this preliminary approach and critique my work. There is so much that I have not seen, and there is so much more that could be articulated about Canada. The national imaginary is often composed of simplified images that reinforce our sense of ourselves as a good and decent people. I am not writing this book to say the opposite; I am saying that the situation is more complicated. Scholars such as Margot Francis have posited the concept of the spectacle to cut through idealistic images of Canada. Alongside spectacle, I am offering a reminder of the literary and its ability to add nuance. These texts highlight what I hope are anomalies in the dream of Canada, nightmare ruptures in the idea of a nation. Public discourse on these books is an attempt to negotiate our ethos. This is not a rational progression towards a better and better populace. This is a messy landscape of desire in which we are perpetually changed, never certain of what might come next. A nuanced representation of Canada needs to be kept at the forefront of our thinking – not to perform shame or guilt but to contemplate seriously what we have been, what we are, and what we aspire to be. We all need spaces in which to explore various desires, cultivate our own identities, and resist the way in which others try to define us. These types of exchanges and openings are happening in the world of Canadian literature. We should be observing.

Works Cited

Abella, Irving, and Harold Troper. *None Is Too Many: Canada and the Jews in Europe 1933–1948*. U of Toronto P, 2012.

Abrams, M.H. *A Glossary of Literary Terms*. 7th ed. 1957. Harcourt Brace, 1999.

Adese, Jennifer. "The New People: Reading for Peoplehood in Métis Literatures." *Studies in American Indian Literatures*, vol. 28, no. 4, 2016, pp. 53–79. https://doi.org/10.5250/studamerindilite.28.4.0053.

Ahearn, Victoria. "'The Antagonist' Author Says Story Catalyst Was Unnerving Book Reading." The Canadian Press, 31 Oct. 2011. https://globalnews.ca/news/171792/the-antagonist-author-says-story-catalyst-was-

Anderson, Benedict R. *Imagined Communities: Reflections on the Origin and Spread of Nationalism*. Rev. ed., Verso, 2006.

Antoniak, Joanna. "A Guarantee of Safety, a Cautionary Tale or a Celebration? Popularity of True Crime Narratives through the Lens of Mary Douglas's Concepts of Pollution and Defilement." *Literatura Ludowa*, vol. 65, no. 2, 2021. https://doi.org/10.12775/ll.2.2021.006.

Antwi, Phanuel. "Rough Play: Reading Black Masculinity in Austin Clarke's 'Sometimes, a Motherless Child' and Dionne Brand's *What We All Long For*." *Studies in Canadian Literature*, vol. 34, no. 2, 2009, pp. 194–222.

Armstrong, Chris. "The Rock Observed: Art and Surveillance in Michael Winter's *This All Happened*." *Newfoundland and Labrador Studies*, vol. 25, no. 1, 2010, pp. 37–53.

Armstrong, Chris, and Herb Wyile. "Firing the Regional Can(n)on: Liberal Pluralism, Social Agency, and David Adams Richards's Miramichi Trilogy." *Studies in Canadian Literature*, vol. 22, no. 1, 1997, pp. 1–18.

Atwood, Margaret. *Survival*. Anansi, 1972.

Babstock, Ken. *On Malice*. Coach House Books, 2015.

Bakhtin, Mikhail. *The Dialogic Imagination*. 1975. Translated by Carol Emerson and Michael Holquist. Texas UP, 1981.

Bala, Sharon. *The Boat People*. McClelland & Stewart, 2018.

Barrett, Paul. *Blackening Canada: Diaspora, Race, Multiculturalism*. U of Toronto P, 2015. https://doi.org/10.3138/9781442668959.

Beebe, Maurice. *Ivory Towers and Sacred Founts: The Artist as Hero in Fiction from Goethe to Joyce*. New York UP, 1964.

Bennett, Colin J., et al. *Transparent Lives: Surveillance in Canada*. Athabasca UP, 2014. https://doi.org/10.15215/aupress/9781927356777.01.

Bentham, Jeremy. "Outline of a Plan for the Management of a Panopticon Penitentiary-House." 1790. *A Bentham Reader*, edited by Mary Peter Mack. Pegasus, 1969, pp. 199–201.

Birkwood, Susan. "Shifting the Narrative of Winnipeg's North End in Katherena Vermette's *The Break*." *Western Humanities Review*, 73, no. 3, 2019, pp. 17–49.

Blake, William. Visions of the Daughters of Albion. Edited by Robert N. Essick, Huntington Library, 2002.

Boon, Marcus. *The Road of Excess: A History of Writers on Drugs*. Harvard UP, 2005.

Booth, Wayne C. *The Company We Keep: An Ethics of Fiction*. U of California P, 1988. https://doi.org/10.1525/9780520351981.

– *The Rhetoric of Fiction*. 1961. UP of Chicago, 1983. https://doi.org/10.7208/chicago/9780226065595.001.0001.

Bradford, Lauren. "My Family Was Traumatised First by a Murder, Then by the TV Serialisation." *The Guardian*, 2 May 2016. https://www.theguardian.com/commentisfree/2016/may/02/the-secret-my-family-traumatised-murder-tv-drama-bereaved.

Brand, Dionne. *A Map to the Door of No Return: Notes to Belonging*. Doubleday Canada, 2001.

– *Thirsty*. McClelland & Stewart, 2002.

Brodeur, Jean-Paul, and Stéphane Leman-Langlois. "Surveillance Fiction or Higher Policing?" *The New Politics of Surveillance and Visibility*, U of Toronto P, 2018, pp. 171–98. https://doi.org/10.3138/9781442681880-008.

Browne, Simone. *Dark Matters: On the Surveillance of Blackness*, Duke UP, 2015. https://doi.org/10.1515/9780822375302.

Brydon, Diana, and Marta Dvořák. *Crosstalk: Canadian and Global Imaginaries in Dialogue*. Wilfrid Laurier UP, 2012. https://doi.org/10.51644/9781554583096.

Butler, Judith. *Giving an Account of Oneself*. Fordham UP, 2005. https://doi.org/10.5422/fso/9780823225033.001.0001.

Carlson, Tim, et al. "Foreign Radical." *Canadian Theatre Review*, vol. 175, 2018, pp. 57–70. https://doi.org/10.3138/ctr.175.011.

CBC. "MV Sun Sea 5 Year Anniversary Reflected upon by Refugees' Lawyer." CBC News, posted 12 Aug. 2015, 15 Aug. 2015. https://www.cbc.ca/news/canada/british-columbia/mv-sun-sea-5-year-anniversary-reflected-upon-by-refugees-lawyer-1.3189314.

– "Tamil Migrant Ship Boarded: Military Sources." CBC News, posted 12 Aug. 2010, updated 13 Aug. 2010. https://www.cbc.ca/news/canada/british-columbia/tamil-migrant-ship-boarded-military-sources-1.972483.

Centola, Damon. "Why Social Media Makes Us More Polarized and How to Fix It." *Scientific American*, 15 Oct. 2020. https://www.scientificamerican.com/article/why-social-media-makes-us-more-polarized-and-how-to-fix-it/.

Chafe, Paul. "Beautiful Losers: The *Flâneur* in St. John's Literature." *Newfoundland and Labrador Studies*, vol. 23, no. 2, 2008, pp. 115–38.

Chariandy, David. *Brother*. McClelland & Stewart, 2018.

– "'Quietly Heroic Lives': Lisa Ray and David Chariandy Discuss His Novel *Brother*." YouTube, uploaded by the CBC, 11 Mar. 2019. https://www.youtube.com/watch?v=QBnCO5WC8t0.

Cheong, Pauline Hope, et al. "Immigration, Social Cohesion and Social Capital: A Critical Review." *Critical Social Policy*, vol. 27, no. 1, 2007, pp. 24–49. https://doi.org/10.1177/0261018307072206.

Chiu, Monica. *Scrutinized!: Surveillance in Asian North American Literature*, U of Hawaii P, 2014. https://doi.org/10.21313/hawaii/9780824838423.001.0001.

Civilian Review and Complaints Commission. *Report into Workplace Harassment in the RCMP*. Apr. 2017. https://www.crcc-ccetp.gc.ca/pdf/harassmentFinR-eng.pdf.

Coady, Lynn. *The Antagonist*. Anansi, 2011.

– *Mean Boy*. Doubleday, 2006.

– "Someone is Recording" *Electric Lit*, 2018. https://electricliterature.com/how-many-emails-does-it-take-to-not-apologize-lynn-coady/.

– *Strange Heaven*. Goose Lane, 2000.

– *Who Needs Books?* U of Alberta P, 2016. https://doi.org/10.1515/9781772121438.

Cole, Desmond. *The Skin We're In: A Year of Black Resistance and Power*. Doubleday, 2020.

Coulthard, Glen Sean. *Red Skin, White Masks: Rejecting the Colonial Politics of Recognition*. U of Minnesota P, 2014. https://doi.org/10.5749/minnesota/9780816679645.001.0001.

Creelman, David. *Setting in the East: Maritime Realist Fiction*. McGill-Queen's UP, 2003. https://doi.org/10.1515/9780773570740.

Crisis of Distrust: Police and Community in Toronto. Directed by Dan Epstein. A Policing Literacy Initiative, 2014.

Critchley, Simon. *The Ethics of Deconstruction: Derrida and Levinas*. 1992. Edinburgh UP, 2014. https://doi.org/10.1515/9780748689330.

– *Infinitely Demanding: Ethics of Commitment, Politics of Resistance*. Verso, 2007.

Cummins, Ian, and Martin King. "'Drowning in Here in His Bloody Sea': Exploring TV Cop Drama's Representations of the Impact of Stress in Modern Policing." *Policing and Society*, vol. 27, no. 8, 2017, pp.832–46. https://doi.org/10.1080/10439463.2015.1112387.

Dawson, Michael. *The Mountie: From Dime Store to Disney*. Between the Lines, 1998.

Derrida, Jacques. "Violence and Metaphysics: An Essay on the Thought of Emmanuel Levinas." *Writing and Difference*, translated by Alan Bass. U of Chicago P, 1978, pp. 97–192.

Dhillon, Sunny. "Sun Sea Anniversary Highlights Canada's Treatment of Refugees." *Globe and Mail*, 9 Aug. 2015. https://www.theglobeandmail.com/news/british-columbia/sun-sea-anniversary-highlights-canadas-treatment-of-refugees/article25900878/.

Djikic, Maja, Keith Oatley, and Mihnea C. Moldoveanu. "Opening the Close Mind: The Effect of Exposure to Literature on the Need for Closure." *Creativity Research Journal*, vol. 25, no. 2, 2013, pp. 149–54. https://doi.org/10.1080/10400419.2013.783735.

Dobson, Kit. "Dystopia Now: Examining the Rach(a)el's in Automaton Biographies and Player One." *Blast, Corrupt, Dismantle, Erase: Contemporary North American Dystopian Literature*, edited by Gisèle Marie Baxter, Gisèle M. Baxter, and Tara Lee, Wilfrid Laurier UP, 2014, pp. 393–408. https://doi.org/10.51644/9781771120562-023.

Dowler, Kenneth, and Valerie Zawilski. "Public Perceptions of Police Misconduct and Discrimination: Examining the Impact of Media Consumption." *Journal of Criminal Justice*, vol. 35, no. 2, 2007, pp. 193–203. https://doi.org/10.1016/j.jcrimjus.2007.01.006

Ericson, Richard V., and Kevin D. Haggerty. *The New Politics of Surveillance and Visibility*, U of Toronto P, 2006, https://doi.org/10.3138/9781442681880.

Ericson, Richard V., and Kevin D. Haggerty. "The New Politics of Surveillance and Visibility." *The New Politics of Surveillance and Visibility*, U of Toronto P, 2006, pp. vi–vi. https://doi.org/10.3138/9781442681880.

Feldman, Gregory. "Essential Crises: A Performance Approach to Migrants, Minorities and the European Nation-State." *Anthropological Quarterly*, vol. 78, no. 1, pp. 213–46. https://doi.org/10.1353/anq.2005.0008.

Fernback, Jan. "Sousveillance: Communities of Resistance to the Surveillance Environment." *Telematics and Informatics*, vol. 30, no. 1, 2013, pp. 11–21. https://doi.org/10.1016/j.tele.2012.03.003.

Fitzgerald, Robin T., and Peter J. Carrington. "Disproportionate Minority Contact in Canada: Police and Visible Minority Youth." *Canadian Journal of Criminology and Criminal Justice*, vol. 53, no. 4, 2011, pp. 449–86, https://doi.org/10.3138/cjccj.53.4.449.

Foley, Rebecca I.M. "(Mis)representing Terrorist Threats: Media Framing of Bill C-51." *Media, War & Conflict*, vol. 11, no. 2, 2018, pp. 204–22. https://doi.org/10.1177/1750635217702557.

Foucault, Michel. *Discipline and Punish: The Birth of the Prison*. Translated by Alan Sheridan. Pantheon, 1977.

Francis, Daniel. *National Dreams: Myth, Memory, and Canadian History*. Arsenal Pulp Press, 2002.

Francis, Margot. *Creative Subversions: Whiteness, Indigeneity, and the National Imaginary*. U of British Columbia P, 2011. https://doi.org/10.59962/9780774820271.

Frye, Northrop. *The Bush Garden: Essays on the Canadian Imagination*. Anansi, 1971.

Ganascia, Jean-Gabriel. "The Generalized Sousveillance Society." *Social Science Information*, vol. 49, no. 3, 2010, pp. 490–507. https://doi.org/10.1177/0539018410371027.

Gilliom, John. "Struggling with Surveillance: Resistance, Consciousness, and Identity." *The New Politics of Surveillance and Visibility*, U of Toronto P, 2018, pp. 111–30, https://doi.org/10.3138/9781442681880-006.

Giroux, Henry A. "Totalitarian Paranoia in the Post-Orwellian Surveillance State." *Cultural Studies*, vol. 29, no. 2, 2015, pp. 108–40. https://doi.org/10.1080/09502386.2014.917118.

Government of Canada. "The Human Rights of Lesbian, Gay, Bisexual, Transgender, Queer, 2-Spirit and Intersex Persons." 30 May 2023. https://www.international.gc.ca/world-monde/issues_development-enjeux_developpement/human_rights-droits_homme/rights_lgbti-droits_lgbti.aspx?lang=eng.

Grainger, James. Review of *Principles to Live By*, by David Adams Richards. *Quill and Quire*, May 2016.

Gregory, Marshall. "Redefining Ethical Criticism: The Old vs. the New." *Journal of Literary Theory*, vol. 4, no. 2, 2010, pp. 273–301. https://doi.org/10.1515/jlt.2010.017.

– *Shaped By Stories: The Ethical Power of Narratives*. U of Notre Dame P, 2009. https://doi.org/10.2307/j.ctvpj78qt.

Haggerty, Kevin D. "Tear Down the Walls: On Demolishing the Panopticon." *Theorizing Surveillance: The Panopticon and Beyond*, edited by David Lyon, Willan, 2006, pp. 23–45.

Hanson, Aubrey Jean. "Holding Home Together: Katherena Vermette's *The Break*." *Canadian Literature*, no. 237, 2019, pp. 27–45.

Haraway, Donna. "A Cyborg Manifesto: Science, Technology, and Socialist Feminism in the Late Twentieth Century." *Simians, Cyborgs and Women: The Reinvention of Nature*, Routledge, 1991. pp.149–81. https://www.sfu.ca/~decaste/OISE/page2/files/HarawayCyborg.pdf.

Hazlitt, William. "Why Distant Objects Please." *Table-Talk, or, Original Essays*, J. Warren, 1821, pp. 219–38.

Herk, Aritha van. "Trembling Strength: Migrating Vulnerabilities in Fiction by Sharon Bala, Yasmin Ladha, and Denise Chong." *Journal of Commonwealth Literature*, vol. 56, no. 3, 2021, pp. 345–58, https://doi.org/10.1177/0021989420972455.

Hewitt, Steve. "Forgotten Surveillance: Covert Human Intelligence Sources in Canada in a Post-9/11 World." *Law, Privacy and Surveillance in Canada in the Post-Snowden Era*, U of Ottawa P, 2015, pp. 45–67. https://doi.org/10.1515/9780776621838-004.

Hills, Thomas, and Filippo Menczer. "Information Overload Helps Fake News Spread, and Social Media Knows It." *Scientific American*, Dec. 2020. https://www.scientificamerican.com/article/information-overload-helps-fake-news-spread-and-social-media-knows-it/.

Hlongwane, Gugu D. "'A Different Economy': Postcolonial Clearings in David Chariandy's *Brother*." *Ariel*, vol. 52, no. 4, 2021, pp. 171–99. https://doi.org/10.1353/ari.2021.0029.

Horeck, Tanya, and Diane Negra. "Reconsidering Television True Crime and Gendered Authority in Allen V. Farrow." *Feminist Media Studies*, vol. 22, no. 6, 2022, pp. 1564–9. https://doi.org/10.1080/14680777.2021.1970608.

Horsman, Yasco. *Theaters of Justice: Judging, Staging, and Working Through in Arendt, Brecht, and Delbo.* Stanford UP, 2010.

Hoy, Helen. "How Should I Read These? Native Women Writers in Canada." *How Should I Read These?*, U of Toronto P, 2001. https://doi.org/10.3138/9781442675896.

Huot, Suzanne, et al. "Constructing Undesirables: A Critical Discourse Analysis of 'Othering' Within the Protecting Canada's Immigration System Act." *International Migration*, vol. 54, no. 2, 2016, pp. 131–43. https://doi.org/10.1111/imig.12210.

Hutcheon, Linda. "The Politics of Postmodernism: Parody and History." *Cultural Critique*, no. 5, 1986, pp. 179–207. https://doi.org/10.2307/1354361.

Hutcheon, Linda, and Mario J. Valdés. "Irony, Nostalgia, and the Postmodern: A Dialogue." Nuevas Poligrafías, Revista de Teoría Literaria y Literatura Comparada, no. 3, 2000, pp. 29–54. https://doi.org/10.22201/ffyl.poligrafias.2000.3.1610.

Iser, Wolfgang. "Indeterminacy and the Reader's Response in Prose Fiction." *Prospecting: From Reader Response to Literary Anthropology*. John Hopkins UP, 1989, pp. 1–30.

Jameson, Fredric. *Postmodernism, or the Cultural Logic of Late Capitalism.* 1991. Duke UP, 1999. https://doi.org/10.1215/9780822378419.

Jiwa, Fazeela. "Fazeela Jiwa in Conversation with Rita Wong and Larissa Lai: *Sybil unrest*." *Lemon Hound: Arts, Letters, Poetry, Prose, An Ever-Evolving Digital Site since 2005.* June 2014. http://lemonhound.com/2014/06/20/fazeela-jiwa-in-conversation-with-rita-wong-and-larissa-lai-sybil-unrest/.

Jones, Katie. "Returning to the Scene: Seriality and the Serial Killer." *Open Screens*, vol. 3, no. 1, 2020, art. 5, https://doi.org/10.16995/os.27.

Jones, Matt. "Forced Entertainment? Gamified Surveillance in Theatre Conspiracy's Foreign Radical." *Canadian Theatre Review*, vol. 175, 2018, pp. 52–6. https://doi.org/10.3138/ctr.175.010.

Justice, Daniel Heath. *Why Indigenous Literatures Matter*. Wilfrid Laurier UP, 2018. https://doi.org/10.51644/9781771121774.

Kamboureli, Smaro. *Scandalous Bodies: Diasporic Literature in English Canada*. Wilfrid Laurier UP, 2009. https://doi.org/10.51644/9781554581665.

Kershaw, Baz. "Curiosity or Contempt: On Spectacle, the Human, and Activism." *Theatre Journal (Washington, D.C.)*, vol. 55, no. 4, 2003, pp. 591–611. https://doi.org/10.1353/tj.2003.0170.

Klauser, Francisco Reto. *Surveillance and Space*. Sage, 2016. https://doi.org/10.4135/9781473983281.

Krüger, Anja. "Sedimenting the Past, Producing the Future: An Interview with Larissa Lai on the Poetics and Politics of Writing." *Zeitschrift für Kanada-Studien*, vol. 31, no. 2, 2011, pp. 93–107.

L'Abbe, Sonnet. "'Infiltrate as Cells' The Biopolitically Ethical Subject of *sybil unrest*." *Canadian Literature*, vol. 210, no. 210, 2011, pp. 169–89.

Lai, Larissa. *Automaton Biographies*. Arsenal Pulp Press, 2009.

– *Iron Goddess of Mercy*. Arsenal Pulp Press, 2021.

Lai, Larissa and Rita Wong. *Sybil unrest*. New Star Books, 2013.

Lawlor, Andrea. "Framing Immigration in the Canadian and British News Media." *Canadian Journal of Political Science*, vol. 48, no. 2, 2015, pp. 329–55, https://doi.org/10.1017/s0008423915000499

Levinas, Emmanuel. *Otherwise than Being Or, Beyond Essence*. 1974. Translated by Alphonso Lingis. Duquesne UP, 2000.

– *Totality and Infinity: An Essay on Exteriority*. 1961. Translated by Alphonso Lingis. Duquesne UP, 2012.

Ling, Justin. *Missing From the Village: The Story of Serial Killer Bruce McArthur, the Search for Justice, and the System That Failed Toronto's Queer Community*. McClelland & Stewart, 2020.

Mann, Steve. "'Sousveillance': Inverse Surveillance in Multimedia Imaging." *ACM Multimedia 2004 – Proceedings of the 12th ACM International Conference on Multimedia*, ACM, 2004, pp. 620–7. https://doi.org/10.1145/1027527.1027673.

Marks, Peter. *Imagining Surveillance : Eutopian and Dystopian Literature and Film*. Edinburgh UP, 2015. https://doi.org/10.3366/edinburgh/9781474400190.001.0001.

Marquis, Greg. *The Vigilant Eye: Policing Canada from 1867 to 9/11*. Fernwood, 2016.

Marx, Gary T. *Windows into the Soul: Surveillance and Society in an Age of High Technology*. U of Chicago P, 2016. https://doi.org/10.7208/chicago/9780226286075.001.0001.

Mathews, Larry. Personal Interview. 20 May 2013.
Mathiesen, Thomas. "The Viewer Society: Michel Foucault's `Panopticon' Revisited." *Theoretical Criminology*, vol. 1, no. 2, 1997, pp. 215–34. https://doi.org/10.1177/1362480697001002003.
Maynard, Robyn. *Policing Black Lives: State Violence in Canada from Slavery to the Present*. Fernwood, 2017.
McKittrick, Katherine. *Dear Science and Other Stories*. Duke UP, 2021. https://doi.org/10.1215/9781478012573.
Miller, D.A. *The Novel and the Police*. 1988. U of California P, 1998. https://doi.org/10.1525/9780520352919.
Milosavljevic, Tatjana. "The Cyborg Continuum: From Myth to Technocapitalism in Larissa Lai's Salt Fish Girl." *Kultura (Belgrade, Serbia)*, no. 152, 2016, pp. 64–79. https://doi.org/10.5937/kultura1652064m.
Monaghan, Jeffrey. "Settler Governmentality and Racializing Surveillance in Canada's North-West." *Canadian Journal of Sociology*, 38, no. 4, 2013, pp. 487–508. https://doi.org/10.29173/cjs21195.
Moore, Lisa. Caught.Anansi, 2014.
Moritz, A.F. *The Garden: A Poem and an Essay*. Gordon Hill Press, 2021.
National Institute for Health and Care Excellence. "Post-Traumatic Stress Disorder." NICE Guideline, No. 116, 2018.
Nguyen, Vinh. *Lived Refuge: Gratitude, Resentment, Resilience*. 1st ed., U of California P, 2023, https://doi.org/10.1525/9780520397279.
Nguyen, Vinh, and Thy Phu. *Refugee States: Critical Refugee Studies in Canada*. U of Toronto P, 2021, https://doi.org/10.3138/9781487541392.
Nix, Justin, and Scott E. Wolfe. "The Impact of Negative Publicity on Police Self-Legitimacy." *Justice Quarterly*, vol. 34, no. 1, 2017, pp. 84–108. https://doi.org/10.1080/07418825.2015.1102954
Nussbaum, Martha. *Poetic Justice: The Literary Imagination and Public Life*. Beacon, 1995.
O'Rourke, James. *Sex, Lies, and Autobiography: The Ethics of Confession*. UP of Virginia, 2006.
Paris, Jamie. "'Men Break When Things Like That Happen': On Indigenous Masculinities in Katherena Vermette's *The Break*." *Canadian Literature*, no. 239, autumn 2019, pp. 68–84.
Perkin, J. Russell. "Learning about the Crucifixion: The Religious Vision of *For Those Who Hunt the Wounded Down*." *Tremblay, David Adams Richards: Essays on His Works*, edited by Tony Tremblay, Guernica, 2005, pp. 119–27.
Porco, Alex. "'The Secular Prophet.': A Review of Ken Babstock, *On Malice*." *Postmodern Culture*, vol. 24, no. 3, 2014. https://doi.org/10.1353/pmc.2014.0017.
Ray, John M. *Rethinking Community Policing*. LFB Scholarly Publishing, 2014.

Razack, Sherene. *Looking White People in the Eye: Gender, Race, and Culture in Courtrooms and Classrooms*. U of Toronto P, 1998. https://doi.org/10.3138/9781442670204.

RCMP. "Missing persons." https://www.rcmp-grc.gc.ca/en/missing-persons.

Reimer, Sharlee. "Troubling Origins: Cyborg Politics in Larissa Lai's *Salt Fish Girl*." *Atlantis*, vol.3, no. 1, 2010, pp. 4–14.

Richards, David Adams. *Blood Ties*. Oberon, 1976.

– *The Coming of Winter*. McClelland & Stewart, 1992.

– *Hope in the Desperate Hour*. McClelland & Stewart, 1996.

– "An Interview with David Adams Richards." With Tony Tremblay. *David Adams Richards: Essays on His Works*, Guernica, 2005, pp. 26–44.

– *Mercy among the Children*. Doubleday, 2000.

– *Principles to Live By*. Doubleday, 2016.

Richler, Noah. *This Is My Country, What's Yours? A Literary Atlas of Canada*. McClelland & Stewart, 2006.

Roach, Kent. "Terrorist Speech Under Bills C-51 and C-59 and the Othman Hamdan Case: The Continued Incoherence of Canada's Approach." *Alberta Law Review*, vol. 57, no. 1, 2019, pp. 203–31. https://doi.org/10.29173/alr2574.

Robbins, Jill. *Altered Reading: Literature and Levinas*. U of Chicago P, 1999.

Rorty, Richard. *Contingency, Irony, and Solidarity*. Cambridge UP, 1989. https://doi.org/10.1017/CBO9780511804397.

Rosen, David, and Aaron Santesso. *The Watchman in Pieces: Surveillance, Literature, and Liberal Personhood*. Yale UP, 2013. https://doi.org/10.12987/yale/9780300155419.001.0001.

Rosenbaum, Dennis P. "The Challenge of Community Policing: Testing the Promises." *The Challenge of Community Policing: Testing the Promises*, Sage, 1994. https://doi.org/10.4135/9781483327006.

Ruti, Mari. *The Call of Character: Living a Life Worth Living*. Columbia UP, 2013. https://doi.org/10.7312/columbia/9780231164085.001.0001.

Saberi, Parastou. "Toronto and the 'Paris Problem': Community Policing in 'Immigrant Neighbourhoods.'" *Race & Class*, vol. 59, no. 2, 2017, pp. 49–69. https://doi.org/10.1177/0306396817717892.

Sanders, Carrie B., and Samantha Henderson. "Police 'Empires' and Information Technologies: Uncovering Material and Organisational Barriers to Information Sharing in Canadian Police Services." *Policing & Society*, vol. 23, no. 2, 2013, pp. 243–60. https://doi.org/10.1080/10439463.2012.703196.

Sanger, Peter. "John Thompson." *New Brunswick Literary Encyclopedia*, edited by Tony Tremblay, St. Thomas U, 2011.

Sarkowsky, Katja. "The Other Side of Citizenship? Narrating Flight and Refugeeism in Sharon Bala's The Boat People." *Parallax (Leeds, England)*, vol. 27, no. 2, 2021, pp. 159–75. https://doi.org/10.1080/13534645.2021.1995950.

Scaggs, John. *Crime Fiction*. Routledge, 2005. https://doi.org/10.4324/9780203598535.

Seitz, David K. "'Missing' Racialized Violence, Disturbing Continuities: Countertopographies of Violence in the Bruce McArthur Murders." *Journal of Canadian Studies*, vol. 54, no. 2, 2020, pp. 459–82. https://doi.org/10.3138/jcs-2019-0005.

Serpell, Namwali. *Seven Modes of Uncertainty*. Harvard UP, 2014. https://doi.org/10.4159/harvard.9780674419674.

Steeves, Rachel. "'Flawed Splendour': A Conversation with Lynn Coady." *Studies in Canadian Literature*, vol. 32, no. 1, 2007, pp. 231–38.

Stephenson, Jenn. *Insecurity: Perils and Products of Theatres of the Real*. U of Toronto P, 2019, https://doi.org/10.3138/9781487514099.

Stroebe, Margaret S., Henk Schut, and Jan van den Bout. *Complicated Grief: Scientific Foundations for Health Care Professionals*. Routledge, 2013. https://doi.org/10.4324/9780203105115.

Swartz, David. "Between-Space, Beforehand and Unseparated: Ken Babstock's *On Malice*." *ARC Poetry Magazine*, 2015.

Taylor, Charles. "The Politics of Recognition." *Multiculturalism: Examining the Politics of Recognition*, edited by Amy Gutmann, Princeton UP, 1994. https://doi.org/10.2307/j.ctt7snkj.6.

Thobani, Sunera. *Exalted Subjects: Studies in the Making of Race and Nation in Canada*. U of Toronto P, 2007.

Thompson, Peter. "Surveillance and the City in Michael Winter's *This All Happened*." *English Studies in Canada*, vol. 36, no. 4, December 2010, pp. 71–90. https://doi.org/10.1353/esc.2010.0044.

Tremblay, Tony, editor. *David Adams Richards: Essays on His Works*. Guernica, 2005.

– *David Adams Richards of the Miramichi: A Biographical Introduction*. U of Toronto P, 2010. https://doi.org/10.3138/9781442687202.

United Nations Refugee Agency Canada. "In Canada." https://www.unhcr.ca/in-canada/.

Vermette, Katherena. *The Break*. Anansi, 2016.

– *The Circle*. Penguin Canada, 2024.

– *The Strangers*. Penguin Canada, 2022.

– *Village of the Missing*. Directed by Michael Del Monte. CBC, 2019.

Wakeham, Pauline. "Outsourcing Reconciliation: The Government of Canada's #IndigenousReads Campaign and the Appropriation of Indigenous Intellectual Labor." *Studies in American Indian Literatures*, vol. 31, nos. 1–2, 2019, pp. 1–30. https://doi.org/10.5250/studamerindilite.31.1-2.0001.

Walcott, Rinaldo. *Black Like Who?: Writing Black Canada*. 2nd ed., Insomniac Press, 2003.

– *On Property: Policing, Prisons, and the Call for Abolition*. Biblioasis, 2021.

Wallace, Cynthia R. "Attention, Representation, and Unsettlement in Katherena Vermette's *The Break*, Or, Teaching and (Re)Learning the Ethics of Reading." *Humanities (Basel)*, vol. 8, no. 4, 2019, pp. 164–179. https://doi.org/10.3390/h8040164.

Welfens, Natalie. "'Promising Victimhood': Contrasting Deservingness Requirements in Refugee Resettlement." *Journal of Ethnic and Migration Studies*, vol. 49, no. 5, 2023, pp. 1103–24. https://doi.org/10.1080/1369183x.2022.2117686.

Winter, Michael. *The Architects Are Here*. Viking, 2007.

– *The Big Why*. Anansi, 2004.

– *The Death of Donna Whalen*. Hamish Hamilton, 2010.

– *This All Happened*. 2001. Anansi, 2013.

Wolfe, Matthew. "Policing The Lost: The Emergence of Missing Persons and the Classification of Deviant Absence." *Theory and Society*, vol. 51, no. 3, 2021, pp. 511–41. https://doi.org/10.1007/s11186-021-09466-w.

Wordsworth, William, et al. *Lyrical Ballads*. 2nd ed., Routledge, 2013. https://doi.org/10.4324/9781315834511.

Wyile, Herb. *Anne of Tim Hortons: Globalization and the Reshaping of Atlantic-Canadian Literature*. Wilfrid Laurier UP, 2011. https://doi.org/10.51644/9781554583706.

– "As for Me and Me Arse: Strategic Regionalism and the Home Place in Lynn Coady's *Strange Heaven*." *Canadian Literature*, vol. 189, no. 189, 2006, pp. 85–101.

– "'The Best Stories … We've Known the End from the Beginning': Lisa Moore's *Caught* and the Rise of the Surveillance Society." *Journal of Newfoundland and Labrador Studies*, vol. 31, no. 2, 2016, pp. 262–85.

– "Laughs in the Desperate Hour." *David Adams Richards: Essays on His Works*, edited by Tony Tremblay, Guernica, 2005, pp. 106–18.

– "Making a Mess of Things: Postcolonialism, Canadian Literature, and the Ethical Turn." *University of Toronto Quarterly*, vol. 76, no. 3, 2007, pp. 821–37. https://doi.org/10.1353/utq.2007.0298

Zappe, Florian and Andrew Gross, editors. *Surveillance | Society | Culture.* Peter Lang, 2020. https://doi.org/10.3726/b16151.

Zuboff, Shoshana. *The Age of Surveillance Capitalism: The Fight for a Human Future at the New Frontier of Power*. Public Affairs, 2019.

Index